```
…ary = 1. Louis XII of France    Margaret ⊤ James IV of Scotland
      ⊤ 2. Charles Brandon,
           D. of Suffolk



  Frances ⊤ Henry, Duke of Suffolk       James V ⊤ Marie de Guise

…ady Jane Grey = Ld. Guild-    Francis II   1. = Mary, Q.o.S.
                ford Dudley   of France
                              Henry, Ld. Darnley   2. ⊤

                              Earl of Bothwell    3. =

                Anne of Denmark ⊤ James VI and I
                                  1567–1625 of Scotland
                                  1603–1625 of England

                              Elizabeth = Frederick, Elector Palatine



  ⊤ James II ⊤ Mary of Modena
    1685–88

  Anne = George      James Edward, Old Pretender
  1702–1714  of
            Denmark

                Charles Edward, Young Pretender
```

THEY SAW IT HAPPEN

THEY
SAW IT HAPPEN

*An Anthology
of Eye-witnesses' Accounts of
Events in British History
1485—1688*

Compiled by
C. R. N. ROUTH

With a foreword by
R. BIRLEY, C.M.G.
Headmaster, Eton College

BASIL BLACKWELL · OXFORD

First Printed 1956
Second Impression 1956
Third Impression 1957
Fourth Impression 1960

BY A. T. BROOME AND SON, 18 ST. CLEMENT'S, OXFORD
AND BOUND BY THE KEMP HALL BINDERY, OXFORD
PRINTED IN GREAT BRITAIN

FOREWORD

Sir Henry Marten, who taught History to generations of Etonians, on entering the Cathedral of St. Vitus in Prague, once startled the worshippers and tourists in the building with a violent exclamation, 'This *is* History'. But is it? 'History', wrote Cicero, is ' the witness of the ages, the light of truth, the life of memory, the mistress of life, the messenger of antiquity '; for Lord Bolingbroke it was ' Philosophy teaching by examples '; for Carlyle, ' the essence of innumerable biographies '. What part is played in all this by those moments when the past suddenly assumes for us such an intense reality ?

We all know them, if we read History. For myself one of the most vivid comes in the first book of Thucydides. The author is writing his introduction; he speaks of the early days of Greece, of the rise of Sparta, of the difficulty in discovering the truth about primitive communities, of the importance of his subject. And then, quite suddenly, we read the words, ' The city of Epidamnus lies on the right-hand side as you sail up the Ionian Gulf '. There is an immediate sense of reality; this, I say to myself, as I settle back in my chair, this *is* history. I am sailing up the gulf; I look out to starboard—there is Epi-damnus. What is going to happen there ?

Of course, Poetry may give it us. Gibbon, in the finest of all his footnotes—and that is saying a great deal—comments on a passage where Procopius refers to a description of archers in Homer. We glance to the bottom of the page, where a line is quoted from the poet—and then, ' How concise—how just— how beautiful is the whole picture! I see the attitudes of the archer—I hear the twanging of the bow '. I have never been able quite to decide what Carlyle meant when he said that ' History after all is true poetry '. But I can understand what Gibbon meant ; the poetry lies in the seeing of the attitudes, the hearing of the bow's twang.

This is what Mr. Routh has enabled us to do for ourselves. He has taken a splendid period of English History, one that anyone interested in History knows something about. There are innumerable books about it, some of them very good ones, from Froude and Gardiner and Macaulay to Professor Neale and Miss Wedgwood and Sir Arthur Bryant. These will often make us see and hear. But we are not going to experience the real joys of History unless we do ourselves what they have done and read the actual accounts of eye-witnesses which gave to these historians those intense moments that they have transmitted to us. They are often difficult to find. Books like Ellis's Original Letters, the State Papers, the Volumes of the Hakluyt Society and others much less wellknown are not easy to come by.

We see and hear. Elizabeth I goes to open Parliament, and ' here the queen dismounted, knelt down at the entrance and said her prayers, entered the church, where prayers were offered and chants performed '. Charles I is on the scaffold and ' the Blow I saw given and can truly say with a sad heart : at the instant whereof, I remember well, there was such a grone by the Thousands then present, as I never heard before, and desire I may never hear again '. James II flees the country, ' but the King kept three large diamond bodkins which belonged to the Queen and the ring which he had worn at his coronation ; which was a valuable ruby, and slipped them down his trousers, hoping thus to save them '. (The subsequent story of those diamond bodkins, which is quite as good as that sentence may lead us to hope, is not to be found in Macaulay's most vivid account of the king's flight nor in such an admirable modern life of James II as that by Mr. F. C. Turner.) We hear what must be one of the grimmest remarks in all History. Rizzio has been murdered. ' The King's dagger was found sticking in his side. The Queen enquired at the King where his dagger was ? who answered that he wist not well. " Well," said the Queen, " it will be known hereafter." '

History may be Philosophy ; History may be Poetry. But this is History.

R. BIRLEY.

CONTENTS

INTRODUCTION

History, by and large, is men and women and children, not coal and railways and wages. This book is for all who enjoy reading history. It is not a selection of passages from the great English historians : it is an anthology of historical events in Tudor and Stuart times, described by men and women who were eye-witnesses of those events. These descriptions are the raw material out of which the historian manufactures his narrative. Eye-witnesses are not always accurate, therefore must the historian balance the veracity of one witness against the veracity of another, estimate the integrity of this man, assess the opportunity of that woman. In the end the trained historian will provide us with a more factually truthful account than we are likely to get from any one eye-witness. But something is lost in the process : the raw material has a quality of its own which the manufactured article too often fails to preserve. These original documents give us original history as the men and women of the past saw, or thought they saw, it happening, either as actors in the events or as bystanders in the crowd. Their letters tell us their inmost thoughts and their deepest feelings, what men they feared, what trials they suffered, in days when life was hazardous and harsh. Read the letter of an unknown Papist, J.A., to his unnamed friend, describing the burning of Archbishop Cranmer (p. 52) : a good Catholic, unshaken in his faith, but sore troubled in his heart. 'I take little pleasure in beholding of such heavy sights . . . and being more than half weary, I make a short end, wishing you a quieter life, with less honour and easier death, with more praise.' Nor is it possible in that letter to read without emotion the last prayer written by Cranmer, to hear the words of our own Litany used by its author in his extremity : ' O Father of Heaven, O Son of God, Redeemer of the world, O Holy Ghost, proceeding from Them both, three Persons and one God, have mercy upon me most wretched caitiff and miserable sinner.'

Or consider the English fisherboy from Swanage, seventeen years old, who found himself suddenly involved in the Spanish

Inquisition in the Canary Islands : ' Questioned, whether this confessant knows what it is to be a Lutheran, Said that he understands that to be a Lutheran means not to attend Mass and to steal, and he could give no other explication whatever ' : not even later under torture (p. 92).

These are living voices unstilled after four hundred years. If life was dangerous and death might be cruel, there were compensations. There were splendid clothes and gorgeous pageants (p. 22) : foreign travellers were struck by the fine shops in London and by the courtesy of the English people, although others thought them naturally hostile to strangers (p. 2). Peter Paul Rubens found England far less barbarous than her climate might warrant (p. 130). A determined and courageous man might at last extract justice even from the hectoring Wolsey (p. 19). There was bear-baiting and the new fashion of smoking tobacco (p. 101). Englishmen were ' going places ', Ralegh to Guiana, the Pilgrim Fathers to North America (pp. 102, 123). These were stirring times, but they were restless and grew ever more restless. The efficient and acceptable government of the Tudors gave place to the disputed theories of the Stuarts. Here in these letters and diaries we may see it all boiling up to Civil War as Englishmen saw it at the time—Crown disputing with Puritans (p. 111), Parliament quarrelling with Crown (p. 137), Cavalier fighting with Roundhead (p. 144). Sometimes it is a participant himself who reports his victories, Cromwell in Ireland or Scotland (pp. 165-6) : sometimes it is the almost chance observer, like the undergraduate who had an exeat from Cambridge and thus saw Charles I executed (p. 153). They were shrewd observers of each other, nor were they reticent in their views. The foreign ambassadors reported to their governments the characters and appearances of the English Kings and Queens : the diarists record for their own satisfaction their opinions of this or that statesman; they tell us how the crowd behaved after Strafford's head was off (p. 136), or how Clarendon took his fall from power (p. 184). It may perhaps be thought that the selection here offered deals too much with the Kings and Queens, the statesmen and the courtiers. Those were the people who counted in Tudor and Stuart times and whose memorials have come down to us. The day of the common man was not yet.

THE SOURCES

At the top of each extract is printed the source from which the account has been drawn. It may perhaps be of interest to readers to know a little bit more about these various sources.

After the destruction of the monasteries in the sixteenth century (see p. 28) most of the libraries and archives were scattered. Some part of them was saved, thanks to the efforts of a few private collectors, of whom the chief were Archbishop Cranmer ; Henry Fitzalan, Earl of Arundel ; his son-in-law John, Lord Lumley; Thomas Howard, Earl of Arundel; Sir Robert Bruce Cotton ; Sir Thomas Bodley ; Archbishop Matthew Parker ; Dr. John Dee. The collections of Cranmer, Fitzalan, Lumley, Howard, Cotton, eventually all went to the British Museum, that of Bodley to Oxford, and Parker's to Corpus Christi College, Cambridge.

In the seventeenth century the chief collectors were Sir Simonds D'Ewes, Sir Julius Caesar, Archbishop Laud, John Selden, Sir Kenelm Digby and Elias Ashmole. D'Ewes's collection was added to the Harleian Collection (see below) and thus went to the British Museum. Sir Julius Caesar's collection was broken up and has been distributed among various other collections, notably the Lansdowne Collection, which also eventually went to the British Museum. The remainder went to increase the bequest to Oxford made by Sir Thomas Bodley and forms now the Bodleian Library.

The eighteenth century saw the foundation and building of the British Museum in 1753, which was completed in 1759. To this Museum came the Cottonian Library, the Harleian Collection, Sir Hans Sloane's Collection, and also the Royal Library, which had been started in the reign of Edward IV. These are the principal sources, outside the Public Record Office which houses all the State Papers, on which historians are able to draw for their original materials.

The Cotton MSS. Collected by Sir Robert Bruce Cotton (1571–1631) and Sir Thomas Cotton (1594–1662), given to the British Museum in 1700 by Sir John Cotton. Sir Robert was deprived of his library by the King in 1629, mainly for political reasons, but it was restored to his son. In 1731 it was badly damaged by fire : out of 958 MSS. 212 were destroyed or seriously injured. Sir Robert kept on the top of each bookcase a bust of a Roman Emperor : the MSS. are now catalogued at the British Museum according to the press in which they are kept, and the name of the Roman emperor is added to the title —e.g. Cotton MS. Caligula, E. iii : Cotton MS. Vitell : etc.

Harleian MSS. Collected by Robert Harley, 1st Earl (1661–1724) and Edward Harley 2nd Earl (1689–1741) of Oxford, including the library of Sir Simonds D'Ewes (1602–1650). Robert Harley was Queen Anne's minister. He began collecting about 1705 and in a few years had amassed at least 6,000 MSS. and over 40,000 printed volumes. His son, Edward, continued the collection, and by his death in 1741 the library contained 7,639 MSS, 14,236 charters and more than 50,000 printed books. His widow sold the books in 1743 for £13,000, far less than they had cost to bind, and the MSS. to the British Museum in 1753 for only £10,000.

Lansdowne MSS. Purchased from the executors of the Marquess of Lansdowne, 1807.

Readers who are interested to pursue this subject further will find the following helpful :

A Student's Guide to the Manuscripts of the British Museum, by Julius P. Gilson. Historical Association, Helps for Students.

English Collectors of Books and MSS.. by De Ricci, C.U.P.

SPELLING AND PUNCTUATION

Where it has seemed to me that something was gained by retaining the original spelling and punctuation, I have retained them, and the choice has been purely arbitrary. For the most part spelling and punctuation have been modernized.

DATING

The dating of original documents presents some difficulties.

Up to 1582 all countries used the Julian Calendar, but by the sixteenth century this calendar was ten days out in its reckonings. Pope Gregory XIII on February 24th, 1582, ordered the use of a reformed calendar—the Gregorian or New Style calendar, by which ten days were cut out between October 4th and 15th and the year was made to start on January the 1st and not on March 25th. Catholic states adopted the new calendar almost immediately, but Protestant states did not do so until the eighteenth century—Great Britain in 1752. (A list of the dates when various states changed over is printed in the C.M.H., vol. iii, p. 770). Two main difficulties arise from the failure of all states to change at the same time :

(1) a discrepancy of 10 days between the Old Style (O.S.) and the New Style (N.S.) of dating. This is clearly illustrated on p. 191

(2) a discrepancy in years between January 1st and March 25th. For example, a document dated in England, March 24th, 1585, shows that it was written on the day after March 23rd, 1585, the last day of that year by O.S. reckoning. But it was also written all but a year *after* a document dated March 25th, 1585, because 1585 began on March 25th, by the Julian (O.S.) reckoning.

Or again, in 1688 Holland used the N.S. calendar, but England still stuck to the Old Style. By Dutch reckoning William III sailed from Holland for England, after his return for refitting, on November 11th, but by English reckoning he landed at Tor Bay on November 5th (see p. 205). In this book almost all dates are O.S. Where difficulty or doubt might arise (O.S.) or (N.S.) has been inserted.

Two useful guides on this subject are :

Methods of Chronology, by A. E. Stamp, Historical Associaton Leaflet, no. 92.

Handbook of Dates. ed. by C. R. Cheney, R.H.S. Guides and Handbooks, no. 4.

ACKNOWLEDGEMENTS

The compiler and the publisher wish to thank the following for permission to reproduce copyright material :

John Lane, The Bodley Head, Ltd., for an extract from the *Fugger Newsletters* and three extracts from *The Great Fire of London* and *The Great Plague*, by W. G. Bell.

The Clarendon Press, Oxford, for a passage from Clarendon's *History of the Great Rebellion*.

Cornish Brothers, Birmingham, for extracts from *The Great Civil War in Midland Parishes*.

Faber and Faber, Ltd., for two passages from *Rubens : Painter and Diplomat* by E. Cammaerts.

The Hakluyt Society for a passage from *New Light on Drake* edited by Z. Nuttall.

Rupert Hart-Davis, Ltd., for two extracts from *The First Night of Twelfth Night* by L. Hotson.

The Public Record Office for extracts from the Spanish and Venetian Calendars.

C. Malfatti for extracts from *Two Italian Accounts of Tudor England*.

The Navy Records Society for documents published in *The Defeat of the Spanish Armada* by J. R. Laughton.

The Nonesuch Press for an extract from the *Journal of Sieur de Maisse*, translated by Harrison and Jones.

The Oxford University Press for extracts from the *Memoirs of Edward Ludlow*.

The Phaidon Press for part of a letter from *Erasmus of Rotterdam*, by J. Huizinga, translated by Barbara Flower.

Farrer, Straus and Cudany Inc., for a passage from *The Autobiography of a Hunted Priest* translated by Philip Caraman. Copyright 1952 by Pellegrini and Cudahy.

E. P. Dutton and Co., Inc. for passages from Everyman's Library Edition of *The Autobiography of Richard Baxter* and the *Life of William Cavendish, Duke of Newcastle*.

The Royal Historical Society for extracts from their transactions and publications of the Camden Society.

The compiler wishes to thank the authorities of the Institute of Historical Research for the use of their library, T. Lyon, Esq., for his help in Eton College Library, and W. A. Barker, Esq., for help in reading proofs.

does not disappear quickly but lasts a long time, in fact nearly the whole year round. The citizens, therefore, in order to remove this mud and filth from their boots, are accustomed to spread fresh rushes on the floors of all houses, on which they clean the soles of their shoes when they come in. . . .

Londoners have such fierce tempers and dispositions that they not only despise the way in which Italians live, but actually pursue them with uncontrolled hatred, and whereas at Bruges foreigners are hospitably received and complimented and treated with consideration by everyone, here the Englishmen use them with the utmost contempt and arrogance, and make them the object of insults. At Bruges we could do as we liked by day as well as by night. But here they look askance at us by day, and at night they sometimes drive us off with kicks and blows of the truncheon. . . .

They eat very frequently, at times more than is suitable, and are particularly fond of young swans, rabbits, deer and sea birds. They often eat mutton and beef, which is generally considered to be better here than anywhere else in the world. This is due to the excellence of their pastures. They have all kinds of fish in plenty and great quantities of oysters which come from the sea-shore. The majority, not to say everyone, drink that beverage[1] I have spoken of before, and prepare it in various ways. For wine is very expensive, as the vine does not grow in the island ; nor does the olive, and the products of both are imported from France and Spain. . . .

They have several harsh laws and customs, one of which, still in force to-day, we would consider the most severe of all. This lays down that, at death, a man must leave all his property to his wife, completely excluding the children, for whom they show no affection, lavishing all their love on their wives. And consequently, since the wives have the same dislike for their children, they choose in the end a husband from among the servants and ignore the children. This custom, apart from being contrary to nature, may also be objected to as impious and profane.

[1] beer

ENGLAND IN THE SIXTEENTH CENTURY

(1) *Source* : Andreas Franciscus. *Itinerarium Britanniae*, a Latin MS. translated into English and published at Barcelona in 1953 by C. V. Malfatti. Franciscus visited England in 1497.

Further Reading : Leland (1506–1552), *Itinerary*. *A Relation, or True Account, of the Island of England*, by an unknown Italian who visited England about 1500. Printed for the Camden Society, 1847.

[London] is defended by handsome walls on the northern side, where they have recently been rebuilt. Within these stands a very strongly defended castle on the banks of the river, where the King of England and his Queen sometimes have their residence. There are also other great buildings, and especially a beautiful and convenient bridge over the Thames, of many marble arches, which has on it many shops built of stone and mansions and even a church of considerable size. Nowhere have I seen a finer or more richly built bridge.

Throughout the town are to be seen many workshops of craftsmen in all sorts of mechanical arts, to such an extent that there is hardly a street which is not graced by some shop or the like, which can also be observed by everyone at Milan. This makes the town exceedingly well-stocked and prosperous, as well as having the immediate effect of adding to its splendour. The working in wrought silver, tin or white lead is very expert here, and perhaps the finest I have ever seen. There are also very many mansions, which do not, however, seem very large from the outside, but inside they contain a great number of rooms and garrets and are quite considerable. Six inch oak beams are inserted in the walls the same distance apart as their own breadth, and walls built in this way turn out to be of the same material as the houses I described at Maastricht.

All the streets are so badly paved that they get wet at the slightest quantity of water, and this happens very frequently owing to the large number of cattle carrying water, as well as on account of the rain, of which there is a great deal in this island. Then a vast amount of evil-smelling mud is formed, which

B

(2) *Source* : *Ritratti del Regno de Inghilterra*,by an unknown Italian, from the MS. in the Library of Monasterio de San Lorenzo El Real del Escorial (X–III–8 Fol. 241–266) published at Barcelona in 1953 by C. V. Malfatti. This Italian visited England in 1553.

Andreas Franciscus misunderstood the legal position about property, which is more accurately set out by this other, unknown Italian who visited England in 1553.

The women of this country have usually little dowry, but, in spite of this, there are many examples of families that have grown rich through women, such as the House of Arundel and several more. This is due to the fact that there exists a law which binds by precedent a third of the husband's estate as soon as he is married ; this part, if the husband dies, the widow has the use of during her lifetime. On her death it is inherited by her eldest son, if there are children ; if not, she is the rightful owner of her part of the estate and can dispose of it as she likes. . . .

On occasions, when the King wishes to enrich one of his servants, and learns that a lady has become a widow and wealthy, it is his custom to give the man a letter for the widow, in which he orders the widow to take him for her husband. If she does not agree to it, the man is entitled, as recently happened, to share the widow's income and enjoy it for life, on the claim that the King intended to make him her companion in the enjoyment of it. The result of this is that many ladies, when they become widows, not wishing to marry at the King's pleasure, immediately after their husband's death, marry again, often one of their servants, as was done lately by the Duchess of Somerset.

KING HENRY VII

Henry Tudor (1457–1509), was the son of Edmund Tudor, Earl of Richmond, and Margaret Beaufort, great-granddaughter of John of Gaunt. He defeated and killed Richard III at the battle of Bosworth Field, 1485, became King of England and reigned until 1509, founding the Tudor dynasty. He married Elizabeth of York, thus uniting the two Houses of York and Lancaster.

(1) *Source* : *A Relation or Rather True Account of the Island of England,* translated from the Italian of an unknown writer and printed by the Camden Society, 1847. Probably the work of some noble Venetian who accompanied the Ambassador to the English Court.

The title of *His Majesty* was never used by English kings until Henry VIII adopted it to put himself on an equality with the Emperor Charles V.

Further Reading : Bacon, *Life of Henry VII.* Morris, *The Tudors.*

From the time of William the Conqueror to the present, no king has reigned more peaceably than he has, his great prudence causing him to be universally feared ; and, though frugal to excess in his own person, he does not change any of the ancient usages of England at his court, keeping a sumptuous table, as I had the opportunity of witnessing twice that your Magnificence dined there, when I judged that there might be from 600 to 700 persons at dinner. And his people say that his Majesty spends upon his table £14,000 sterling annually, which is equal to 70,000 crowns. And it is possible that his own personal expenses, those of the queen and of his children, and the military escorts who compose his guard, and are from 150 to 200 in number, besides the many civilities that he pays to foreigners, may amount to £20,000 sterling, as it is said they do. And, although this appears a large sum, it forms a very small item in the revenue of the crown.

(2) *Source* : Extract from a letter from Ayala, the Spanish Ambassador, to the Spanish King and Queen, Ferdinand and Isabella : Spanish Calendar, i, 177. Written Wednesday, July 25th, 1498.

His crown is, nevertheless, undisputed and his government is strong in all respects. He is disliked, but the Queen is beloved, because she is powerless. They love the Prince [*Arthur*] as much as themselves, because he is the grandchild of his grandfather [*Edward IV*]. Those who know him love him also for his own virtues. The King looks old for his years, but young for the sorrowful life he has led. One of the reasons why he leads a good life is that he has been brought up abroad. He would like to govern England in the French fashion, but he can not. He is subject to his Council, but has already shaken off some, and got rid of some part of this subjection. Those who have received the greatest favours from him are the most discontented. He knows all that. The King has the greatest desire to employ foreigners in his service. He can not do so, for the envy of the English is diabolical and, I think, without equal. He likes to be much spoken of and to be highly appreciated by the whole world. He fails in this because he is not a great man. Although he professes many virtues, his love of money is too great. He spends all the time he is not in public or in his Council, in writing the accounts of his expenses with his own hand.

ARCHBISHOP MORTON

John Morton (?1420–1500) Archbishop of Canterbury and Cardinal, was famous as the alleged inventor of ' Morton's Fork ', although in fact at the Council meetings he usually tried to moderate the King's desire for money. He was probably the real author of the Latin version of the *History of Richard III*, generally attributed to Sir Thomas More, whose intimate friend he was and who probably translated the History into the English version. A less favourable picture is drawn in *The Daughter of Time*, by Josephine Tey.

Source : More, *Utopia*, Book I.

' I pray you, Sir ' (quoth I), ' have you been in our country? ' ' Yea forsooth ' (quoth he), ' and there I tarried for the space of four or five months together, not long after the insurrection, that the western English men made against their king ; which by their own miserable and pitiful slaughter was suppressed and ended. In the mean season I was much bound and beholden to the right reverend father John Morton, Archbishop, and Cardinal of Canterbury, and at that time also Lord Chancellor of England ; a man, master Peter (for master More knoweth already that I will say), not more honourable for his authority than for his prudence and virtue. He was of a mean stature, and though stricken in age yet bare he his body upright. In his face did shine such an amiable reverence, as was pleasant to behold. Gentle in communication, yet earnest and sage. He had great delight many times with rough speech to his suitors to prove, but without harm, what prompt wit and what bold spirit were in every man. In the which, as in a virtue much agreeing with his nature, so that therewith were not joined impudency, he took great delectation ; and the same person, as apt and meet to have an administration in the weal public, he did lovingly embrace. In his speech he was fine, eloquent and pithy. In the law he had profound knowledge ; in wit he was incomparable ; and in memory wonderful excellent. These qualities, which in him were by nature singular, he by learning and use had made perfect.

The King put much trust in his counsel : the weal public also in a manner leaned unto him, when I was there. For even in the chief of his youth he was taken from school into the Court, and there passed all his time in much trouble and business, and was continually tumbled and tossed in the waves of divers misfortunes and adversities. And so by many and great dangers he learned the experience of the world, which so being learned can not easily be forgotten.

PERKIN WARBECK

Perkin Warbeck was the son of John Osbeck or De Werbecque, controller of Tournay. He was born in 1474 and was hanged in 1499. He went in 1491 to Ireland, where he found support from the Earls of Desmond and Kildare as a pretender to the English throne. He gave out that he was Richard, Duke of York, son of Edward IV, was accepted by Margaret, the Dowager Duchess of Burgundy as her nephew, was financed by the Emperor Maximilian, tried to land at Deal but was repulsed, and again at Waterford. He was welcomed by James IV of Scotland, and in 1497 he landed in Cornwall. The following letters cover his subsequent exploits.

(1) *Source* : A letter from Raimondo de Soncino, a member of the large and important Venetian colony in London, to the Duke of Milan, dated September 30th, 1497. *Milanese Cal.*, i. 327.

Further Reading : Gairdner, *The Story of Perkin Warbeck*, from the original documents appended to his *Richard III*.

On the 19th inst., by Vadino Gambarana of Saona, I advised your Excellency of the coming of Perkin to this realm and what was the general opinion about it ; and on the 25th by way of the Genoese at Bruges, I sent word that Perkin had fled. Now with the arrival of the Venetian packet I will send a detailed account of what has taken place according to the relation of Messer Fra Zoan Antonio de Carbonariis of Milan, who was actually present in the city of Exeter.

On the 6th of this month Perkin landed in Cornwall at a port called Mount St. Michael with three small ships and about three hundred persons of various nationalities, who had followed him for some time before. As he had so few with him, it is thought that the Cornishmen must have invited him. In fact eight thousand peasants were forthwith in arms with him, although ill disciplined and without any gentlemen, who form the governing class of England.

They proclaimed Perkin as King Richard, and they paid for the victuals with which the commune provided them, as they had done when the Cornishmen were routed at London. They marched towards his Majesty, who did not hear of this movement until the 10th. . . .

Without waiting the royal command, the Earl of Devon, a lord of the County, opposed these people with about 1,500 men, but owing to the multitude of the enemy he withdrew to the city of Exeter. Perkin arrived at that place at the 22nd hour of the 17th of the month, and being refused admission, he began the attack on two of the gates. He burned one, but the Earl drove him off with stones, so that at the second hour on the following day Perkin asked for a truce for six hours. This was granted on the understanding that no one of Exeter should be allowed to follow him. The moment the truce was made, Perkin departed and went to a village called Minet, ten miles from Exeter, where he passed the night. On the 19th he came to another good village called Taunton, twenty-four miles from Exeter, and stayed there until the 21st. Among other things he published certain apostolic bulls affirming that he was the son of King Edward and that he meant to coin money and give money to all.

In the meantime his Majesty had sent the Lord Chamberlain against him with a good number of men, and announced that he would pardon all who laid down their arms. Accordingly the numbers with Perkin constantly lessened. He began to declare that he had a close understanding with some lords of the realm. As the bridges on the straight road were cut, he proposed to turn somewhat to the right and take another way. Subsequently at the fourth hour of the night, he silently departed from the camp with some ten thousand persons and at dawn the next morning the unfortunate Cornishmen discovered their plight and took to flight, to such an extent that by the third hour of the day not one was left in Taunton. . . .

(2) *Source*: Raimondo de Soncino to the Duke of Milan, dated October 21st, 1497. *Milanese Cal.* i, 329.

I will also relate what was told me by the royal herald Richmond, who is a man of wit and discretion. When Perkin fled from Taunton, in the company of John Aeron [*Heron*], sometime a merchant of London, and two other English gentlemen, he came to an abbey called Diodle [*Beaulieu*]. . . . The abbot of this happened to know the said John and the two gentlemen, and sent word to his Majesty about them, feeling sure that the youth

must be with them, as indeed he was. Some of the Royal Council
sent thither, and came to the following arrangement with John
and his fellows, to wit, that John should go to his Majesty and
either bring back a pardon for himself and his companions, or
should be put back into sanctuary, while in the meantime the
two companions should stay behind and guard the youth, so
that he should not escape. . . .

John, who swore to the King that he had never known
Perkin except as Richard II [*sic*] son of King Edward, returned
with the offer of a pardon to the young man if he would go to
the King's presence. The youth agreed to go. . . . He tells me
that the young man is not handsome, indeed his left eye rather
lacks lustre, but he is intelligent and well spoken.

The young man was brought into the royal presence, where
many nobles of the realm were assembled, some of whom had
been companions of Richard, Duke of York. He kneeled down
and asked for mercy. The King bade him rise and then spoke as
follows : We have heard that you call yourself Richard, Son of
King Edward. In this place are some who were companions of
that lord, look and see if you recognise them. The young man
answered that he knew none of them, he was not Richard, he
had never come to England except that once, and he had been
induced by the English and Irish to commit this fraud and to
learn English. For quite two years he had longed to escape from
these troubles, but Fortune had not allowed him.

Richmond was not present at this interview, at which there
were none besides princes, but I believe it all, because he is a
wise man, and because he shewed me a sheet, written in French,
signed in a different hand, thus ' Per Pero Osbeck ', which he
says is Perkin's hand. . . .

I asked Richmond if Perkin would escape with his life. He
told me that he would, but it was necessary to guard him well,
in order that the men of Cornwall may not murder him, as they
are incensed since they have learned from the King that they have
been worshipping a low born foreigner as their sovereign. . . .

(3) *Source* : Raimondo de Soncino to the Duke of Milan, dated
December 6th, 1497. *Milanese Cal.* 1, 335.

Perkin has been made a spectacle for everybody and every day he is led through London, in order that everyone may perceive his past error. In my opinion he bears his fortune bravely.

(4) *Source* : Agostino de Spinula, Milanese agent in England, to the Duke of Milan, *Milanese Cal.* i, 348.

There is little fresh to advise except that on the 12th inst. (*sic.*: *9th correct*) at midnight Perichino Oxbeke, when sleeping between two warders in the wardrobe of the King's palace at Westminster, escaped through a window, but was found on the following day in the Carthusian monastery of Sheen, seven miles from that place. He was brought here, and after receiving much contumely, he remains in the Tower of London, under better guard.

(5) *Source* : de Puebla, Spanish ambassador in London, to Ferdinand and Isabella of Spain. *Spanish Cal.* i, 185.

With respect to the observations of your Hignesses on Perkin, there is nothing to be said, except that he is kept with the greatest care in a tower, where he sees neither sun nor moon. The Bishop of Cambrai, ambassador of the Archduke, wished to see Perkin, because he had formerly transacted business with him. The King, therefore, sent a few days ago for Perkin, and asked him in my presence why he had deceived the Archduke and the whole country. Perkin answered as he had done before, and solemnly swore to God that the Duchess, Madame Margaret, knew as well as himself that he was not the son of King Edward. . . . I saw how much altered Perkin was. He is so much changed that I, and all other persons here, believe his life will be short. He must pay for what he has done.

(6) *Source* : John Pullan to Sir Robert Plumpton (1453–1523): *The Plumpton Correspondence*, ed. for the Camden Society by Thomas Stapleton, 1838–9. p. 141. Spelling modernisned. ' From Lincoln's Inn at London, this xxi day of November.'

Sir, so it was that Parkin Warbek and other three were arraigned, on Saturday next before the making hereof, in the Whitehall at Westminster, for their offences, afore Sir John Sygly, knight marshall, and Sir John Trobilfeild ; and there they were all attainted, and judgement given that they should be drawn on hurdles from the Tower throughout London to the Tyburn, and there to be hanged, and cut down quick [*alive*] and their bowells to be taken out and burned, their heads to be struck off, and quartered, their heads and quarters to be disposed of at the King's pleasure.

(7) *Source* : Kingsford's *Chronicles*, p. 227. Saturday, November 1499. Spelling modernised.

And upon the Saturday following next, being St. Clement's day, was drawn from the Tower unto Tyburn Perkyn or Peter Warbek, and one John a Water, sometime Mayor of Cork, as before is said, at which place of execution was ordained a small scaffold, whereupon the said Perkyn standing shewed to the people there in great multitude being present, that he was a stranger born according unto his former confession. . . . After which confession he took his death meekly, and was there upon the gallows hanged, and with him the said John a Water. And when they were dead, stricken down and their heads stricken off ; and after, their bodies brought to the friary Augustinian, and there buried, and their heads set after upon London Bridge.

THE MEETING OF HENRY VII AND PHILIP, KING OF CASTILE

SATURDAY, JANUARY 17TH, 1506

In January 1506, Philip of Burgundy, son of the Hapsburg ruler and Holy Roman Emperor, Maximilian I, with his wife Joanna, the daughter of Ferdinand and Isabella of Spain, on the death of her mother set out from the Netherlands to take over their new kingdom of Castile. They were shipwrecked and forced to land in Dorsetshire. Henry VII invited them to Windsor, and there he entertained them and made Philip a Knight of the Garter, but he also compelled him to sign the *Intercursus Malus*, a trade agreement which earned its name from the fact that the clauses were so greatly in favour of the English merchant at the expense of the Fleming.

Source : A letter from William Makefyrr to Darcy and Alington, dated January 17th, 1506, taken from the *Paston Letters*, vol. iii, letter 953. Spelling has been modernised.

To the right worshipful Master Roger Darcy and Master Giles Alington being at the George, in Lombard Street, be this delivered in haste.

Right worshipful masters, I recommend me unto you, certifying you that the King's Grace and the King of Castile met this day at three of the clock, upon Cleworth Green, two miles out of Windsor, and there the King received him in the goodliest manner that ever I saw, and each of them embraced other in arms.

To show you the King's apparel of England, thus it was :— his horse of bay, trapped with needle work ; a gown of purple velvet, a chain with a George of diamonds, and a hood of purple velvet, which he put not off at the meeting of the said King of Castile ; his hat and his bonnet he avaled,[1] and the King of Castile in like case. And the King of Castile rode upon a sorrel hobby,[2] which the King gave unto him ; his apparel was all black, a gown of black velvet, a black hood, a black hat, and his horse harness of black velvet.

To show you of the King's company, my Lord Harry of Stafford rode in a gown of cloth of tissue, tucked, furred with sables, a hat of goldsmith work, and full of stones, diamonds, and rubies, riding upon a sorrel courser barded[3] with a bard of goldsmith's work, with roses and dragons red.

And my Lord Marquis,[4] riding upon a bald[5] sorrel horse, with a deep trapper[6] full of long tassels of gold of Venice, and upon the crupper of his horse a white feather, with a coat upon his back, the body goldsmith's work, the sleeves of crimson velvet, with letters of gold.

My Lord of Kent, upon a sorrel horse, bald, the harness of Venice gold, with a deep fringe of half zerd[7] of length. My Lord of Kent's coat was one bar of cloth of gold, another of crimson velvet, purled with a demi-manche[8] cut off by the elbow. These be the lords that bare the bruit.[9]

[1] doffed. [2] horse. [3] caparisoned. [4] Thomas Grey, Marquis of Dorset.
[5] with head unadorned. [6] cloth. [7] yard. [8] embroidered at the edge and with a short sleeve. [9] outshone the others.

Sir Hugh Vaughan upon a bay horse trapped with crimson velvet full of gilt bells, a gown of black velvet, and a chain of gold, baldricwise,[1] worth five hundred pounds. . . .

Of the King of Castile's party, the Lord Chamberlain chief, I cannot tell his name as yet ; his apparel was sad, and so was all the residue of his company with cloaks of sad tawny black, guarded, some with sarsenet and some with velvet, not passing a dozen in number. It is said there is many behind, which comes with the Queen of Castile, which shall come upon Tuesday.

When the King rode forth to Windsor Castle, the King rode upon the right hand of the King of Castile, howbeit the King's Grace offered him to take him upon the right hand, the which he refused. And at the lighting the King of Castile was off his horse a good space or our King was alight ; and then the King's Grace offered to take him by the arm, the which he would not, but took the King by the arm, and so went to the King of Castile's chamber, which is the richliest hanged that ever I saw ; seven chambers together hanged with cloth of Arras wrought with gold as thick as could be ; and as for three beds of estate, no king christened can shew such three.

This is as far as I can show you of this day, and when I can know more, ye shall have knowledge.

From Windsor this Saturday, at five of the clock,

By yours,

WILLIAM MAKEFYRR.

[1] worn like a sash across the shoulder.

KING HENRY VIII

Source : The following descriptions of Henry VIII were written by the Venetian ambassadors to the Seignory at Venice. The first two were sent by the ambassador Pasqualigo, the third by Giustinian, and are taken from Giustinian's *Despatches*, i, 86 and ii, 312. cf. Brewer, *The Reign of Henry VIII*, i, 8–10.

(1) His Majesty is the handsomest potentate I ever set eyes on : above the usual height, with an extremely fine calf to his leg ; his complexion very fair and bright, with auburn hair combed straight and short in the French fashion, and a round face, so very beautiful that it would become a pretty woman, his throat being rather long and thick.

(2) He wore a cap of crimson velvet, in the French fashion, and the brim was looped up all round with lacets and gold enamelled tags. His doublet was in the Swiss fashion, striped alternately with white and crimson satin, and his hose were scarlet, and all slashed from the knee upwards. Very close round his neck he had a gold collar, from which there hung a rough cut diamond, the size of the largest walnut I ever saw, and to this was suspended a most beautiful and very large round pearl. His mantle was of purple velvet lined with white satin, the sleeves open, with a train more than four Venetian yards long. This mantle was girt in front like a gown, with a thick gold cord, from which there hung large golden acorns like those suspended from a cardinal's hat ; over this mantle was a very handsome gold collar, with a pendant St. George entirely of diamonds. Beneath the mantle he wore a pouch of cloth of gold, which covered a dagger ; and his fingers were one mass of jewelled rings.

(3) His Majesty is twenty-nine years old, and extremely handsome. Nature could not have done more for him. He is much handsomer than any other sovereign in Christendom ; a great deal handsomer than the King of France ; very fair, and his whole frame admirably proportioned. On hearing that Francis I wore a beard, he allowed his own to grow ; and as it

is reddish, he has now got a beard that looks like gold. He is very accomplished; a good musician; composes well; is a most capital horseman; a fine jouster; speaks good French, Latin, and Spanish; is very religious; hears three masses daily when he hunts, and sometimes five on other days. He hears the Office every day in the Queen's Chamber; that is to say, vesper and compline. He is very fond of hunting, and never takes his diversion without tiring eight or ten horses, which he causes to be stationed beforehand along the line of country he means to take; and when one is tired he mounts another, and before he gets home they are all exhausted. He is extremely fond of tennis, at which game it is the prettiest thing in the world to see him play, his fair skin glowing through a shirt of the finest texture.

DEFENDER OF THE FAITH

Friday, Oct. 11th, 1521

Henry VIII had been carefully educated in his youth and he was well versed both in Latin and in theology. In 1520 Martin Luther published his *De Captivitate Babylonica*, in which he made a violent attack on the accepted Sacraments of the Catholic church. Tunstal, later Bishop of Durham, wrote, ' I pray God keep that book out of England '. But the book found its way here, and it is that book which Henry is reading in the following letter. Henry wrote an answer to refute Luther, and it was published in 1521 under the title *Assertio Septem Sacramentorum*. Perhaps the literary style was polished by other hands, but the substance of the book was certainly written by Henry. On October 2nd it was presented formally to Pope Leo X. On October 11th Leo published the Bull by which he conferred on the English King the title of *Fidei Defensor, Defender of the Faith*. Richard Pace (1482?–1536), was made Henry's secretary in 1515. 1519 he became Dean of St. Paul's.

Source : Ellis, *Original Letters*, 2nd series, Letter LXXXI, printed from the original letter in the Cotton MSS. Vitell. B. iv fol. 96.

the which he most commonly smelt unto, passing amongst the
press, or else when he was pestered with many suitors. There
was also borne before him first, the great seal of England, and
then his cardinal's hat, by a nobleman or some worthy gentleman,
right solemnly, bareheaded. And as soon as he was entered into
his chamber of presence, where there was attending his coming
to await upon him to Westminster Hall, as well noblemen and
other worthy gentlemen, as noblemen and gentlemen of his own
family ; thus passing forth with two great crosses of silver borne
before him ; with also two great pillars of silver, and his pur-
suivant at arms with a great mace of silver gilt. Then his gentlemen ushers cried, and said : ' On, my lords and masters, on
before ; make way for my Lord's Grace '. Thus passed he down
from his chamber through the hall ; and when he came to the
hall door, there was attendant for him his mule, trapped all
together in crimson velvet, and gilt stirrups. When he was
mounted, with his cross bearers, and pillar bearers, also upon
great horses trapped with fine scarlet. Then marched he forward,
with his train and furniture in manner as I have declared, having
about him four footmen, with gilt pollaxes in their hands ;
and thus he went until he came to Westminster Hall door. And
there alighted, and went after this manner, up through the hall
into the chancery ; howbeit he would most commonly stay
awhile at a bar, made for him, a little beneath the chancery on the
right hand, and there commune sometime with the judges, and
sometime with other persons. And that done he would repair
into the chancery, sitting there till eleven of the clock, hearing
suitors, and determining of divers matters. And from thence,
he would divers times go into the star chamber, as occasion did
serve ; where he spared neither high nor low, but judged every
estate according to their merits and deserts. . . . [see next extract.]

Thus in great honour, triumph, and glory, he reigned a long
season, ruling all things within this realm, appertaining unto the
king, by his wisdom, and also all other weighty matters of foreign
regions, with which the king of this realm had any occasion to
intermeddle. All ambassadors of foreign potentates were always
dispatched by his discretion, to whom they had always access

for their dispatch. His house was also always resorted and furnished with noblemen, gentlemen, and other persons, with going and coming in and out, feasting and banqueting all ambassadors diverse times, and other strangers right nobly. . .

CARDINAL WOLSEY IN STAR CHAMBER

Sir Hugh Vaughan was Governor of Jersey from 1502 to 1532. A young Welshman of no birth, originally a tailor by trade, handsome, brave and high-spirited, he attracted the attention of Henry Tudor, Earl of Richmond. He became a gentleman usher to Henry when Henry became King; he was knighted in 1503 when Henry VIII was made Prince of Wales. He had caused a sensation by killing his opponent in a tournament at Richmond. He was a ruthless, unscrupulous and dishonest Governor of Jersey and quarrelled with everybody, including the Bailiff, Helier de Carteret. Carteret came over to England to try to get justice in Star Chamber. The machinations of Vaughan with Wolsey resulted in Carteret's being kept waiting in London for nearly four years, during which time he lost all his official income and the revenues of his manor, so that he was by 1528 destitute. He determined to brave Wolsey in Star Chamber. The following extract shows how he did it, and also the hatred felt for the Cardinal by all the nobility of England.

Source : Chroniques des Iles de Jersey, Guernesey, Auregny et Serk, by George S. Syvret, pub. by Thomas James Manger, Guernesey, 1832, chapter XIX. (B.M. 10388 dd 2). The original *Chronicle* is very vague in its dates : probably these events took place in the first half of 1528. The account is almost certainly Carteret's own account.

When the Bailiff perceived that the trick and cunning of the Cardinal were as great as those of Sir Hugh Vaughan, and that Sir Hugh Vaughan was always feeding the Cardinal with more and more gifts and bribes, he came to the conclusion that in the face of such methods he would never reach the end of his suit. He made up his mind, as the saying goes, to risk all or win all, seeing that he had been kept waiting the whole of the Term

without his case being expedited or despatched, and neither he
nor his counsel had been able to secure a hearing. It was the
last day of the Term, and if by then his case was not settled, he
would have to wait for another Term, a thing which he could not
well do, since his money was all but exhausted by the long delay.
When, therefore, his barrister and solicitor began to open his
case, and the Cardinal, as was his habit, refused to give them a
hearing but began to open another case, the Bailiff plucked up
courage to speak himself to the Cardinal. The whole council
was sitting in plenary session in the Star Chamber. The Bailiff,
commending himself to God and praying for His help, began to
speak at the top of his voice so that everybody should hear him.
' Sir, I beg and beseech you for justice.' The Cardinal heard him
perfectly well, but all the time, as his habit was, he turned a deaf
ear, pretending not to hear him at all. He gave orders for another
case to be dealt with and he had already begun to open it when the
Bailiff began again to shout as loudly as he could, ' Sir, I require
justice at your hands, or at any rate some show of justice '. The
Cardinal could no longer pretend to be deaf in the presence of all
the Lords, especially also since the Bailiff was shouting so loudly
and calling for ' Justice, justice '. The Cardinal said to him. 'You
want justice : if you had justice and got what you deserve, you
would be punished as a man who, unlike everybody else, brings
an outrageous action and who causes much trouble in his own
country '. The Bailiff plucked up his courage and said, ' Sir, if I
were such as you say I am, I should certainly deserve to be
punished, but you wrong me, Sir, in accusing me of something
which you can not make good.' Then the Cardinal rose up in a
great fury and said to the Lords of the Council who were present,
' Have you ever seen such a perverse fellow? He must lord
it in word and deed in his own country, seeing how ill-mannered
he is here.'

Thereupon the Cardinal called for the keeper of the Fleet,
which is a very expensive prison to which are sent those gentlemen who offend against any of the Council. A meal there usually
costs an angel a time. When they saw that the Cardinal wanted
to send the Bailiff there, everybody said that the Bailiff must keep

his mouth shut or he was like to be ruined. But the Bailiff boldly answered, ' Sir, I prefer to be imprisoned in the Fleet rather than to lose my life, but before you send me there, I beg and beseech you, Sir, to explain to me why you want to send me there, whether it is because I am asking for justice or because I want to vindicate myself, as is my right to do. If it is for anything else, Sir, I beg you to divulge it here and now in the presence of all. Sir, you have kept me waiting in this city for three years and more by your express command and all this time I have never been given a hearing. You have sequestrated all my livelihood, all my money is eaten up, and I am a poor gentleman with wife and children dependent on me, and I can not help them in any way. You see, then, Sir, whether I have cause to speak out or not.' Everybody was astounded to hear the Bailiff speak so boldly. Then the Cardinal replied, ' I told you that you are an outrageous fellow, unworthy of holding any office or Government post in the island.' The Bailiff answered, ' Sir, you can not prove that.' The Cardinal said he would demonstrate this under the Seal of the island. The Bailiff said, ' Sir, you can not demonstrate that, because I have the custody of the Seal of the island myself, and therefore, Sir, I demand justice from you.' The Cardinal, not knowing what to answer, broke up the Court in a great rage, saying, ' You'll get nothing more for the present,' and so he went off, and all the Lords of the Council, who were much put out by the unfairness with which the Cardinal treated the Bailiff.

Afterwards the Duke of Norfolk sent to fetch the Bailiff, and clapping him on the shoulder said to him, ' I am delighted with you : you are a proper sort of man : don't you be afraid that you may be short of money. If you have any business on hand and are in need of £500 sterling, you shall have the money from me. I shall never cease to like you, because you have behaved and spoken like a true and proper man.' Mr. Compton also spoke to him and assured him that he would go bail for £200, if he had need of it. These two personages had an incredible hatred for the Cardinal. Therefore the Bailiff waited until the Cardinal had dined and then met him and accompanied him to his lodgings. ' Sir,' he said, ' I ask for justice at your hands.' The Cardinal answered him quite gently and politely.[1] ' You will have to wait, but I promise you that on the first day of next Term I will deal with your suit, for indeed I think that you have been badly treated.' The Bailiff said to him, ' Sir, the remedy lies with you.' And thus they parted from each other until the next Term.

QUEEN ANNE BOLEYN. HER CORONATION

WHIT-SUNDAY, JUNE 1ST, 1533

Henry VIII's first wife, Katharine of Aragon, failed to provide a male heir to the throne. Henry persuaded himself that this was divine judgement on an illegal marriage. He therefore sought an annulment from the Pope. He had also fallen in love with Anne Boleyn. When he found that the annulment would not be completed in time to make Anne's child legitimate, on St. Paul's Day, January 25th, 1533, he secretly married Anne. On May 23rd Archbishop Cranmer pronounced Henry's marriage with Katharine null and void. On Whit-Sunday, June 1st, Anne was crowned Queen.

Source : Cranmer's own account contained in a letter from him to Mr. Hawkyns, English Ambassador at the court of the Emperor, Charles V. Ellis, *Original Letters* 1st series, vol. ii, pp. 33 sqq. Printed here from the Harleian MSS., B.M. 6148. Spelling modernized.

Further Reading : Froude, *History of England*, vols. i and ii.

Croydon, June 17th, 1533.

. . . The Thursday next before the Feast of Pentecost, the King and the Queen being at Greenwich, all the Crafts of London thereunto well appointed, in several barges decked after the most gorgeous and sumptuous manner, with divers pageants thereunto belonging, repaired and waited all together upon the Mayor of London ; and so, well furnished, came all unto Greenwich, where they tarried and waited for the Queen's coming to her

---

[1] I have inserted the word *politely* to mark the Cardinal's use for the first time of the French word *vous* in place of the insulting *tu* which he had used all the time in Court.

barge; which so done, they brought her unto the Tower, trumpets, shawms, and other divers instruments playing and making great melody, which, as is reported, was as comely done as never was like in any time nigh to our remembrance. And so her Grace came to the Tower on Thursday at night, about five of the clock, where also was such a peal of guns as hath not been heard the like a great while before. And the same night, and Friday all day, the King and Queen tarried there; and on Friday at night the King's Grace made eighteen knights of the Bath, whose creation was not only so strange to hear of, as also their garments stranger to behold or look upon; which said knights, the next day, which was Saturday, rode before the Queen's Grace throughout the City of London towards Westminster Palace, over and besides the most part of the nobles of the realm, which like accompanied her Grace throughout the said city; she sitting in her hair [*i.e. her hair flowing down*], upon a horse litter, richly apparelled, and four knights of the Five Ports bearing a canopy over her head. And after her came four rich chariots, one of them empty, and three other furnished with divers ancient old ladies; and after them came a great train of other ladies and gentlewomen; which said progress, from the beginning to the ending, extended half a mile in length by estimation or thereabout. To whom also, as she came along the City, were shewn many costly pageants, with divers other encomiums spoken of children to her; wine also running at certain conduits plenteously. And so proceeding throughout the streets, passed further unto Westminster Hall, where was a certain banquet prepared for her, which done, she was conveyed out of the back side of the Palace into a barge, and so unto York Place, where the King's Grace was before her coming, for this you must ever presuppose that his Grace came always before her secretly in a barge as well from Greenwich to the Tower as from the Tower to York Place.

Now then on the Sunday was the Coronation, which also was of such a manner.

In the morning there assembled with me at Westminster Church the Bishop of York, the Bishop of London, the Bishop of Winchester, the Bishop of Lincoln, the Bishop of Bath, and the Bishop of St. Asaph, the Abbot of Westminster with ten or eleven more Abbots, which all revestred ourselves in our pontificalibus, and, so furnished, with our Crosses and Croziers, proceeded out of the Abbey in a procession into Westminster Hall, where we received the Queen apparelled in a robe of purple velvet, and all the ladies and gentlewomen in robes and gowns of scarlet according to the manner used beforetime in such business ; and so her Grace sustained of each side with two bishops, the Bishop of London and the Bishop of Winchester, came forth in procession unto the Church of Westminster, she in her hair, my Lord of Suffolk bearing before her the Crown, and two other Lords bearing also before her a sceptre and a white rod, and so entered up into the High Altar, where divers ceremonies used about her, I did set the Crown on her head, and then was sung *Te Deum* &c. And after that was sung a solemn Mass, all which while her Grace sat crowned upon a scaffold which was made between the High Altar and Choir in Westminster Church ; which Mass and ceremonies done and finished, all the assembly of noblemen brought her into Westminster Hall again, where was kept a great solemn feast all that day ; the good order thereof were too long to write at this time to you.

But now, Sir, you may not imagine that this Coronation was before her marriage, for she was married much about St. Paul's Day last, as the condition thereof doth well appear by reason she is now somewhat big with child. Notwithstanding it hath been reported throughout a great part of the realm that I married her[1]; which was plainly false, for I myself knew not thereof a fortnight after it was done. And many other things be reported of me, which be mere lies and tales. . . .

[1] Dr. Rowland Lee, later Bishop of Chester, married Henry and Anne.

QUEEN ANNE BOLEYN. ON THE DAY OF HER EXECUTION

FRIDAY, MAY 19TH, 1536

Within three months of her Coronation, Henry's affection for Anne had died. He had been attracted by Jane Seymour. On Jan. 7th, 1536, Katharine of Aragon died. Only one thing could have saved Anne—the birth of a son, but her son was stillborn. On May 2nd she was arrested and on the 19th she was executed on charges of adultery. The executioner was specially brought over from St. Omer. She spent the night before her execution in the same room in the Tower as she had used the night before her Coronation.

Source : A letter from Sir W. Kingston, Constable of the Tower, to Thomas Cromwell, May 19th, 1536. Printed by Ellis in *Original Letters*, Series I, vol. ii.

This morning she sent for me, that I might be with her at such time as she received the good Lord, to the intent I should hear her speak as touching her innocency alway to be clear. And in the writing of this she sent for me, and at my coming she said, ' Mr. Kingston, I hear I shall not die afore noon, and I am very sorry therefore, for I thought to be dead by this time and past my pain '. I told her it should be no pain, it was so little. And then she said, ' I heard say the executioner was very good, and I have a little neck ', and then put her hands about it, laughing heartily. I have seen many men and also women executed, and that they have been in great sorrow, and to my knowledge this lady has much joy in death. Sir, her almoner is continually with her, and had been since two o'clock after midnight.

PORTRAIT OF SIR THOMAS MORE
BY ERASMUS

Sir Thomas More (1478–1535) was Lord Chancellor in the reign of Henry VIII. Author of Utopia, he was executed on a charge of high treason, for refusing to take any oath which denied the supreme powers of the Pope. His great friend was Desiderius Erasmus, the Dutch scholar and one of the chief figures in the Renaissance in Northern Europe.

Source : A letter from Erasmus to Ulrich von Hutten, a German knight, dated Antwerp, 23 July 1519.

Further Reading : for Sir Thomas More, Chambers, *Life of Sir Thomas More*. For Erasmus, Huizinga, *Erasmus of Rotterdam*.

. . . To begin with that side of More of which you know nothing, in height and stature he is not tall, nor again noticeably short, but there is such symmetry in all his limbs as leaves nothing to be desired here. He has a fair skin, his complexion glowing rather than pale, though far from ruddy, but for a very faint rosiness shining through. His hair is of a darkish blond, or if you will, a lightish brown, his beard scanty, his eyes bluish grey, with flecks here and there. . . . His expression corresponds to his character, always shewing a pleasant and friendly gaiety, and rather set in a smiling look ; and, to speak honestly, better suited to merriment than to seriousness and solemnity, though far removed from silliness and buffoonery. His right shoulder seems a little higher than the left, particularly when he is walking : this is not natural to him but due to force of habit, like many of the little habits which we pick up. There is nothing to strike one in the rest of his body ; only his hands are somewhat clumsy but only when compared with the rest of his appearance. He has always from a boy been very careless of everything to do with personal adornment, to the point of not greatly caring for those things which according to Ovid's teaching should be the sole care of men. One can tell even now, from his appearance in maturity, how handsome he must have been as a young man ;

although when I first knew him he was not more than three and twenty years old, for he is now barely forty.

His health is not so much robust as satisfactory, but equal to all tasks becoming an honourable citizen, subject to no, or at least very few, diseases : there is every prospect of his living long, as he has a father of great age—but a wondrously fresh and green old age. I have never yet seen anyone less fastidious in his choice of food. Until he grew up he liked to drink water ; in this he took after his father. But so as to avoid irritating anyone over this, he would deceive his comrades by drinking from a pewter pot ale that was very nearly all water. Wine— the custom in England is to invite each other to drink from the same goblet—he would often sip with his lips, not to give the appearance of disliking it, and at the same time to accustom himself to common ways. He preferred beef, salt fish, and bread of the second quality, well risen, to the foods commonly regarded as delicacies : otherwise he was by no means averse from all sources of innocent pleasure, even to the appetite. He has always had a great liking for milk foods and fruit : he enjoys eating eggs. His voice is neither strong nor at all weak, but easily audible, by no means soft or melodious, but the voice of a clear speaker : for he seems to have no natural gift for vocal music, although he delights in every kind of music. His speech is wonderfully clear and distinct, with no trace of haste or hesitation.

He likes to dress simply, and does not wear silk or purple or gold chains, excepting where it would not be decent not to wear them. . . .

In social intercourse he is of so rare a courtesy and charm of manners that there is no man so melancholy that he does not gladden, no subject so forbidding that he does not dispel the tedium of it. From his boyhood he has loved joking, so that he might seem born for this, but in his jokes he has never descended to buffoonery, and has never loved the biting jest. . . .

In human relations he looks for pleasure in everything he comes across, even in the gravest matters. If he has to do with intelligent and educated men, he takes pleasure in their brilliance ; if with the ignorant and foolish, he enjoys their folly. He is not put out by perfect fools, and suits himself with marvellous dexterity to all men's feelings. For women generally, even for his wife, he has nothing but jests and merriment. . . .

He takes an especial pleasure in watching the appearance, characters and behaviour of various creatures; accordingly there is almost no kind of bird which he does not keep at his home, and various other animals not commonly found, such as apes, foxes, ferrets, weasels and their like. Added to this, he eagerly buys anything foreign or otherwise worth looking at which comes his way, and he has the whole house stocked with these objects, so that wherever the visitor looks there is something to detain him; and his own pleasure is renewed whenever he sees others enjoying these sights. . . .

He diligently cultivates true piety, while being remote from all superstitious observance. He has set hours in which he offers to God not the customary prayers but prayers from the heart. With his friends he talks of the life of the world to come so that one sees that he speaks sincerely and not without firm hope. Such is More even in the Court. And then there are those who think that Christians are to be found only in monasteries! . . .

THE DISSOLUTION OF THE MONASTERIES. GLASTONBURY

Wednesday, September 22nd, 1539

The logical conclusion of the Reformation, by which Henry VIII transferred the government of the Church into the hands of the laity, was to transfer to the same hands the property of the Church. This was accomplished by the Dissolution of the Monasteries. Cromwell sent round his agents on Visitations to the monasteries, who sent in to him reports on the state of the Houses which they visited. The following letter provides such a report.

Source : from the Tanner MSS. in the Bodleian Library, Oxford : printed by the Camden Society in Thomas Wright's *Suppression of the Monasteries*, 1843. Also to be found in Burnet's *History of the Reformation*, vol. iii, p. 160.

Further Reading : Baskerville, *English Monks*. Pickthorn, *Early Tudor Government*.

Please it your lordship to be advertised, that we came to Glastonbury on Friday last past, about ten of the clock in the forenoon; and for that the abbot was then at Sharpham, a place of his a mile and somewhat more from the abbey, we, without any delay, went into the same place, and there examined him in certain articles. And for that his answer was not then to our purpose, we advised him to call to his remembrance that which he had then forgotten, and so declare the truth, and then came with him the same day to the abbey, and there anew proceeded that night to search his study for letters and books ; and found in his study secretly laid, as well a written book of arguments against the divorce of the king's majesty and the lady dowager, which we take to be a great matter, as also divers pardons, copies of bulls, and the counterfeit life of Thomas Becket in print ; but we could not find any letter that was material. And so we proceeded again to his examination concerning the articles we received from your lordship, in the answers whereof, as we take it, shall appear his cankered and traitorous heart and mind against the king's majesty and his succession. And so with as fair words as we could, we have conveyed him from hence into the tower, being but a very weak man and sickly. And as yet we have neither discharged servant nor monk ; but now the abbot being gone, we will, with as much celerity as we may, proceed to the despatching of them. We have in money £300 and above ; but the certainty of plate and other stuff there as yet we know not, for we had not opportunity for the same, but shortly we intend—God willing—to proceed to the same ; whereof we shall ascertain your lordship as shortly as we may.

This is also to advertise your lordship, that we have found a fair chalice of gold, and divers other parcels of plate, which the abbot had hid secretly from all such commissioners as have been there in times past ; and as yet he knoweth not that we have found the same. It may please your lordship to advertise us of the king's pleasure by this bearer, to whom we shall deliver the custody and keeping of the house, with such stuff as we intend to leave there convenient to the king's use. We assure your lordship it is the goodliest house of that sort that we ever have seen. We would that your lordship did know it as we do ; then we doubt not but your lordship would judge it a house meet for the king's majesty and for no man else : which is to our great comfort ; and we trust verily that there shall never come any double hood within that house again.

Also this is to advertise your lordship, that there is never a one doctor within that house ; but there be three bachelors of divinity, which be but meanly learned, as we can perceive. And thus our Lord preserve your good lordship.

From Glastonbury, the 22nd day of September, 1539,

Yours to command,

RICHARD POLLARD,
THOMAS MOYLE
RICHARD LAYTON.

To the right honorable
and their singular good
lord, my lord Privy Seal,
this be delivered.

HOW THE LORD CROMWELL HELPED ARCHBISHOP CRANMER'S SECRETARY

When Henry VIII made his break with Rome, he wanted only two things : to be rid of the Pope as head of the Church, and to get for himself the Pope's power and wealth in this country. He in no way wished to alter the religious teachings of the Church. He was strongly opposed to the views of Luther, but other reformers wanted to go further than he did. Some of the Protestants began to attack ancient teaching, and to stop them, Henry had Six Articles passed by Parliament in 1539. There were to be heavy punishments for all those who would not accept them. Among these Protestants was the Archbishop Cranmer who set out in a book his views and his opposition to the Six Articles. Ralph Morice was his secretary and he had to make a fair copy of Cranmer's book to send to the King. In this passage Morice recounts an adventure which befell him and the fair copy of Cranmer's book.

Source: John Foxe, the Martyrologist, *The Ecclesiastical History*, containing the *Actes and Monuments, etc.*, 2nd edition, 1570 pp. 1355–6. Punctuation modernized.

This book was written in his Secretary's Chamber ; where in a by-chamber, lay the Archbishop's Almoner.

When this book was fair written, and while the Secretary was gone to deliver the same unto the Archbishop his Master, who was, as it chanced, ridden to Croydon, returning back to his chamber, he found his door shut, and the key carried away to London by the Almoner.

At this season also chanced the father of the said Secretary to come to the city ; by whose occasion it so fell out that he [*Morice*] must needs go to London. The book he could not lay in his chamber, neither durst he commit it to any other person to keep, being straitly charged, in any condition, by the Archbishop his Master, to be circumspect thereof : so he determined to go to his father, and to keep the Book about him.

And so, thrusting the Book under his girdle, he went over unto Westminster Bridge, with a sculler, where he entered into a wherry that went to London : wherein were four of the Guard, who meant to land at Paul's Wharf, and to pass by the King's

Highness who was then in his barge, with a great number of barges and boats about him, then baiting of bears in the water, over against the Bank.[1]

The aforesaid Yeomen of the Guard, when they came against the King's barge, they durst not pass by towards Paul's Wharf, lest they should be espied : and therefore entreated the Secretary to go with them to the Bearbaiting, and they would find the means, being of the Guard, to make room and see all the pastime.

The Secretary, perceiving no other remedy, assented thereto.

When the wherry came nigh the multitude of boats, they with the poleaxes got the wherry so far that, being encompassed with many other wherries and boats, there was no refuge if the bear should break loose and come upon them : as, in very deed, within one *Paternoster* while, the bear brake loose and came into the boat where the Yeomen of the Guard were and the said Secretary.

The Guard forsook the wherry, and went into another barge, one or two of them leaping short, and so fell into the water.

The bear and the dogs so shaked the wherry wherein the Secretary was, that the boat being full of water sank to the ground; and being, also, as it chanced, an ebbing tide, he sat there in the end of the wherry up to the middle in water. To whom came the bear and all the dogs. The bear, seeking as it were aid and succour of him, came back with his hinder parts upon him ; and so, rushing upon him, the Book was loosed from the Secretary's girdle, and so fell into the Thames out of his reach.

The flying of the people, after that the bear was loose, from one boat to another, was so cumbrous that divers persons were thrown into the Thames : the King commanding certain men, that could swim, to strip themselves naked, and to help to save them that were in danger.

This pastime so displeased the King, that he bade, 'Away, away with the bear! and let us all go hence!'

The Secretary, perceiving his Book to fleet away in the Thames, called to the Bearward to take up the Book.

---

[1] Bank Side in Southwark.

When the Bearward had the Book in his custody, being an arrant Papist, far from the religion of his Mistress (for he was the Lady Elizabeth's bearward, now the Queen's Majesty), ere that the Secretary could come to land, he had delivered the Book to a Priest of his own affinity in religion standing on the bank : who, reading the Book and perceiving that it was a manifest refutation of the *Six Articles*, made much ado ; and told the Bearward that whosoever claimed the Book should surely be hanged.

Anon, the Secretary came to the Bearward for his Book.

' What,' quoth the Bearward, ' dare you challenge this Book? Whose servant be you? '

' I am servant to one of the Council,' said the Secretary, ' and my Lord of Canterbury is my master.'

' Yea, marry,' quoth the Bearward, ' I thought as much. You be like, I trust, to be both hanged for this Book.'

' Well,' said he, ' it is not so evil as you take it : and, I warrant you, my Lord will avouch the book to the King's Majesty. But I pray you let me have my Book, and I will give you a crown[1] to drink.'

' If you will give me 500 crowns, you shall not have it,' quoth the Bearward. . . .

When that the Secretary saw the matter so extremely to be used against him, he then thought it expedient to . . . make the Lord Cromwell privy of the chance that happened.

So, on the next day, as the Lord Cromwell went to the Court, the Secretary declared the whole matter unto him, and how he had offered the Bearward 20s. for the finding thereof.

' Where is the fellow? ' quoth the Lord Cromwell.

' I suppose,' said the Secretary, ' that he is now in the Court, attending to deliver the book unto some of the Council.'

' Well,' said the Lord Cromwell, ' it maketh no matter. Go with me thither, and I shall get you your book again! '

When the Lord Cromwell came into the Hall of the Court, there stood the Bearward with the Book in his hand. . . . To whom the Lord Cromwell said, ' Come hither, fellow! What

---

[1] 6 shillings, or about £4 in present money.

D

Book hast thou there in thy hand?' and with that snatched the
Book out of his hand : and looking in the Book, said, ' I know
this hand well enough. This is your hand,' said he to the Secretary.

' But where hadst thou this Book?' quoth the Lord Cromwell
to the Bearward.

' This gentleman lost it two days ago in the Thames,' said the
Bearward.

' Dost thou know whose servant he is?' said the Lord
Cromwell.

' He saith,' quoth the Bearward, ' that he is my Lord of
Canterbury's servant.'

' Why then didst thou not deliver to him the Book when he
required it?' said the Lord Cromwell. ' Who made thee so bold
as to detain or withhold any Book or writing from a Councillor's
servant, especially being his Secretary? It is more meet for thee
to meddle with thy bears than with such writing : and were it
not for thy Mistress's sake, I would set thee fast by the feet, to
teach such malapert knaves to meddle with Councillors' matters.'
. . .

And with those words the Lord Cromwell went up into the
King's Chamber of Presence, and the Archbishop's Secretary with
him : where he found, in the Chamber, the Lord of Canterbury.
To whom he said, ' My Lord, I have here found good stuff for
you,' showing to him the paper book that he had in his hand,
' ready to bring both you, and this good fellow your man, to the
halter : namely,[1] if the knave Bearward, now in the Hall, might
have well compassed it.'

At these words the Archbishop smiled and said, ' He that
lost the Book is like to have the worst of the bargain : for,
besides that he was well washed in the Thames, he must write
the Book fair again.' . . .

' Surely, my Lord, it somewhat rejoiceth me,' quoth the Lord
Cromwell, ' that the varlet might have had of your man 20s.
for the Book : and now I have discharged the matter with never

[1] especially.

a penny; and shaken him well up for his overmuch malapertness.'

'I know the fellow well enough,' quoth the Archbishop, ' there is not a ranker Papist within this realm than he is ; most unworthy to be a servant unto so noble a Princess.'

THE DEBASEMENT OF THE COINAGE, 1540

The sixteenth century was a period of immense inflation. Between 1500 and 1540 prices rose by a half, and in the next twenty years were more than doubled, very largely owing to a huge increase in minted bullion. In England inflation was aggravated by the debasement in the coinage undertaken between 1544 and 1551 by Henry VIII and the Duke of Northumberland, although Northumberland did begin to stabilise the coinage in 1551. In the following extract Latimer uses the economic evil of the times as a kind of text for a sermon in which he goes on to deal with the debased currency of Christian behaviour.

Source : Master Hugh Latimer, *Seven Sermons before Edward VI.* Edited by E. Arber, English Reprints, 1869.

Further Reading : Elton, *England under the Tudors*, pp. 224–229.

8th March, 1549.

We have now a pretty little shilling, indeed a very pretty one. I have but one, I think, in my purse, and the last day I had put it away almost for an old groat, and so I trust some will take them. The fineness of the silver I can not see. But therein is printed a fine sentence : that is, *Timor Domini fons vitae vel sapientiae.* The fear of the Lord is the fountain of life or wisdom. I would God this sentence were always printed in the heart of the King in choosing his wife, and in all his officers.

ARCHBISHOP CRANMER

Thomas Cranmer (1489–1556) was the only servant of Henry VIII for whom the King had an unfailing affection and in whom he put unshakeable confidence, and against whom he refused to listen to any accusations, as the following extract illustrates. Ralph Morice (fl. 1523–1570) was Cranmer's secretary, and it was largely on Morice's information that Foxe relied for his narrative of Cranmer in his *Actes and Monuments*.

Source : Morice's *Anecdotes and Character of Archbishop Cranmer*, printed by the Camden Society, *Narratives of the Reformation*, vol. lxvii, 1860, from the MS. in the Library of Corpus Christi College, Cambridge.

Further Reading : for a summary of the events of Cranmer's life, see the *Concise Dictionary of National Biography*.
Maynard Smith, *Henry VIII and the Reformation*.

And for because the king would have amity always nourished between the lords of the Council and him [*Cranmer*], the king would send them divers times to dinner unto my lord of Canterbury's . . . and at that dinner I heard the Lord Cromwell say to my lord Cranmer, 'You were born in a happier hour I suppose, (said he), for, do or say what you will, the king will always well take it at your hand. And I must needs confess that in some things I have complained of you unto his Majesty, but all in vain, for he will never give credit against you, whatsoever is laid to your charge ; but let me or any other of the Council be complained of, his Grace will most seriously chide and fall out with us. And therefore you are most happy, if you can keep you in this estate.' . . .

Now, as concerning the manner and order of his hospitality and house-keeping. . . . They found means to put into the king's head, that the Archbishop of Canterbury kept no hospitality or house correspondent unto his revenues and dignity, but sold his woods, and by great incomes and fines maketh money to purchase lands for his wife and children. And to the intent the king should with more facility believe this information, Sir Thomas Seymour, the Duke of Somerset's brother, being of the

Privy Chamber, was procured to take this matter in hand. And before he informed the king thereof, he blasted it abroad in the Court, insomuch that mine eldest brother, being one of the gentlemen ushers, and he fell out for the same, my brother declaring that his report was manifest false, as well for the keeping of his house as for purchasing of lands for his wife and children. This notwithstanding, mr. Seymour went through with his said information, and declared unto the king as is before declared. The king, hearing this tale, . . . said, ' I do marvel that it is said that my Lord of Canterbury should keep no hospitality, for I have heard the contrary.' And so with a few words more in commendation of my Lord, as one that little regarded the suit, but yet, as it appeared afterwards, something smelling what they went about, left off any further to talk of that matter, and converted his communication to another purpose. Notwithstanding, within a month after, whether it was of chance or of purpose it is unknown, the king, going to dinner, called mr. Seymour unto him and said, ' Go ye straightways unto Lambeth, and bid my Lord of Canterbury come and speak with me, at two of the clock at afternoon.' Incontinently mr. Seymour came to Lambeth, and being brought into the hall by the porter, it chanced the hall was set for dinner, and when he was at the screen, and perceived the hall furnished with three principal messes, besides the rest of the tables thoroughly set, having a guilty conscience of his untrue report made to the king, recoiled back and would have gone into my Lord by the chapel way. Mr. Nevill being steward, perceiving that, rose up and went after him, and declared unto him that he could not go that way, and so brought him back unto my Lord throughout the hall ; and when he came to my Lord, and had done his message, my Lord caused him to sit down and dine with him. But, making a short dinner because he would bring the king word again of his message, he departed and came to the king before he was risen from the table. When he came to the king's presence, said the king, ' Will my Lord of Canterbury come to us? ' ' He will wait on your Majesty (said mr. Seymour), at two of the clock.' Then said the king, ' Had my Lord dined before ye came? ' ' No forsooth (said mr. S.) for I found him at dinner.' ' Well (said the king), what cheer made he you? ' With those words mr. Seymour kneeled down and besought the king's Majesty of pardon. ' What is the matter? ' (said the king). ' I do remember (said mr. Seymour), that I told your Highness that my Lord of Canterbury kept no hospitality correspondent unto his dignity ; and now I perceive that I did abuse your Highness with an untruth, for, besides your Grace's house, I think he be not in the realm of none estate or degree that hath such a hall furnished, or that fareth more honorably at his own table.' 'Ah (quoth the king), have you espied your own fault now? ' ' I assure your Highness (said mr. Seymour) it is not so much my fault as other men's who seemed to be honest men that informed me hereof, but I shall henceforth the worse trust them whiles they live.'. . .

THE BIBLE IN ENGLISH

In 1526 Tyndale had translated the New Testament into English, but Henry VIII and Wolsey hunted it out of England because of its heresies. After the breach with Rome Henry decided that the more men knew the Bible the less they would put up with the claims of the Pope. Coverdale's translation appeared in 1536 and was licensed by the King in 1537. Matthew's Bible was recommended by Cranmer, 1537. A new version of Matthew's Bible, known as the Great Bible, was published in 1539. On May 6th, 1541, a royal proclamation ordered every parish to provide itself with a Bible in English of the largest size. How this new Bible was received is described in the following passage.

Source : *The Narrative of William Maldon of Newington* written for Foxe's *Actes and Monuments*. B. M. Harleian MS. 590 folio 77.

Further Reading : Maynard Smith, *Henry VIII and the Reformation*, Part II chapters 2 and 3, from which this abbreviated passage is quoted.

When the King had allowed the Bible to be set forth to be read in all churches, immediately several poor men in the town of Chelmsford in Essex, where his father lived and he was born, bought the New Testament and on Sundays sat reading of it in the lower end of the church : many would flock about them to hear their reading : and he among the rest, being then but fifteen years old came every Sunday to hear the glad and sweet tidings of the Gospel. But his father observing it once angrily fetched him away, and would have him say the latin matins with him, which grieved him much. And as he returned at other times to have the Scripture read, his father still would fetch him away. This put him upon the thoughts of learning to read English that so he might read the New Testament himself; which, when he had by diligence effected, he and his father's apprentice bought the New Testament, joining their stocks together, and to conceal it laid it under the bedstraw, and read it at convenient times. One night his father being asleep, he and his mother chanced to discourse concerning the crucifix, and kneeling down to it, and knocking on the breast then used, and holding up the hands to it when it came in by procession. This he told his mother was plain idolatry, and against the commandment of God, when He saith, *Thou shalt not make any graven image, nor bow down to it, nor worship it.* His mother, enraged at him for this, said ' Wilt thou not worship His cross, which was about thee when thou wast christened, and must be laid on thee when thou art dead? ' In this heat the mother and son went to their beds. The sum of this evening's conference she presently repeats to her husband, which he impatient to learn, and boiling in fury against his son for denying worship to be due to the cross, arose up forthwith, and goes into his son's chamber, and like a mad zealot, taking him by the hair of his head with both his hands, pulled him out of the bed, and whipped him unmercifully. And when the young man bore this beating, as he related, with a kind of joy, considering it was for Christ's sake, and shed not a tear, his father seeing that was more enraged, and ran down and fetched a halter, and put it about his neck, saying he would hang him. At length, with much entreaty of the mother and brother, he left him almost dead.

A DESCRIPTION OF THE SCOTS ARMY AFTER THE BATTLE OF PINKIE CLEUGH

SATURDAY, SEPTEMBER 10TH, 1547

In March 1543 the Scots Parliament accepted a treaty of marriage between the Prince Edward of England and the infant Mary, Queen of Scots. In December they turned away from England and made an alliance with France. Henry VIII attacked Scotland, but war with France ensued and the Scottish war was given up. Henry died in a few months. Protector Somerset, the Regent for the young king, Edward VI, took his stand on the original marriage treaty, but the French party in Scotland was too strong. A Scots army gathered on the Border, and Somerset led an English army north in order to prevent a Scottish invasion of England. He destroyed the Scots at Pinkie Cleugh, but in so doing he destroyed any hope of a union of the English and Scottish crowns. Mary was sent to France, where later she married the Dauphin.

Source: An account of the battle by William Patten, who was employed in the provost-marshal's court. He was present at the battle and wrote one of the earliest and most detailed of military tracts, complete with plans and sketch-maps. Printed in Arber's *English Garner*. Punctuation modernized.

Further Reading: Pollard, *England under Protector Somerset*, ch. 6.

Their armour among them so little differed and their apparel was so base and beggarly, wherein the Lurdein[1] was, in a manner, all one with the Lord, and the Lound[2] with the Lairde : all clad alike in jacks covered with white leather, doublets of the same or of fustian, and most commonly all white hosen. Not one ! with either chain, brooch, ring, or garment of silk that I could see, unless chains of latten[3] drawn four or five times along the thighs of their hosen, and doublet sleeves for cutting : and of that sort I saw many. This vileness of port[4] was the cause that so many of their great men and gentlemen were killed and so few saved. The outward show, the semblance and sign whereby a stranger might discern a villain from a gentleman, was not to be seen among them. As for words and goodly proffer of great ransoms, they were as common and rife in the mouths of the one

---

[1] a heavy, dull fellow.   [2] a loon, a term of abuse.   [3] pewter.   [4] dress.

as the other : and therefore it came to pass that after, in the examination and counting of the prisoners, we found we had taken above twenty of their villains to one of their gentlemen, whom no man need to doubt we had rather have spared than the villains, if we could have known any difference between them in the taking. . . .

Here now, to say somewhat of the manner of their camp. As they had no pavilions or round houses of a commendable compass, so were there few other tents with posts, as the used manner of making is ; and of these few also, none of above twenty foot in length, but most far under. For the most part, they were all sumptuously beset, after their fashion, with fleur de lys, for the love of France, some of blue buckram, some of black, and some of other colours.

These white ridges, as I called them, that as we stood on Fauxside Bray, did make so great a muster towards us, which I did then take to be a number of tents, when we came, we found them to be a linen drapery, of the coarser camerick[1] indeed, for it was all of canvas sheets.

They were the tenticles or rather cabins and couches of their soldiers : which (much after the common building of their country besides) they had framed of four sticks, about an ell long a piece, whereof two fastened together at one end aloft, and the two ends beneath stuck in the ground an ell asunder, standing in fashion like the bow of a sow's yoke. Over two such bows, one, as it were, at their head, the other at their feet, they stretched a sheet down on both sides, whereby their cabins became roofed like a ridge, but scant shut at both ends ; and not very close beneath, on the sides, unless their sticks were the shorter, or their wives the more liberal to lend them larger napery. Howbeit within they had lined them, and stuffed them so thick with straw, that as the weather was not very cold, when they were once couched, they were as warm as they had been in horsedung. . . .

Nigh the place of onset, where the Scots, at their running away, had let fall their weapons, there found we, besides their common manner of armour, certain nice instruments of war, as

[1] cambric.

we thought. They were new boards' ends cut off, being about a
foot in breadth and half a yard in length, having on the inside,
handles made very cunningly of two cords' ends. These, a
God's name! were their targets against the shot of our small
artillery; for they were not able to hold out a cannon.

And with these found we great rattles, swelling bigger than
the belly of a pottle[1] pot, covered with old parchment or double
paper, small stones in them to make a noise, and set upon the
end of a staff of more than two ells long. And this was their fine
device to fray[2] our horses, when our horsemen should come at
them. Howbeit, because the riders were no babies, nor their
horses any colts, they could neither duddle the one, nor affray
the other. So that this policy was as witless as their power
forceless. . . .

Thus, through the favour of God's bounty, by the valiance
and policy of my Lord Protector's Grace, by the forward endea-
vour of all the nobles and council there besides, and by the
willing diligence of every captain, officer, and true subject else,
we, most valiantly and honourably, wan the victory over our
enemies.

KING EDWARD VI

Edward VI was the only son of Henry VIII and Jane Seymour
He was born in 1537 and died in 1553. He succeeded his father on the
throne in 1547. He was a rather heartless boy and an ardent Protestant.
His *Journal*, a daily chronicle of his life from his accession down to
Nov. 28th, 1552, is in the Cotton Library at the British Museum. It
has been printed by Burnet in his *History of the Reformation*.

(1) *Source*: the following character of the King was written by
Giralamo Cardano, a well-known Milanese physician, who visited
him in September or October, 1552. He cast his horoscope and fore-
told that the King would reach middle age. This extract is taken from
Burnet, *History of the Reformation*, vol. ii, p. 3 1823 ed. O.U.P.
(modernized).

[1] half gallon. [2] frighten.

Further Reading: there is no modern full scale biography. An interesting study is in Morris, *The Tudors*.

All the graces were in him. He had many tongues when yet but a child ; together with the English, his natural tongue, he had both Latin and French ; nor was he ignorant, as I hear, of the Greek, Italian and Spanish, and perhaps some more. But for the English, French and Latin, he was great in them and apt to learn everything. Nor was he ignorant of logic, of the principles of natural philosophy, nor of music. The sweetness of his temper was such as became a mortal, his gravity becoming the majesty of a King, and his disposition suitable to his high degree. In sum, that child was so bred, had such parts, was of such expectation, that he looked like a miracle of a man. These things are not spoken rhetorically and beyond the truth, but are indeed short of it. He was a marvellous boy. When I was with him he was in the 15th year of his age, in which he spake Latin as politely and as promptly as I did. He asked me what was the subject of my books, *De Rerum Varietate*, which I dedicated to him. I answered that in the first chapter I gave the true cause of comets, which had long been enquired into, but was never found out before. ' What is it ? ' said he. I said it was the concourse of the light of wandering stars. He answered, ' How can that be, since the stars move in different motions ? How comes it that the comets are soon dissipated, or do not move after them according to their motions ? ' To this I answered, ' They do move after them, but much quicker than they, by reason of the different aspect, as we see in a crystal, or when a rainbow rebounds from the wall : for a little change makes a great difference of place.' But the King said, ' How can that be, where there is no subject to receive that light, as the wall is the subject for the rainbow ? ' To this I answered that this was as in the Milky-way, or where many candles were lighted, the middle place where their shining met was white and clear. From this little taste it may be imagined what he was. And indeed the ingenuity and sweetness of his disposition had raised in all good and learned men the greatest expectation of him possible. He began to love the liberal arts before he knew them, and to know them before he could use them : and in him there was such an attempt of nature, that not only England, but the world has reason to lament his being so early snatched away. How truly was it said of such extraordinary persons, that their lives are short and seldom do they come to be old. He gave us an essay of virtue, though he did not live to give a pattern of it. When the gravity of the King was needful, he carried himself like an old man ; and yet he was always affable and gentle, as became his age. He played on the lute, he meddled in affairs of state, and for bounty he did in that emulate his father ; though he, even when he endeavoured to be too good might appear to have been bad : but there was no suspecting any such thing in the son, whose mind was cultivated by the study of philosophy.

(2) *Source* : Letter from John Hooper, Bishop of Gloucester to Bullinger, son-in-law of the Swiss Protestant leader, Zwingli. Hooper was burnt for heresy in 1555. Tuesday, March 27th, 1550. Printed by the Parker Society.

Believe me, my much esteemed friend, you have never seen in the world for these thousand years so much erudition united with piety and sweetness of disposition. Should he live and grow up with these virtues, he will be a terror to all the sovereigns of the earth. He receives with his own hand a copy of every sermon that he hears, and most diligently requires an account of them after dinner from those who study with him. Many of the boys and youths who are his companions in study are well and faithfully instructed in the fear of God and in good learning.

MARY TUDOR

Mary Tudor was the daughter of Henry VIII and Katharine of Aragon. She was born in 1516 (N.S.), succeeded to the throne in 1553 on the death of her step-brother, Edward VI, and in 1554 she married her cousin, Philip II of Spain. She died in 1558.

Source : From the Report of England made to the Senate in Venice by Giacomo Soranzo, Ambassador from Venice to Edward VI and Queen Mary. Dated Saturday, August 18th, 1554. *Venetian Calendar*, vol. 4, p. 532.

Further Reading : Prescott, *Mary Tudor*. Morris, *The Tudors*.

The Most Serene Madame Mary is entitled Queen of England and of France, and Defendress of the Faith. She was born on 18th Feb. 1515 [1516 *N.S.*] so she yesterday completed her 38th year and six months. She is of low stature, with a red and white complexion, and very thin ; her eyes are white and large, and her hair reddish ; her face is round, with a nose rather low and wide ; and were not her age on the decline, she might be called handsome rather than the contrary. She is not of a strong constitution, and of late she suffers from headache and serious affection of the heart, so that she is often obliged to take medicine, and also to be blooded. She is of very spare diet, and never eats until 1 or 2 p.m., although she rises at daybreak, when, after saying her prayers and hearing mass in private, she transacts business incessantly, until after midnight, when she retires to rest ; for she chooses to give audience not only to all the members of her Privy Council, and to hear from them every detail of public business, but also to all other persons who ask it of her. Her Majesty's countenance indicates great benignity and clemency, which are not belied by her conduct, for although she has had many enemies, and though so many of them were by law condemned to death, yet had the executions depended solely on her Majesty's will, not one of them perhaps would have been enforced. . . . She is endowed with excellent ability, and more than moderately read in Latin literature, especially with regard to Holy Writ ; and besides her native tongue she speaks

Latin, French and Spanish, and understands Italian perfectly, but does not speak it. She is also very generous, but not to the extent of letting it appear that she rests her chief claim to commendation on this quality.

She is so confirmed in the Catholic religion that although the King her brother and his Council prohibited her from having mass celebrated according to the Roman Catholic ritual, she nevertheless had it performed in secret, nor did she ever choose by any act to assent to any other form of religion. . . . Her Majesty takes great pleasure in playing on the lute and spinet, and is a very good performer on both instruments ; and indeed before her accession she taught many of her maids of honour. But she seems to delight above all in arraying herself elegantly and magnificently. . . . She also makes great use of jewels . . . in which she delights greatly.

THE MARRIAGE OF QUEEN MARY AND PHILIP II

JULY 25TH, 1554

Mary Tudor married her cousin Philip II, King of Spain, in Winchester Cathedral, July 25th, 1554.

Source : The best first-hand account of Philip II's arrival in England, of his marriage to Mary and of their entry into London, will be found in a letter written by John Elder to Lord Robert Stuart, Bishop of Caithness and brother to Matthew, Earl of Lennox, printed entire for the Camden Society, vol. xlviii, 1849. The following extract is taken from the *Wriothesley's Chronicle*, vol. 2, p. 120, Camden Society, 1875, which appears to be a compressed version of Elder's letter and is more suitable for quotation.

The 25th of Julie, beinge Weddensdaye and St. James daye, about XI of the clocke the Kinge and Queene came from their lodgings towardes the churche all the way on foote, verie richelye apparelled in gownes of cloth of golde sett with riche stones, he with his gentlemen and garde and she with hers, eache of them havinge a sworde borne before them, the Earle of Darbye bearinge the sworde before her Maiestie, and the Earle of Pembroke before the Kinge ; and when they were come into the churche he went into one traveys and the Queene to another richlye hunge, where they were shriven. This done they came forth of their traveys to the place appointed for the marriage, where the Lord Chancellor, being before with 5 other bishops assistinge him, used all thinges, both in the banes-biddinge and otherwise, as hath bene in all marriages of old time, and spoke it both in Latin and Englishe, her Grace on the right syde standinge and the King on the left syde. Her marriage ring was a rownd hoope of gould without anye stone, which was her desire, for she said she would be married as maydens were in the olde tyme, and so she was.

After the marriage knott thus knitt the King and Queen came hand in hand under a riche canopie, beinge borne over them with 6 knightes and 2 swordes before them, all the lordes both Englishe and strangers richly apparelled goeinge afore them, the trumpetts then blowinge till they came into the quier, where all the priestes and singinge men all in riche copes began to singe a psalm used in marriages, the King and Queen kneeling awhile before the aulter, eche of them having a taper before them ; then after her Majestie went into her traveys on the right syde, and the King into another on the left syde ; after the gospell they came owt and kneeled before the alter openlye all the masse time, and then the care-cloth was holden ouer them ; and he kissed the bishop at the Agnus and then her Majestie. The masse done the Kinge of Herroldes openlye in the churche, and in the presence of the King, the Queen, the lords and ladies, and all the people, solemnlye proclaymed their Maiesties Kinge and Queene, with their title and style, in manner as followeth :

Philippe and Marie, by the grace of God Kinge and Queene of Englande, France, Naples, Jerusalem and Irelande, Defender of the Faythe, Princes of Spayne and Sicilie, Archdukes of Austriche, Dukes of Mylan, Burgundye, and Brabant, Countes of

Aspurge,[1] Flaunders, and Tyrrole. Which proclamation ended, the trumpetts blue and other noyses playde. And then the Kinge and Queene came forthe hand in hand, with their lordes, ladies, and gentlemen waytinge on them, and 2 swordes borne afore them in manner as aforesayde; and so went on foote to the courte, and there dined openlye in the hall, both together at one table.

LADY JANE GREY

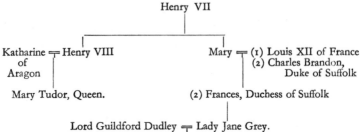

On the death of Edward VI the Duke of Northumberland tried to put his daughter-in-law, Lady Jane Grey, on the throne and to keep Mary Tudor off it. His plot failed, Lady Jane Grey and her husband, Lord Guilford Dudley, were sent to the Tower by Queen Mary, and both were eventually executed. Probably a rebellion led by the Duke of Suffolk, Lady Jane Grey's father, against Mary sealed Lady Jane's fate.

Source: *The Chronicle of Queen Jane*, compiled perhaps by Rowland Lea, who may have been employed in the Mint, which at that time was conducted in the Tower of London. Printed by the Camden Society, vol. xlviii, 1849. Spelling modernized.

Further Reading: Froude, *History of England*, vol. iv.

[1] Hapsburg.

On Tuesday the 29th of August, I dined at Partrige's house with my lady Jane, being there present, she sitting at the board's end, Partrige, his wife, Jacob my lady's gentlewoman, and her man. She commanding Partrige and me to put on our caps, amongst our communication at the dinner, this was to be noted : after she had once or twice drunk to me and bade me heartily welcome, saith she, ' The Queen's Majesty is a merciful princess ; I beseech God she may long continue, and send His bountiful grace upon her '. After that we fell in discourse of matters of religion ; and she asked what he was that preached at St. Paul's on Sunday before ; and so it was told her to be one (*blank in MS.*). ' I pray you,' quoth she, ' have they Mass in London ? ' ' Yea, forsooth,' quote I, ' in some places.' ' It may be so,' quoth she, ' it is not so strange as the sudden conversion of the late Duke (Northumberland) ; for who would have thought,' said she, ' he would have so done ? ' It was answered her, ' Perchance he thereby hoped to have had his pardon.' ' Pardon ! ' quoth she ; ' woe worth him ! he hath brought me and our stock in most miserable calamity and misery by his exceeding ambition. But for the answering that he hoped for life by his turning, though other men be of that opinion, I utterly am not ; for what man is there living, I pray you, although he had been innocent, that would hope of life in that case ; being in the field against the Queen in person as general, and after his taking so hated and evil spoken of by the commons ? and at his coming into prison so wondered at as the like was never heard by any man's time. Who was judge that he should hope for pardon, whose life was odious to all men ? But what will ye more ? like as his life was wicked and full of dissimulation, so was his end thereafter. I pray God, I, nor no friend of mine, die so. Should I, who am young and in my few years, forsake my faith for the love of life ? Nay, God forbid ! much more he should not, whose fatal course although he had lived his just number of years, could not have long continued. But life was sweet, it appeared ; so he might have lived, you will say, he did not care how. . . .

E

THE EXECUTION OF LADY JANE GREY

Monday, February 12th, 1554

Source : *The Chronicle of Two Years of Queen Mary*. (A continuation of the Chronicle of Queen Jane.) This account ends at the words, ' whereon when she was mounted, etc.,' but it is probable that the rest of this extract is by the same hand. Camden Society, vol. xlviii, 1849, and *Archaeologia*, vol. 13. Spelling modernized.

The Monday, being the 12th of February, about ten of the clock, there went out of the Tower to the scaffold on Tower Hill, the Lord Guildford Dudley, son to the late Duke of Northumberland, husband to the Lady Jane Grey, daughter to the Duke of Suffolk, who at his going out took by the hand Sir Anthony Browne, master John Throgmorton, and many other gentlemen, praying them to pray for him ; and without the bulwark Offley the Sheriff received him and brought him to the scaffold, where, after a small declaration, having no ghostly father with him, he kneeled down and said his prayers ; and then holding up his eyes and hands to God many times, he laid himself along, and his head upon the block, which was at one stroke of the axe taken from him.

Note, the lord Marquis (Northampton) stood upon the Devil's tower, and saw the execution. His carcass thrown into a cart, and his head in a cloth, he was brought into the chapel within the Tower, where the Lady Jane, whose lodging was in Partrige's house, did see his dead carcass taken out of the cart, as well as she did see him before on life going to his death,—a sight to her no less than death.

By this time was there a scaffold made upon the green over against the White Tower, for the said Lady Jane to die upon. Who with her husband was appointed to have been put to death the Friday before, but was stayed till then, for what cause is not known, unless it were because her father was not then come into the Tower. The said lady, being nothing at all abashed, neither with fear of her own death, which then approached, neither with the sight of the dead carcass of her husband, when he was brought into the chapel, came forth, the lieutenant leading her, in the same gown wherein she was arraigned, her countenance nothing abashed, neither her eyes anything moistened with tears, although her two gentlewomen, mistress Elizabeth Tilney and mistress Eleyn, wonderfully wept, with a book in her hand, whereon she prayed all the way till she came to the said scaffold, whereon when she was mounted etc.

THE END OF THE LADY JANE DUDLEY, DAUGHTER OF THE DUKE OF SUFFOLK, upon the scaffold, at the hour of her death.

First, when she mounted upon the scaffold, she said to the people standing thereabout : ' Good people, I am come hither to die, and by a law I am condemned to the same. The fact, indeed, against the Queen's Highness was unlawful, and the consenting thereunto by me : but touching the procurement and desire thereof by me or on my behalf, I do wash my hands thereof in innocency, before God, and the face of you, good Christian people, this day,' and therewith she wrung her hands, in which she had her book. Then she said, ' I pray you all, good Christian people, to bear me witness that I die a true Christian woman, and that I look to be saved by none other mean, but only by the mercy of God in the merits of the blood of his only son Jesus Christ : and I confess, when I did know the word of God I neglected the same, loved myself and the world, and therefore this plague or punishment is happily and worthily happened unto me for my sins ; and yet I thank God of his goodness that he hath given me a time and respite to repent. And now, good people, while I am alive, I pray you to assist me with your prayers.' And then, kneeling down, she turned to Feckenham, saying, ' Shall I say this psalm ? ' And he said, ' Yea.' Then she said the psalm of *Miserere mei Deus* in English, in most devout manner, to the end. Then she stood up, and gave her maiden mistress Tilney her gloves and handkercher, and her book to master Bruges, the lieutenant's brother ; forthwith she untied her gown. The hangman went to help her off therewith ; then she desired him to let her alone, turning towards her two gentlewomen, who helped her off therewith, and also with her frose paast[1] and neckercher, giving to her a fair handkercher to knitt about her eyes.

Then the hangman kneeled down, and asked her forgiveness, whom she forgave most willingly. Then he willed her to stand upon the straw : which doing, she saw the block. Then she said, ' I pray you dispatch me quickly.' Then she kneeled down, saying, ' Will you take it off before I lay me down? ' and the hangman answered her, ' No, madam.' She tied the kercher about her eyes ; then feeling for the block, said, ' What shall I do ? Where is it ? ' One of the standers-by guiding her thereunto, she laid her head down upon the block, and stretched forth her body and said : ' Lord, into thy hands I commend my spirit.' And so she ended.

THE BURNING OF ARCHBISHOP CRANMER

SATURDAY, MARCH 21ST, 1555 (O.S.)

Thomas Cranmer was appointed Archbishop of Canterbury by Henry VIII, who regarded himself as a true son of the Catholic Church. Edward VI was a Protestant and Cranmer carried out a full Protestant Reformation in England. The accession of Mary brought a violent Roman Catholic to the throne, one who repudiated the political changes made by her father, Henry VIII, and the doctrinal changes of Edward VI, and brought England back into the old Catholic Church,

---

[1] Probably matronly head-dress : the paste being a head attire worn by brides.

acknowledging the supremacy of the Papacy. Cranmer was in a dilemma. He made seven recantations, but his death had been determined on. It was thought that he would speak at the very end in defence of the old Catholic Faith and would condemn his own errors. When he found he was to die in any case, he spoke out at the end in defence of Protestantism. The following letter was written by a bystander at his burning. The author was a Papist, who detested everything to do with Cranmer, but he found it difficult to withold admiration for Cranmer's end. Who J.A. was we do not know, nor to whom the letter was written.

Source : a letter signed J.A. in the Harleian MS. 422. It is printed in Strype's *Memorials of Archbishop Cranmer*, p. 384 sqq. with one mistake, which has been rectified in this version from the original MS. The date of the letter is 23rd of March 1555 (O.S.), two days after the burning. Spelling and punctuation have been modernized.

But that I know for our great friendship and long-continued love you look, even of duty, that I should signify to you of the truth of such things as here chanceth among us, I would not at this time have written to you the unfortunate end and doubtful tragedy of T.C. late Bishop of Canterbury, because I little pleasure take in beholding of such heavy sights. And when they are once overpassed, I like not to rehearse them again, being but a renewing of my woe and doubling my grief. For although his former life and wretched end deserves a greater misery (if any greater might have chanced than chanced unto him), yet setting aside his offences to God and his country, and beholding the man without his faults, I think there was none that pitied not his case and bewailed his fortune, and feared not his own chance, to see so noble a prelate, so grave a counsellor, of so long-continued honour, after so many dignities, in his old years to be deprived of his estate, adjudged to die and in so painful a death to end his life. I have no delight to increase it . . . . But to come to the matter : on Saturday last, being the 21st of March was his day appointed to die. And because the morning was rainy, the sermon appointed by Mr. Dr. Cole to be made at the stake was made in S. Mary's church. . . .

When he had ended his sermon, he desired all the people to pray for him, Mr. Cranmer kneeling down with them and praying for himself. I think there was never such a number so earnestly praying together. For they that hated him before now loved him for his conversion and hope of continuance. They that loved him before could not suddenly hate him, having hope of his confession again of his fall. So love and hope increased on every side. . . .

When praying was done, he [*Cranmer*] stood up, and having leave to speak said, 'Good people, I had intended to desire you to pray for me, which, because Mr. Dr. hath desired and you have done already, I thank you most heartily for it. And now will I pray for myself, as I could best devise for mine own comfort, and say the prayer, word for word, as I have here written it.'And he read it standing, and after kneeled down and said the Lord's Prayer, and all the people on their knees devoutly praying with him. His prayer was thus :

O Father of Heaven, O Son of God, Redeemer of the World, O Holy Ghost, proceeding from them both, three Persons and one God, have mercy upon me most wretched caitiff and miserable sinner. I who have offended both Heaven and earth, and more grievously than any tongue can express, whither then may I go, or whither shall I fly for succour ? To Heaven I may be ashamed to lift up mine eyes, and in earth I find no refuge. What shall I then do ? Shall I despair ? God forbid. O good God, Thou art merciful, and refusest none that come unto Thee for succour. To Thee therefore do I come. To Thee do I humble myself, saying, O Lord God, my sins be great, but yet have mercy upon me for Thy mercy is great. O God the Son, Thou wast not made man, this great mystery was not wrought, for few or small offences. Nor didst Thou give Thy Son unto death, O God the Father, for our little and small sins only, but for all the greatest sins of the world, so that the sinner return unto Thee with a penitent heart, as I do here at present. Wherefore have mercy upon me, O Lord, whose property is always to have mercy. For although my sins be great, yet Thy mercy is greater. I crave nothing, O Lord, for mine own merits, but for Thy name's sake, that it may be glorified thereby, and for Thy dear Son Jesus Christ's sake. And now therefore, Our Father, which art in Heaven etc. . . .

Then rising he said, 'Every man desireth, good people, at the time of their deaths to give some good exhortation, that other may remember after their deaths and be the better thereby. So I beseech God grant me grace that I may speak something at this my departing, whereby God may be glorified and you edified. . . .

And now I come to the great thing that troubleth my conscience more than any other thing that ever I said or did in my life ; and that is, the setting abroad of writings contrary to the truth. Which here now I renounce and refuse as things written with my hand, contrary to the truth which I have in my heart, and writ for fear of death and to save my life, if it might be : and that is all such bills which I have written or signed with mine own hand since my degradation, wherein I have written many things untrue. And forasmuch as my hand offended in writing contrary to my heart, therefore my hand shall first be punished. For if I may come to the fire, it shall be first burned. And as for the Pope, I refuse him as Christ's enemy and Antichrist, with all his false doctrine.'

And here being admonished of his recantation and dissembling, he said, 'Alas, my lord, I have been a man that all my life loved plainness and never dissembled till now against the truth, which I am most sorry for.' He added hereunto, that for the Sacrament, he believed as he had taught in his book against the Bishop of Winchester. And here he was suffered to speak no more.

Then he was carried away, and a great number that did run to see him go so wickedly to his death, ran after him, exhorting him, while time was, to remember himself. And one Friar John, a godly and well-learned man, all the way travelled with him to reduce him. But it would not be. What they said in particular I cannot tell, but the effect appeared in the end. For at the stake he professed that he died in all such opinions as he had taught, and oft repented him of his recantation.

Coming to the stake with a cheerful countenance and willing mind, he put off his garments with haste, and stood upright in his shirt. And a Bachelor of Divinity, named Elye, of Brasenose College, laboured to convert him to his former recantation, with the two Spanish friars. But when the friars saw his constancy, they said in Latin one to another, 'Let us go from him, we ought not to be nigh him, for the devil is with him.' But the Bachelor in Divinity was more earnest with him. Unto whom he answered, that as concerning his recantation he repented it right sore, because he knew it to be against the truth, with other words more. Whereupon the Lord Williams cried, 'Make short, make short.' Then the bishop took certain of his friends by the hand. But the bachelor of divinity refused to take him by the hand, and blamed all others that did so, and said he was sorry that ever he came in his company. And yet again he required him to agree to his former recantation. And the bishop answered (shewing his hand), 'This is the hand that wrote it, and therefore shall it suffer first punishment.'

Fire being now put to him, he stretched out his right hand and thrust it into the flame, and held it there a good space, before the fire came to any other part of his body, where his hand was seen of every man sensibly burning, crying with a loud voice, 'This hand hath offended.' As soon as the fire was got up, he was very soon dead, never stirring or crying all the while.

His patience in the torment, his courage in dying, if it had been taken either for the glory of God, the wealth of his country, or the testimony of truth, as it was for a pernicious error and subversion of true religion, I could worthily have commended the example and matched it with the fame of any father of ancient time : but seeing that not the death, but the cause and quarrel thereof, commendeth the sufferer, I cannot but much dispraise his obstinate stubbornness and sturdiness in dying, and specially in so evil a cause. Surely his death much grieved every man, but not after one sort. Some pitied to see his body so tormented with the fire raging upon the silly carcass, that counted not of the folly. Other that passed not much of the body, lamented to see him spill his soul wretchedly, without redemption, to be plagued for ever. His friends sorrowed for love, his enemies for pity, strangers for a common kind of humanity whereby we are bound one to another. Thus I have enforced myself, for your sake, to discourse this heavy narration, contrary to my mind :

and being more than half weary, I make a short end, wishing you a quieter life, with less honour and easier death, with more praise. The 23rd of March.

Yours J.A.

CALAIS IN 1497

At this date Calais was the last possession in France held by the English. Henry VIII gave it representation in Parliament 1545. It was captured by the French in Queen Mary's reign and was surrendered by the Treaty of Cateau Cambrésis, 1559. (See next extract).

Source: Andreas Franciscus, *Itinerarium Britanniae*, a Latin MS. translated into English and published by C. V. Malfatti at Barcelona, 1953.

Further Reading: Sandeman, *Calais under English Rule*. (Oxford 1908).

We came to Calais, which is called ' Calisia ' in our language, and is fifty miles from Bruges. Its circumference is scarcely more than a mile. It stands on the sea coast just opposite the island of Britain, and is carefully guarded by a very large garrison, as Henry, King of England, hardly possesses any other land on the continent.

Every day in the afternoon, when the inhabitants take their rest, the gates are closed ; and this also happens on holidays, only, instead of once, as on working days, it is done twice, the first time when services are being held in the churches, and the second time, as before, when the people are having lunch. At these times sentries and guards keep watch from the town's walls on all sides, so much so that I never heard of a guard being kept anywhere else with such care. . . .

From Britain, which rises out of the sea at a distance of thirty miles, they import a vast quantity of wool, which is conveyed later to Italy, or into France or anywhere else by land. In fact, if the merchants want to buy English wool, and do not want to go to the island themselves, they have to buy it at Calais.

THE LOSS OF CALAIS

WEDNESDAY, JANUARY 5TH, 1558

When England was dragged into the Spanish war against France through Mary's marriage with Philip II, her conduct of the war was a failure, with the result that the French captured and retained Calais, the last English possession on French soil. (See last extract).

Source : An account by John Highfield, Master of the Ordnance at Calais. Lord Hardwick's Miscellaneous State Papers, i, 114, ed. 1788. Printed by Arber, in *An English Garner*.

Further Reading : Prescott, *Mary Tudor*, ch. xxi.

On Wednesday [*5th January*], the enemy continued their battery on the town, without great hurt done, because they could not beat the foot of the wall, for that the *contremure* was of a good height, and we reinforced the breach, in the night, with timber, wool, and other matter sufficiently ; and we looked that the enemy would have attempted the assault the same evening; whereupon I caused two flankers to be made ready, and also placed two bombards, by the help of the soldiers, appointing weapons and fireworks to be in readiness at the said breach. At which time, my Lord commanded the soldiers of the garrison to keep their ordinary wards, and Master GRIMSTON to the breach with the residue of the best soldiers. And then my Lord exhorted all men to fight, with other good words as in such cases appertaineth. And my Lord told me, divers times, that ' although there came no succour ; yet he would never yield, nor stand to answer the loss of such a town.'

On Thursday, began one other battery to the Castle ; which being a high and weak wall without ramparts, was made saultable the same day. Whereupon, the Captain of the Castle desired some more help to defend this breach, or else to know what my Lord thought best in that behalf. Then, after long debating, my Lord determined to have the towers overthrown, which one SAULLE took upon him to do ; notwithstanding, I said openly that ' if the Castle were abandoned, it should be the loss of the Town.'

The same night, my Lord appointed me to be at the breach of the town with him : and, about eight of the clock, the enemy waded over the haven, at the low water, with certain harque-bussiers, to view the breaches ; and coming to the Castle, found no resistance, and so entered. Then the said SAULLE failed to give fire unto the train of powder.

Then my Lord, understanding that the enemy were entered into the Castle, commanded me to give order for battering of the Castle : whereupon incontinent there were bent three cannons and one saker before the gate, to beat the bridge ; which, being in the night, did not greatly annoy.

The same time, Master Marshall with divers soldiers, came towards the Castle, lest the enemy should enter the town also. And after we had skirmished upon the bridge, seeing no remedy to recover the Castle, we did burn and break the said bridge : and there was a trench immediately cast before the Castle, which was only help at that time.

Within one hour after, upon a necessity of things [my Lord] determined to send a trumpet with a herald, declaring that ' If the Frenchmen would send one gentleman, then he would send one other in gage '. Whereupon my Lord sent for me, and commanded that I should go forth of the town for the same purpose ; wherein I desired his Lordship that he would send some other, and rather throw me over the walls. Then he spake likewise to one WINDEBANKE, and to MASSINGBERD, as I remember, which were both to go unto such service.

Then my Lord sent for me again, in PEYTON's house ; and being eftsoons commanded by the Council there, I went forth with a trumpet, and received in a French gentleman : who, as I heard, was brought to my Lord Deputy's house, and treated upon some articles ; which were brought, within one hour, by one HALL, merchant of the staple.

Then Monsieur D'ANDELOT entered the town with certain French gentlemen ; and the said HALL and I were brought to Monsieur DE GUISE, who lay in the sand hills by Rysbank, and there the said HALL delivered a bill : we were sent to Monsieur D'ESTREES' tent.

The Friday after [7th January], Monsieur D'ESTREES told me that my Lord Deputy had agreed to render the town with loss of all the goods, and fifty prisoners to remain. . . .

THE LOSS OF GUISNES, FOLLOWING ON THE LOSS OF CALAIS

Source : An account by Thomas Churchyard, the poet, who took part in the siege, 11th–22nd January, 1558, from *A General Rehearsal of Wars*, 1579. Printed by Arber in *An English Garner*.

And now we, that were without the Castle, might hear great business and stir throughout the whole body and heart of the piece.[1]

For, the next morning,[2] which was the third day we were assaulted, our General looked for a general assault, and to be roundly assailed : as, of troth, he was. In the meanwhile, we might speak one to another afar off, and our friends answered us over the wall ; for nearer together we might not come : and for succour or aid to our soldiers in Mary Bulwark, we hoped not after. Every man was occupied with his own business and charge ; that no one person might be spared from his place.

Well, as God would permit, the poor Spaniards and such Burgundians as were left alive in Mary Bulwark, fell to make a counterscarf, to beat out the enemy from the Braie, when the Bulwark should be won : as it was likely to be lost, the breach was so bare, and the entry for the enemy was so large ; for in a manner they might assault our Bulwark round about, on all sides. And they did lodge at the very edge of the breach, to the number of 2,000, of their bravest bands : minding to assail us, as soon as the day began to peep out of the skies.

[1]fortress. [2] Jan. 20th, 1558.

Which they performed, when the third day approached. For a general assault was given to every place of the Castle : which assault endured till the very night came on. The French, in this assault, wan the Base Court ; and were ready to set fire under the gate, and blow it up with powder.

Monsieur D'ANDELOT, in his own person, with 2,000 soldiers, entered the Mary Bulwark ; who slew the Spaniards in the Braie : and forced as many Burgundians and English as were left alive, which were but 15 (Captain Andrea, Captain Lambert, and Myself; with twelve common soldiers) out of 400, to leap down the dykes, and so to scramble for their lives ; and to creep into a hole of a brick wall that my Lord Grey had broken out to receive such as escaped from the assault. But when we had entered the hole in the wall, the French followed at our heels ; and we, to save our lives, turned again, bending pikes against the passage, and so shot off one haragaboze ; by which means, the enemy followed no further.

And yet we were in as great distress as before. For we were between two gates : and at the gate we should have entered, were two great cannon, ready charged to be shot off, to drive them back that would have set fire on the gate. And the cry and noise was so great and terrible, on all sides, that we could not be heard to speak. But, as God would, Master LEWIS DIVE (now a man of worship in Bedfordshire) heard my voice. Then I plied the matter so sore, for life : so that, with much ado, Master Dive received us into the heart of the Castle. And yet, in the opening of the gate, the French were like to enter pelley melley with us, if a cannon shot had not made place, whiles the gate was a shutting.

But now, we were no sooner come before my Lord Grey : but all the soldiers cried, ' Yield up the Castle, upon some reasonable composition! ' And when the soldiers saw they could not have the Castle yielded ; they threatened ' to fling my Lord Grey over the walls! ' : and that was determined ; if my Lord had not prevented them with a policy. Whereupon the Captains were called together ; and there they agreed to send me to Monsieur DE GUISE, with an offer, that ' If we might all march, with bag and baggage, ensign displayed, and six pieces of ordnance : we would yield the Castle into the hands of the French '.

Now it was night, and I must be let out at Master HARRY NOR-
WITCH his Bulwark ; but neither Drum nor Trumpet went with
me : because a Trumpeter was slain as he sounded to have a
parley ; and, as I heard say, a Drum that would have followed me,
was shot in the leg. But there was no remedy I must wade over
the water, in which there lay certain galthroppes, as they term
them, which were great boards, full of long spikes of iron ; on
the which, having good boots and a stay in my hand, I was
taught daintily to tread : and the night was so dark, that the
enemy might not take any good mark of me, albeit they shot
divers times.

So, with some hazard and no great hope to attain that I was
sent for, I was taken by the watch ; and brought to Monsieur
DE GUISE's tent, where the Duke D'AUMALE and many great
Estates were in presence.

[After some parleying] They concluded ' that the soldiers
should march away with bag and baggage : and the Captains
and Officers should remain prisoners ' : which I knew would
not be liked : and so desired to be sent to my Lord Grey.

But when I came into the Castle, and the soldiers had gotten
word that they might march away at their will : they came to
me, and threatened me with great words, commanding me, ' To
make despatch, and yield up the fort ! ' For they said, ' Since the
matter is in talk, and likely to be brought to a good purpose ;
they would cut my throat, if I made not hastily, an end of the
case '. And thereupon had they made a great hole in a wall ;
and so they thrust me out among the Almains, who rudely
handled me. . . . I was come to Monsieur DE GUISE . . . and had
told him my message. And he, like a noble Prince and faithful
Captain, rode to the gate (causing me to mount behind Master
HARRY DUDLEY) ; where the Almains were busily occupied about
some naughty practice : and, with a great truncheon, he stroke
divers of the Almains and others to make them retire ; and laying
a load[1] about him he made such way, that the gate was free, and
the capitulation was, at leisure, talked of. . . . And to say the
truth, I think our peace was not so dishonourable, as some report.

[1] of blows.

QUEEN ELIZABETH I

Elizabeth I was the daughter of Henry VIII and Anne Boleyn. She was born in 1536, succeeded her sister Mary as Queen in 1558, and died in 1603.

(1) *Source* : *The Annals of Queen Elizabeth*, by Sir John Hayward, Kt. edited for the Camden Society by John Bruce from a MS. in the Harleian Collection, 1840. Spelling and punctuation have been modernized. Sir John Hayward was born in 1564? and died in 1627. He was a historian of some repute in his own day.

Further Reading : on Elizabeth, Neale, *Elizabeth* ; and Clapham, *Elizabeth of England*, edited by Read : on Hayward, Bruce, introduction to the *Annals*, and the article in the D.N.B.

Now, if ever any person had either the gift or the style to win the hearts of people, it was this Queen ; and if ever she did express the same, it was that present, in coupling mildness with majesty as she did, and in stately stooping to the meanest sort. All her faculties were in motion, and every motion seemed a well guided action ; her eye was set upon one, her ear listened to another, her judgement ran upon a third, to a fourth she addressed her speech ; her spirit seemed to be everywhere, and yet so entire in herself as it seemed to be nowhere else. Some she pitied, some she commended, some she thanked, at others she pleasantly and wittingly jested, contemning no person, neglecting no office, and distributing her smiles, looks and graces so artificially that thereupon the people again so redoubled the testimonies of their joy ; and afterwards, raising everything to the highest strain, filled the ears of all men with immoderate extolling of their Prince.

She was a lady upon whom nature had bestowed and well placed many of her fairest favours : of stature mean,[1] slender, straight and amiably composed ; of such state in her carriage as every motion of her seemed to bear majesty ; her hair was inclined to pale yellow, her forehead large and fair, a seeming seat for princely grace ; her eyes lively and sweet, but shortsighted ; her nose somewhat rising in the midst ; the whole compass of her countenance somewhat long, but yet of admirable

[1] i.e. of medium height.

beauty, not so much in that which is termed the flower of youth, as in a most delightful composition of majesty and modesty in equal mixture. But without good qualities of mind, the gifts of nature are like painted flowers, without either virtue or sap ; yea, sometimes they grow horrid or loathsome. Now her virtues were such as might suffice to make an Ethopian beautiful, which, the more a man knows and understands, the more he shall admire and love. In life, she was most innocent ; in desires, moderate ; in purpose, just ; of spirit, above credit and almost capacity of her sex ; of divine wit, as well for depth of judgement as for quick conceit and speedy expedition ; of eloquence, as sweet in the utterance, so ready and easy to come to the utterance : of wonderful knowledge both in learning and affairs ; skilful not only in the Latin and Greek, but also in divers other foreign languages ; none knew better the hardest art of all others, that is, of commanding men, nor could more use themselves to those cares without which the royal dignity could not be supported. She was religious, magnanimous, merciful and just ; respective of the honour of others, and exceeding tender in touch of her own. She was lovely and loving, the two principal bands of duty and obedience. She was very ripe and measured in counsel and experience, as well not to let go occasions as not to take them when they were green. She maintained Justice at home and Arms abroad with great wisdom and authority in either place. Her Majesty seemed to all to shine through courtesy : but as she was not easy to receive any to especial grace, so she was most constant to those whom she received, and of great judgement to know to what point of greatness men were fit to be advanced. She was rather liberal than magnificent, making good choice of the receivers ; and for this cause was thought weak by some against the desire of money. But it is certain that beside the want of treasure which she found, her continual affairs in Scotland, France, the Low Countries and in Ireland did occasion great provision of money, which could not be better supplied than by cutting off either excessive or unnecessary expense at home. Excellent Queen ! what do my words but wrong thy worth? what do I but gild gold? what but show the sun with a candle, in attempting to praise thee, whose honour doth fly over the whole world upon the two wings of Magnanimity and Justice, whose perfection shall much dim the lustre of all other that shall be of thy sex?

(2) *Source* : From the account given by André Hurault, Sieur de Maisse, Ambassador Extraordinary from Henry IV of France to Queen Elizabeth. He was sent to discover whether the Queen was willing to join in negotiations for peace with Spain. He landed on Wednesday, November 30th, 1597 (O.S.). He saw Shakespeare's company act at Court, but his only comment was ' the sixth day they began to dance in the presence of the Queen, and to act comedies which was done in the Great Chamber.' Translated by Harrison and Jones. Nonesuch Press, 1931.

I reached London in the evening of the second day of the month of December, night having fallen, and was lodged in a house that the Queen had commanded for me wherein Drake had formerly lodged. What I learned of the Queen and of the principal of her Council before I had seen either her or any of them is that when a man speaks to her, and especially when he says something displeasing, she interrupts not seldom ; and by reason of her interruptions very often she misunderstands what is said to her and misreports it to her Council. Hence comes the custom of delivering to the Council in writing what has been said to her. She is a haughty woman, falling easily into rebuke. . . . In her own nature she is very avaricious and when some expense is necessary her Councillors must deceive her before embarking her on it little by little. She thinks highly of herself and has little regard for her servants and Council, being of opinion that she is far wiser than they ; she mocks them and often cries out upon them. On their part, they, even the Earl of Leicester, have given her a high opinion of her wisdom and prudence. she thinks also this is due to her age, saying quite freely that she was intended for affairs of state, even from her cradle ; she told me so herself. She is sixty years old, and since the seventh of November last, 1597, in the fortieth year of her reign.

8th December : [*de Maisse had an audience of the Queen*].
She was strangely attired in a dress of silver cloth, white and crimson, or silver ' gauze ', as they call it. This dress had slashed

F

sleeves lined with red taffeta, and was girt about with other little sleeves, that hung down to the ground, which she was for ever twisting and untwisting. She kept the front of her dress open, and one could see the whole of her bosom, and passing low, and often she would open the front of this robe with her hands as if she was too hot. The collar of the robe was very high, and the lining of the inner part all adorned with rubies and pearls, very many, but quite small. She had also a chain of rubies and pearls about her neck. On her head she wore a garland of the same material and beneath it a great reddish-coloured wig, with a great number of spangles of gold and silver, and hanging down over her forehead some pearls, but of no great worth. On either side of her ears hung two great curls of hair, almost down to her shoulders and within the collar of her robe, spangled as the top of her head. Her bosom is somewhat wrinkled, as well as one can see for the collar that she wears round her neck, but lower down her flesh is exceeding white and delicate, so far as one could see.

As for her face, it is and appears to be very aged. It is long and thin, and her teeth are very yellow and unequal, compared with what they were formerly, so they say, and on the left side less than on the right. Many of them are missing, so that one cannot understand her easily when she speaks quickly. Her figure is fair and tall and graceful in whatever she does ; so far as may be she keeps her dignity, yet humbly and graciously withal.

All the time she spoke she would often rise from her chair and appear to be very impatient with what I was saying. She would complain that the fire was hurting her eyes, though there was a great screen before it and she six or seven feet away ; yet did she give orders to have it extinguished, making them bring water to pour on it. She told me she was well pleased to stand up, and that she used to speak thus with ambassadors who came to seek her, and used sometimes to tire them, of which they would on occasion complain. I begged her not to overtire herself in any way, and I rose when she did ; and then she sat down again, and so did I.

(3) *Source*: from *A Journey into England in the Year M.D. XCVIII* by Paul Hentzner, translated by Horace Walpole for the Aungervylle Society, 1757, p. 31. Hentzner was tutor to a young German nobleman.

Next came THE QUEEN, in the Sixty-fifth Year of her Age, as we were told, very Majestic; her Face oblong, fair, but wrinkled; her Eyes small, yet black and pleasant; her Nose a little hooked; her Lips narrow; and her Teeth black (a defect the English seem subject to, from their too great Use of Sugar); she had in her Ears two Pearls, with very rich Drops; she wore false Hair, and that red . . . her Hands were small, her Fingers long, and her Stature neither tall nor low; her Air was stately, her Manner of speaking mild and obliging.

AN EMBASSY TO QUEEN ELIZABETH I

1564 (probably October)

Sir James Melville of Hallhill (1535–1617), was sent by Mary, Queen of Scots, to try to win over Queen Elizabeth I to Mary's marriage to Lord Darnley. Later he tried to prevent the murder of Mary's secretary, Rizzio, and later still he tried to dissuade Mary from marrying Bothwell. In this extract from his memoirs he is describing an interview with Queen Elizabeth. The word 'sister' is used here in its then customary sense when one queen was speaking of any other. Elizabeth and Mary were in fact cousins.

Source: *The Memoirs of Sir James Melville*, 3rd edition, pub. 1752 p. 96.

She (Elizabeth) appeared to be so affectionate to the Queen her good sister, that she expressed a great desire to see her. And because their so much, by her, desired meeting could not be so hastily brought to pass, she appeared with great delight to look upon her Majesty's picture. She took me to her bed-chamber, and opened a little cabinet, wherein were divers little pictures wrapt within paper, and their names written with her own hand upon the papers. Upon the first that she took up was written, ' My Lord's picture '. I held the candle and pressed to see that picture so named. She appeared loath to let me see it ; yet my importunity prevailed for a sight thereof, and found it to be the Earl of Leicester's picture. I desired that I might have it to carry home to my Queen ; which she refused, alledging that she had but that one picture of his. I said, Your Majesty hath here the original, for I perceived him at the farther part of the chamber, speaking with Secretary Cecil. Then she took out the Queen's picture, and kissed it ; and I adventured to kiss her hand, for the great love therein evidenced to my mistress. She shewed me also a fair ruby, as great as a tennis-ball. I desired that she would either send it, or my Lord Leicester's picture, as a token unto the Queen. She said, if the Queen would follow her counsel, that she would in process of time get all she had ; that in the mean time she was resolved in a token to send her with me a fair diamond. It was at this time late for supper ; she appointed me to be with her next morning by eight of the clock, at which time she used to walk in her garden.

THE MURDER OF RIZZIO

Saturday, March 9th, 1565 (o.s.)

David Rizzio—or more correctly Riccio—(1533?–1566) was the son of an Italian musician. Recommended to Mary, Queen of Scots, as a bass singer for her choir, he rapidly rose in the estimation of the Queen, until he was virtually the Prime Minister of a sovereign who intended to be independent of the Scottish nobility. In July 1565 Mary married the worthless Lord Darnley. She soon discovered her mistake, and the influence of Rizzio grew at the expense of Darnley, who was excluded from all political importance. Rizzio was haughty and hated by the whole of the nobility, who determined to be rid of him, but also to make the murder appear to be the wish and work of Darnley.

Source : *The Narrative* of Lord Ruthven, MS. Cotton, Calig. bk. ix, f. 219–222, printed in the Appendix (vol. 3) of Keith's *History of the Affairs of Church and State of Scotland.* Spelling modernized.

Further Reading : Froude, *History of England*, vol. vii.

Upon Saturday the 9th of March, conform to the King's ordinance and device, the said Earl of Morton, Lord Ruthven, and Lord Lindsay, having their men and friends in a readiness, abiding the King's advertisement ; the King having supped the sooner for the same purpose ; and the Queen's Majesty in her cabinet, within her inner-chamber at supper, the King sent for the said Earl, Lords, and their accomplices, and desired them to make haste and come to the Palace, for he should have the door of the privy-chamber open, and should be talking with the Queen before their coming. The said Earl Morton, Lords Ruthven and Lindsay, with their accomplices, entering the Palace by the King's commandment, and the said Earl Morton to the King's outer-chamber, and certain with him ; and the said Lord Ruthven the other way, through the King's chamber to the cabinet, up to the privy way to the Queen's chamber, as the King directed them, and through the chamber to the cabinet, where they found her Majesty at supper, at a little table, the Lady Argyll at the one end, and David at the other end, his cap on his head, the King speaking with her Majesty, with his hand about her waist.

The said Lord Ruthven at his entering in, said unto the Queen's Majesty, ' let it please your Majesty that yonder man David come forth of your privy chamber, where he hath been overlong '. The Queen answered, ' what offence hath he done ? ' Ruthven answered, that he made a greater and more heinous offence to her Majesty's honour, the King her husband, the Nobility and the Commonwealth. ' If it please your Majesty, he hath offended your honour, which I dare not be so bold to speak of. As to the King your husband's honour, he hath hindered him of the Crown-Matrimonial, which your Grace promised him, besides many other things which are not necessary to be expressed ; and hath caused your Majesty to banish a great part of the Nobility, and to forfeit them, that he might be made a Lord '. . . .

Then the said Lord Ruthven said to the King, ' Sir, take the Queen your wife and sovereign to you ', who stood all amazed, and wist not what to do. Then her Majesty rose upon her feet, and stood before David, he holding her Majesty by the plates of her gown, leaning back over the window, his dagger drawn in his hand, and Arthur Erskine, and the Abbot of Holyrood-house, and the Lord Keith, master of the household, with the French pothecary ; and one of the chamber began to lay hands on the Lord Ruthven, none of the King's party being there present. Then the said Lord Ruthven pulled out his dagger, and defended himself until more came in, and said to them, ' Lay no hands on me, for I will not be handled.' At the coming in of others into the cabinet, the said Lord Ruthven put up his dagger ; and with the rushing in of men, the board fell into the wall, meat and candles being thereon, and the Lady of Argyll took one of the candles in her hand. At the same instant the Lord Ruthven took the Queen in his arms and put her into the King's arms, beseeching her Majesty not to be afraid, for there was no man there that would do her body any more harm than they would do their own hearts ; and assured her Majesty that all that was done was the King's own deed. And the remnant of the gentlemen being in the cabinet took David out of the window, and after they had him out of the Queen's chamber, the said Lord Ruthven followed, and bade take him away down to the King's chamber the privy way ; and the said Lord returned to the cabinet, thinking that the said David had been taken down to the King's chamber ; the press of the people hurled him forth to the outer-chamber, where there was a great number standing who were vehemently moved against him, so that they could not abide any longer, but slew him at the Queen's fore-door in the other chamber. . . .

and David was thrown down the stairs from the Palace where he was slain, and brought to the Porter's lodge, who taking off his clothes said, ' this was his destiny ; for upon this chest was his first bed when he came to this place, and now he lieth a very niggard and misknown knave '. The King's dagger was found sticking in his side. The Queen enquired at the King where his dagger was? who answered that he wist not well. ' Well,' said the Queen, ' it will be known hereafter.'

THE REBELLION OF THE NORTHERN EARLS, 1569

The arrival of Mary, Queen of Scots, in England in 1568 raised the hopes of the Catholics. A marriage between her and the most powerful of the English nobles, Thomas Howard, 4th Duke of Norfolk, was mooted. Elizabeth was much against the plan. Norfolk at first rejected it, but later lent himself to it. He was about to join the Catholic and discontented Lords in the north of England in a plot against Cecil, when he was arrested and sent to the Tower. The northern Earls carried out their rising, but it was a failure, partly owing to the resistance put up by Sir George Bowes (1527–1580). Had the Earl of Sussex, Lord President of the North, listened to the warnings Bowes sent him, the rising might have been nipped in the bud.

Source : *Memorials of the Rebellion of* 1569, compiled by Sir C. Sharp from the Bowes MSS. at Streatlam, contain the following letter written by Sir George Bowes to Secretary Cecil, dated 14th of December, 1569. The spelling and punctuation have been modernized.

Further Reading : Froude, *History of England*, vol. ix.

It may please your honourable mastership : yesternight I received a letter from the Queen's Majesty, of the 26th of Nov. last, with another letter from you of the same date . . . being then commanded by her Grace's several commissions to me and others direct, to levy power, to be in readiness to attend upon the Lord Lieutenant, to suppress this rebellion. I had gathered together both horsemen and also footmen, and keeping them at Barnard Castle with me, to repair to the Lord Lieutenant upon his Lordship's call, as he had directed me. I was, in the meantime, besieged by the rebels, and continuing there in straight siege, with very hard diet and great want of bread, drink and water, which was our only drink, save I mixed it with some wine.

I found the people in the Castle in continual mutinies, seeking not only by great numbers to leap the walls and run to the rebels, but also by all means to betray the piece, and with open force to deliver it and all in it, to the rebels. So far, as in one day and night, two hundred and twenty-six men leaped over the walls and opened the gates and went to the enemy, of which number thirty-five broke their necks, legs or arms in the leaping. Upon which especial extremities, and that day our water that we had, by the intelligence of them that fled from us, being straight or taken away, and by other great occasions, I was forced, by composition offered, to leave the piece, taking with me all the men, armour, weapons and horses, leaving my household stuff, which I made no account of in this time of service, though the value were great, so as the enemies received only the bare piece and stuff aforesaid, which, by the causes aforesaid, I could hold no longer. And I am come with my whole number, which this day will be three hundred horse and one hundred footmen, to the Lo. Lieutenant to serve her Highness with all my force and ready heart, trusting it will please her Grace's goodness to accompt in good part these my doings, intended only to save her Grace's good subjects from the force of the rebels, and to bring them again in place of service rather than to preserve my life, the danger whereof shall never draw me any whit back from her Highness' service with my full duty. . . . At my coming abroad, my storers and keepers of my houses repaired to me with the same speech that Job's servants to him (save only my children) : for I am utterly spoiled of all my goods, both within and without : my houses fully defaced by pulling away of the doors, windows, irons of the windows, ceiling, and all my brew vessels and other vessels and chimneys appertaining to my kitchen, so that now I possess nothing but my horse, armour and weapon brought out from Barnard Castle, which I more esteem than twenty times so much of other things, for that by it I am enabled to serve my good Queen, whom God preserve, and I weigh not all my losses. And thus I pray God preserve you.

From Sysaye the 14th of December, 1569.

ELIZABETH I OPENS PARLIAMENT
WEDNESDAY, NOVEMBER 25TH, 1584

Source : *A Journey through England and Scotland,* by Leopold von Wedel, 1584 and 1585. Von Wedel was born in 1544 and died 1615. The original MS. is in the library of Graf von der Osten in Plathe, Pomerania. Printed in the R.H.S. Transactions, vol. ix, 1895. The diary of von Wedel is full of information, much of it wholly wrong, as may be seen from the opening sentence of the following extract.

The Queen has reigned already twenty-six years, and during her reign Parliament has never been held. This year she enters her fifty-third year, as it is said, and she has sent orders through the whole realm to convoke Parliament. The principal cause is, I am told, that the English do not wish the King of Scotland, who is the next to the throne, to be King of England, and wish to know who after the queen's death is to wear the crown. I have forgotten the exact date, but I believe the opening of Parliament took place on November 25th. All the streets and lanes in Westminster were well cleaned and strewn with sand when the queen made her entrance into the house, for it is a custom that on the first and last day of the session the king or queen shall be present in the assembly. At the head of the procession rode, two by two, eighteen lords and gentlemen of the court, after them fifteen trumpets, two gentlemen, each with 100 soldiers uniformly clad ; now came fifteen members of Parliament in long red cloth coats, lined with white rabbit and reverses of the same almost down to the girdle. Next followed two gentlemen, the first with the queen's mantle, the other with her hat, their horses were led by servants. Now came two heralds, each in a blue mantle with two wings on it of beaten gold bearing the queen's arms, then three pairs of gentlemen of the Parliament in their usual robes, two heralds like those before followed by thirteen gentlemen of the Parliament, counts and barons, like the former, two heralds, seven pairs of bishops in long red robes with broad reverses of white linen and square caps of black stuff on their heads, then came five pairs of gentlemen of the Parliament in long red coats set with four stripes of rabbit fur. Now followed the Chancellor of the realm, behind him the Treasurer and the Secretary in their usual robes, with broad golden collars hanging down in the front and back to the saddle. Followed four men with sceptres, each ornamented with a crown, followed some gentlemen of the Parliament like the others. All these, I have mentioned, had gold and silver trappings on their horses, the least valuable being velvet. Followed the huntsmen, about fifty in number, all of noble birth, with small spears. These marched on foot. Now followed a horse, led by a gentleman, the trappings, saddle and bridle all of gold covered with pearls, the latter being set with precious stones. On the forehead an ornament was fixed with one large diamond, and on the ears hung pearls. Now followed the queen in a half-covered sedan chair, which looked like a half-covered Bed. The chair and the cushions on which the queen was seated were covered with gold and silver cloth. The queen had a long red velvet parliamentary mantle, down to the waist, lined with ermine, white with little black dots, and a crown on her head. The sedan chair was carried by two cream-coloured horses with yellow manes and tails, on the heads and tails yellow and white plumes were fastened, and they had saddles and trappings of golden stuff. Behind the queen another horse was led, having trappings of red velvet fringed with gold and ornamented with plumes. . . . On both sides of the queen marched her guard, not in their daily suit, but clad in red cloth, covered with beaten gold. The procession took its way to Westminster Church, where all the kings are buried. Here the queen dismounted, knelt down at the entrance and said her prayers, entered the church, where prayers were offered and chants performed. Then the queen went to the house of Parliament close by, and was led into a separate chamber, on the platform of which was a splendid canopy of golden stuff and velvet, embroidered with gold, silver and pearls, and below it a throne, arranged with royal splendours, on which the queen seated herself. The benches in this chamber had their seats as well as the backs covered with red silk, in the midst four woolsacks of red cloth were laid square. The walls were entirely hung with royal tapestry. In front of the woolsacks opposite the door a low bar was fixed right across the chamber, also covered with red silk. On the woolsack nearest to the queen's throne sits the Chancellor, turning his back to the queen, on that to the right hand sit three judges, on that to the left three secretaries. Close to the bar, but outside of it, sit two [writing] clerks, on the benches around to the right side twenty bishops, two viscounts or peers, one marquis, to the left twenty counts and twenty barons. Thus the sitting of this Parliament began, they had sittings every day until Christmas, but the queen, as I said before, was present only on the first and last day. During the holy feast the sitting was suspended, but afterwards it began again and lasted until Easter, when it was again suspended, though not closed, and was to begin again. Meanwhile I left the country.

THE EXECUTION OF MARY, QUEEN OF SCOTS

TUESDAY, FEBRUARY 8TH, 1586 (O.S.)

Mary Stuart was the daughter of James V of Scotland and Marie de Guise, and great-granddaughter of Henry VII of England. She was thus a cousin to Elizabeth I. The chief facts in her life are these : born 1542 : succeeded to Scottish throne 1542 : sent to France 1548 : married the Dauphin, later Francis II, 1558, who died 1560 : returned to Scotland, 1561 : married Henry, Earl of Darnley, 1565 : connived at his murder, generally suspected to be the work of James Hepburn, 4th Earl of Bothwell : married Bothwell, 1567 : imprisoned in Lochleven Castle, 1568 : escaped, defeated at Langside, fled to England, imprisoned by Elizabeth, 1568 : executed 1587 (N.S.)

Source : A report sent to William Cecil, Lord Burghley, and endorsed in his hand *8th Feb.* 1586. *The Manner of the Q. of Scotts death at Fodrynghay, wr. by Ro. Wy.'* Landsdowne MSS 51 *art.* 46. Printed in Ellis, *Original Letters*, 2nd series, iii, 113–118. The author was probably R. Wynkfielde. Spelling modernized.

Further Reading: Froude, *History of England*, vol. xii,

. . . Her prayers being ended, the executioners, kneeling, desired her Grace to forgive them her death : who answered, ' I forgive you with all my heart, for now, I hope, you shall make an end of all my troubles.' Then they, with her two women, helping her up, began to disrobe her of her apparel : then she, laying her crucifix upon the stool, one of the executioners took from her neck the *Agnus Dei*, which she, laying hands off it, gave to one of her women, and told the executioner he should be answered money for it. Then she suffered them, with her two women, to disrobe her of her chain of pomander beads and all other her apparel most willingly, and with joy rather than sorrow, helped to make unready herself, putting on a pair of sleeves with her own hands which they had pulled off, and that with some haste, as if she had longed to be gone.

All this time they were pulling off her apparel, she never changed her countenance, but with smiling cheer she uttered these words, ' that she never had such grooms to make her unready, and that she never put off her clothes before such a company '. . . .

This done, one of the women having a Corpus Christi cloth lapped up three-corner-ways, kissing it, put it over the Q. of Sc. face, and pinned it fast to the caule of her head. Then the two women departed from her, and she kneeling down upon the cushion most resolutely, and without any token or fear of death, she spake aloud this Psalm in Latin, *In Te Domine confido, non confundar in eternam*, etc. Then, groping for the block, she laid down her head, putting her chin over the block with both her hands, which, holding there still, had been cut off had they not been espied. Then lying upon the block most quietly, and stretching out her arms cried, *In manus tuas, Domine*, etc. three or four times. Then she, lying very still upon the block, one of the executioners holding her slightly with one of his hands, she endured two strokes of the other executioner with an axe, she making very small noise or none at all, and not stirring any part of her from the place where she lay : and so the executioner cut off her head, saving one little gristle, which being cut asunder, he lift up her head to the view of all the assembly and bade *God save the Queen.* Then, her dress of lawn falling from off her head, it appeared as grey as one of threescore and ten years old, polled very short, her face in a moment being so much altered from the form she had when she was alive, as few could remember her by her dead face. Her lips stirred up and down a quarter of an hour after her head was cut off. . . .

Then one of the executioners, pulling off her garters, espied her little dog which was crept under her clothes, which could not be gotten forth but by force, yet afterward would not depart from the dead corpse, but came and lay between her head and her shoulders, which being imbrued with her blood was carried away and washed. . . .

TWELFTH NIGHT, JANUARY 6th, 1600 (O.S.)

On this day Queen Elizabeth I entertained the Russian Ambassador to dinner. Later she entertained Don Virginio Orsino, Duke of Bracciano, at the first performance of Shakespeare's *Twelfth Night.*

Source : These two accounts are taken from *The First Night of Twelfth Night* by Leslie Hotson, published by Rupert Hart-Davis, London, 1954.

(1) An account of his entertainment by Grigóri Ivánóvich Mikúlin, ambassador from the Lord Tsar and Great Prince of all Russia, Boris Fedórovich.

And when they came to the principal Chamber Lord Bedford spake to Grigori : ' Please you ', quoth he, ' to sit here for a little '. And at the same time there came from the Queen a higher person, an earl, the Lord Chamberlain of the Household, and shook hands with Grigori, and spake to Grigori : ' Let it not displease you,' quoth he, ' that I have not yet spoken to the Queen of you.' And the Lord Chamberlain went to the Queen, and Lord Windsor with him ; but Lord Bedford and Sir Jerome sat with Grigori ; and after a little while, Lord Windsor arrived from the Queen, and spake from her Majesty, putting off his hat : ' Our Lady,' quoth he, ' Elizabeth the Queen, hath commanded that you go to her '.

And then Grigori and Ivashko entered the Queen's chamber and prostrated themselves to her Majesty. And the Queen, rising from her place, bowed, and questioned Grigori about his health, and spake : ' For love of our brother ', quoth she, ' your great Lord, Tsar, and mighty Prince Boris Fedorovich, Monarch of all Russia, and in favour to you, I have this day summoned you to me on this Feast, to eat bread. But now I go to divine service, and you shall go along, and witness our ceremonies, how in our religion we pray to God, and how in our country the Communion Service is sung.' And she bade Grigori to go before her with her greatest lords. And the Queen passed out of the room to the entry.

And at that instant, at the entrance, on the threshold, there bowed low to the Queen an Italian nobleman ; and the Queen chatted with him, and appointed him to eat bread with her ; and the officers said that he was an Italian, the Florentine Duke Virginio degli Orsini, called brother-in-law to the French King ; he was come, said they, to make his obeisance to the Queen, to see the English realm, and to observe her Majesty's ceremonies ; and the Queen invited him to dine. ' However,' said they,' he is not to sit together with you at table in the Queen's dining-chamber, but is to dine in another chamber with the lords '.

Then the Queen passed to the Chapel ; and before the Queen went the courtiers, and after the courtiers the lords, and following the Queen, went many ladies and maidens ; and in the chambers and passages people stood on both sides ; on the right hand stood courtiers, and on the left ladies and maidens. And the Queen, going out of her chambers, passed to the Chapel. And at that moment in the Chapel they began to play on the organ, and on wind instruments, with much other music and song. The officers said, ' They are singing the psalms of David '.

And in the place where the priests serve is set a dais, and on the dais is placed a table covered with a damask cloth, and on the table lie two books covered with gold, which they call the Apostles and the Gospel ; and also on the tables are two unlighted candles. The priests were in golden copes, and at the sides stood subdeacons in white surplices. And as they began to celebrate the Eucharist, the Queen, approaching the place where the priests minister, knelt down, and gave the priest a dish with three things in papers ; and the officers said that the Queen in her religion at every Feast[1] brings as an offering to God gold, and frankincense, and myrrh. And having made her offering, she went back to her lodging. . . .

And to Grigori and Ivashko in the chamber came the nobleman and courtier, the Lord Chamberlain, and spake to Grigori and Ivashko : ' The Queen,' quoth he, ' hath commanded that you go to the dining chamber, and at table await her coming.'

And after that, with little delay, the Queen came to the dining chamber, and commanded the Archbishop and the priests to say before dinner ' Our Father ' ; and she sat down to table ; but she gave order for Grigori, Ivashko, and the interpreter Andrei to be seated by themselves at a special table on the left hand. . . .

And as we sat at dinner, the Queen sent by the Carver a gift to Grigori—a white loaf on a dish covered with a napkin, and he spake to Grigori : ' Our great Lady,' quoth he, ' Elizabeth the Queen, of her grace bestows on you this loaf. And moreover,' quoth he, ' she graces you with this napkin.' And Grigori prostrated himself to the Queen's favour in the gift and the napkin. . . .

Then drink was brought before the Queen ; and her Majesty, rising, drank a cup to the health of the great Lord, Tsar, and mighty Prince Boris Fedorovich, Monarch of all Russia ; and having drunk the cup, she commanded the Tsar's cup to be given to Grigori ; and Grigori, coming out from the table, drank the Tsar's cup, and having drunk it said : ' I see, your Majesty, your

[1] The Epiphany.

love to our great Lord, the great Tsar; and when I (which God grant) shall be with the great Tsar, I shall inform his Majesty of your love.' . . .

And when the Queen's board was removed, the Queen rose from the table and began to wash her hands; and having washed, she ordered the silver ewer with water to be taken to Grigori; and to her Majesty's favour Grigori prostrated himself, but did not wash his hands, and said, 'Our great Lord the Tsar calls Elizabeth the Queen his beloved sister; and it doth not befit me, his bond-slave, to wash my hands in her presence. Thereupon the Queen waxed merry, and commended Grigori that he honoured her so highly as not to wash his hands before her.

After that, the Queen summoned Grigori and Ivashko and the interpreter Andrei to her hand, and commanded them to go to their house.

(2) An Account of his entertainment, by Don Virginio Orsino, Duke of Bracciano.

When her Majesty had entered her chamber, I was conducted into the hall where her Majesty was to dine: the which hall, together with many other rooms, was hanged with tapestries of gold. On a dais at the head was her Majesty's table; at the opposite end, a great court-cupboard all of vessels of gold; on the right hand, a great cupboard of vessels with gold and jewels; and on the left, a low table with three little services for the Muscovite ambassador and two who were with him; it being the custom of Muscovy that if he had not been seen eating in the Queen's presence, his Great Duke would have had him beheaded.

Meanwhile came the viands of her Majesty, borne by knights, and the Sewer was of the great Order.[1] These did the same honour to her Majesty's chair of state as they would have done had she been present; and as soon as the table was prepared came the Queen. I reserve for telling by word of mouth the manner of the many cloths, and of her hand-washing, for this description alone would fill four sheets. Presently after her Majesty had sat down to table, the Muscovite ambassador (of whose ridiculous manners I shall give an account) fell to dining; and I was

[1] Of the Garter.

conducted by the Lord Admiral . . . and many other great officers of the Crown and Knights of the Order,[1] into a hall where there was prepared for me a most noble banquet, at the end of which appeared a good music. . . .

. . . To sup with me came the Master of the Horse, and also the Earl of Cumberland; and with him I had some speech which will be to the taste of his Highness,[2] since that man is the greatest corsair in the world. Presently after supper I was taken to the lodgings of her Majesty, where in a hall the Secretary of State caused me to salute all the ladies of title after the French fashion.[3] With one I spoke Italian, with divers French; and with the rest he himself played the interpreter for me.

Hereupon the Queen came in, and commanded me to go along discoursing with her. Her Majesty mounted the stairs, amid such sounding of trumpets that methought I was on the field of war, and entered a public hall, where all round about were rising steps with ladies, and divers consorts of music. As soon as her Majesty was set at her place, many ladies and knights began a grand ball. When this came to an end, there was a mingled comedy,[4] with pieces of music and dances, and this too I am keeping to tell by word of mouth. The Muscovite ambassador was not present. I stood ever near her Majesty, who bade me to be covered, and withal caused a stool to be fetched for me; and although she willed me a thousand times to sit, I would however never obey her. She conversed continually with me; and when the comedy was finished, I waited upon her to her lodgings, where there was made ready for her Majesty and for the ladies a most fair collation, all of confections. The Queen, after having first taken but two morsels, gave order that it should all be put to the spoil; which was done amid a graceful confusion. After the Queen had gone into her chamber, those ladies who could speak Italian and French fell into conversation with me, and at the end of half an hour we took our leave of one another, and I went away home, it being already two hours after midnight.

[1] Of the Garter.   [2] his uncle, the Grand Duke Ferdinand of Tuscany
[3] 'first, kiss the fingers; next, kiss the lips; then embrace the waist.'
[4] Shakespeare's *Twelfth Night*.

G

THE TRUE MANNER OF TAKING OF EDMUND CAMPION AND HIS ASSOCIATES

JULY 17TH, 1581

The ecclesiastical settlement made by Elizabeth in 1559 finally established England as a Protestant country. The foundation of the English seminary college at Douai in 1568 marks the moment when the Counter-Reformation began upsetting that settlement. From about 1575 English Catholic priests trained at Douai began to arrive secretly in England and to travel the countryside in disguise, living secretly with Catholic families, always in danger of arrest and martyrdom. Of these priests two of the most notable were Campion and Gerard.

Source : *A very True Report of the Apprehension and Taking of that arch-Priest Edmund Campion, the Pope his right hand* : *by George Elliott, one of the Ordinary Yeomen of Her Majesty's Chamber.* From a MS. in Lambeth Palace Library xxx, 8, 17. Printed in Arber's *An English Garner.*

Further Reading : Allen, *Death and Martyrdom of Father Edmund Campion.*

It pleased my Lords of Her Highness's most honourable Privy Council to grant the Commission . . . to myself and to the said David Jenkins for the apprehension of certain lewd Jesuit Priests. . . . We were utterly ignorant where, or in what place, certainly to find out the said Campion or his compeers. . . . It then presently came to my remembrance of certain acquaintance which I once had with one THOMAS COOPER, a Cook, who in November [1578] was two years, served Master THOMAS ROPER of Kent; where at that time I in like manner served: and both of us, about the same month, departed the said Master ROPER his service ; I into Essex, and the said COOPER to Lyford in Berkshire, to one Master YATE. From whence, within one half year after, I was advertised, in Essex, that the said Cook was placed in service ; and that the said Master YATE was a very earnest Papist, and one that gave great entertainment to any of that sect. . . . Hereof I informed the said DAVID JENKINS, being my fellow in Commission, and told him it would be our best way to go thither first. . . . Upon this determination we set from London on the 14th day of July last; and came to the said Master YATE's House, the 16th of the same month [1581], being Sunday, about eight of the clock in the morning. . . . The Cook came forth presently to us where we sat still upon horseback. And after a few speeches, as betwixt friend and friend when they have been long asunder, were passed; still sitting upon our horses, I told him That I longed to see him; and that I was travelling into Derbyshire to see my friends, and came so far out of my way to see him. And said I, ' Now I have seen you, my mind is well satisfied; and so fare you well ! '

' No,' saith he, ' that shall you not do before dinner.'

I made the matter very earnest to be gone; and he, more earnest and importune to stay me. But in truth I was as willing to stay as he to have me.

And so, perforce, there was no remedy but stay we must. And having lighted from horseback; and being by him brought into the house, and so into the buttery, and there caused to drink : presently after, the Cook came and whisepered with me, and asked, Whether my friend (meaning the said Jenkins) were within the Church or not? Therein meaning, Whether he were a Papist or no?

To which I answered, ' He was not; but yet,' said I, ' he is a very honest man, and one that wisheth well that way.'

Then said the Cook to me, ' Will you go up? ' By which speech I knew he would bring me to a Mass.

And I answered him and said, ' Yea, for God's sake, that let me do : for seeing I must needs tarry, let me take something with me that is good.'

And so we left Jenkins in the buttery; and I was brought by the Cook through the hall, the dining parlour, and two or three other odd rooms, and then into a fair large chamber : where there was, at the same instant, one Priest, called SATWELL, saying Mass; two other Priests kneeling by, whereof one was CAMPION and the other called PETERS *alias* COLLINGTON; three Nuns and 37 other people. . . .

During the time that the Masses and the Sermon were made, JENKINS remained still beneath in the buttery or hall ; not knowing of any such matter until I gave him some intelligence what I had seen.

And so we departed, with as convenient expedition as we might, and came to one Master FETTIPLACE, a Justice of the Peace in the said country whom we made privy of our doings therein ; and required him that, according to the tenour of our Commission, he would take sufficient Power, and with us thither.

Whereupon the said Justice of Peace, within one quarter of an hour, put himself in a readiness, with forty or fifty men very well weaponed : who went in great haste, together with the said Master FETTIPLACE and us, to the said Master YATE his house.

Where at our coming upon the sudden, being about one of the clock in the afternoon of the same day . . . we beset the house with our men round about the moat in the best sort we could devise : and then knocked at the gates, and were presently heard and espied ; but kept out by the space of half an hour.

In which time, as it seemeth, they had hidden CAMPION and the other two priests in a very secret place within the said house ; and had made reasonable purveyance for him as is hereafter mentioned : and then let us into the house.

Where came presently to our sight, Mrs. YATE, the good wife of the house ; five Gentlemen, one Gentlewoman, and three Nuns : the Nuns being then disguised in Gentlewomen's apparel, not like unto that they heard Mass in. All which I well remembered to have seen, the same morning, at the Masses and Sermon aforesaid : yet every one of them a great while denied it. And especially the said Mistress YATE ; who could not be content only to make a plain denial of the said Masses and Priests : but with great and horrible oaths, forsware the same, betaking herself to the Devil if any such there were ; in such sort as, if I had not seen them with mine own eyes, I should have believed her.

But knowing certainly that these were but bare excuses, and that we should find the said CAMPION and his compeers if we made narrow search; I eftscons put Master FETTIPLACE in remembrance of our Commission : and so he, myself, and the said JENKINS Her Majesty's Messenger, went to searching the house; where we found many secret corners. . . .

It then drew something towards evening, and doubting lest we were not strong enough; we sent for some further aid. . . .

And so the said house was beset the same night with at the least three score men well weaponed; who watched the same very diligently.

And the next day, being Monday, in the morning very early . . . began a fresh search for the said Priests; which continued with very great labour until about ten of the clock in the forenoon of the same day : but the said Priests could not be found, and every man almost persuaded that they were not there.

Yet still searching, although in effect clean void of any hope for finding of them, the said DAVID JENKINS, by God's great goodness, espied a certain secret place, which he quickly found to be hollow; and with a pin of iron which he had in his hand much like unto a harrow tine, he forthwith did break a hole into the said place : where then presently he perceived the said Priests lying all close together upon a bed, of purpose there laid for them; where they had bread, meat, and drink sufficient to have relieved them three or four days together.

The said JENKINS then called very loudly, and said, ' I have found the traitors!'; and presently company enough was with him: who there saw the said Priests, when there was no remedy for them but *nolens volens*, courteously yielded themselves.

THE TORTURING OF FATHER JOHN GERARD

April, 1597

Gerard was born in 1564 and died in Rome in 1637. One of the most active of the seminary priests in England, he was betrayed by a servant, imprisoned and tortured. He escaped from prison, and later was suspected of complicity in Gunpowder Plot, 1605. Director of the English College in Rome 1627–1637. He wrote a narrative of Gunpowder Plot.

Source: *John Gerard, The Autobiography of an Elizabethan*: translated from the Latin by Philip Caraman. Longmans, 1951, from chapter 15.

On the third day the warder came to my room straight from his dinner. Looking sorry for himself, he said the Lords Commissioners had arrived with the Queen's Attorney-General and that I had to go down to them at once.

'I am ready,' I said, 'but just let me say an *Our Father* and *Hail Mary* downstairs.'

He let me go, and then we went off together to the Lieutenant's lodgings inside the walls of the Tower. Five men were there waiting for me, none of whom, except Wade, had examined me before. He was there to direct the charges against me. . . .

'You say,' said the Attorney-General, 'you have no wish to obstruct the Government. Tell us, then, where Father Garnet is. He is an enemy of the state, and you are bound to report on all such men.'

'He isn't an enemy of the state,' I said. . . . 'But I don't know where he lives, and if I did, I would not tell you.'

'Then we'll see to it that you tell us before we leave this place.'

'Please God you won't,' I answered.

Then they produced a warrant for putting me to torturé. They had it ready by them and handed it to me to read. (In this prison a special warrant is required for torture.)

I saw the warrant was properly made out and signed, and then I answered: 'With God's help I shall never do anything which is unjust or act against my conscience or the Catholic faith. You have me in your power. You can do with me what God allows you to do—more you cannot do.'

Then they began to implore me not to force them to take steps they were loath to take. They said they would have to put me to torture every day, as long as my life lasted, until I gave them the information they wanted.

' I trust in God's goodness,' I answered, ' that He will prevent me from ever committing a sin such as this—the sin of accusing innocent people. We are all in God's hands and therefore I have no fear of anything you can do to me.'

This was the sense of my answers, as far as I can recall them now.

We went to the torture-room in a kind of solemn procession, the attendants walking ahead with lighted candles.

The chamber was underground and dark, particularly near the entrance. It was a vast place and every device and instrument of human torture was there. They pointed out some of them to me and said I would try them all. Then they asked me again whether I would confess.

' I cannot,' I said.

I fell on my knees for a moment's prayer. Then they took me to a big upright pillar, one of the wooden posts which held the roof of this huge underground chamber. Driven into the top of it were iron staples for supporting heavy weights. Then they put my wrists into iron gauntlets and ordered me to climb two or three wicker steps. My arms were then lifted up and an iron bar was passed through the rings of one gauntlet, then through the staple and rings of the second gauntlet. This done, they fastened the bar with a pin to prevent it slipping, and then, removing the wicker steps one by one from under my feet, they left me hanging by my hands and arms fastened above my head. The tips of my toes, however, still touched the ground, and they had to dig away the earth from under them. They had hung me up from the highest staple in the pillar and could not raise me any higher, without driving in another staple.

Hanging like this I began to pray. The gentlemen standing around asked me whether I was willing to confess now.

' I cannot and I will not,' I answered.

But I could hardly utter the words, such a gripping pain came over me. It was worst in my chest and belly, my hands and arms. All the blood in my body seemed to rush up into my arms and hands and I thought that blood was oozing from the ends of my fingers and the pores of my skin. But it was only a sensation caused by my flesh swelling above the irons holding them. The pain was so intense that I thought I could not possibly endure it, and added to it, I had an interior temptation. Yet I did not feel any inclination or wish to give them the information they wanted. The Lord saw my weakness with the eyes of His mercy, and did not permit me to be tempted beyond my strength. With the temptation He sent me relief. Seeing my agony and the struggle going on in my mind, He gave me this most merciful thought : the utmost and worst they can do is to kill you, and you have often wanted to give your life for your Lord God. The Lord God sees all you are enduring—He can do all things. You are in God's keeping. With these thoughts, God in His infinite goodness and mercy gave me the grace of resignation, and with a desire to die and a hope (I admit) that I would, I offered Him myself to do with me as He wished. From that moment the conflict in my soul ceased, and even the physical pain seemed much more bearable than before, though it must, in fact, I am sure, have been greater with the growing strain and weariness of my body. . . .

Sometime after one o'clock, I think, I fell into a faint. How long I was unconscious I don't know, but I think it was long, for the men held my body up or put the wicker steps under my feet until I came to. Then they heard me pray and immediately let me down again. And they did this every time I fainted—eight or nine times that day—before it struck five. . . .

A little later they took me down. My legs and feet were not damaged, but it was a great effort to stand upright. . . .

A MEETING WITH SIR FRANCIS DRAKE AT SEA

SATURDAY, APRIL 4TH, 1579

On November 15th, 1577, Drake set sail on the voyage which was to take him round the world. On June 19th, 1578, he entered St. Julian's Bay, where he executed Doughty for stirring up mutiny in the ships. He then sailed through the Straits of Magellan, and went up the west coast of South America. Off the coast of Guatemala he fell in with the ship belonging to Francisco da Zarate.

Source : A letter from Don Francisco da Zarate to Don Martin Enriquez, Viceroy of New Spain. The original is in Atchivo General de Indias, Patronato, E. 1, C. 5, L. 2–21 : an English translation, from which this extract is taken, was published in *New Light on Drake*, p. 201 sqq, edited by Z. Nuttall for the Hakluyt Society, 1914.

Further Reading : Corbett, *Drake and the Tudor Navy*, vol. i, ch. x.

Realejo, Nicaragua, 16th of April, 1579.

I sailed out of the port of Acapulco on the 23rd of March and navigated until Saturday, the fourth of April, on which date, half an hour before dawn, we saw, by moonlight, a ship very close to ours. Our steersman shouted that she was to get out of the way and not come alongside of us. To this they made no answer, pretending to be asleep. The steersman then shouted louder, asking them where their ship hailed from. They answered ' from Peru ', and that she was ' of *Miguel Angel* ', which is the name of a well-known captain of that route. . . .

The ship of the adversary carried her bark at her prow as though she were being towed. Suddenly, in a moment, she crossed our poop, ordering us ' to strike sail ' and shooting seven or eight arquebuse shots at us.

We thought this as much of a joke as it afterwards turned out to be serious.

On our part there was no resistance, nor had we more than six of our men awake on the whole boat, so they entered our ship with as little risk to themselves as though they were our friends. They did no personal harm to any one, beyond seizing the swords and keys of the passengers. Having informed themselves as to who were on board ship, they ordered me to go in their boat to where their general was—a fact I was glad of, as it appeared to me that it gave me more time in which to recommend myself to God. But in a very short time we arrived where he was, on a very good galleon, as well mounted with artillery as any I have seen in my life.

I found him promenading on deck and, on approaching him, I kissed his hands. He received me with a show of kindness, and took me to his cabin, where he bade me be seated and said: ' I am a friend of those who tell me the truth, but with those who do not I get out of humour. Therefore you must tell me (for this is the best road to my favour) how much silver and gold does your ship carry? ' I said to him, ' None '. He repeated his question. I answered, ' None, only some small plates that I use and some cups—that is all that is in her.' He kept silent for a while, then renewing the conversation asked me if I knew Your Excellency, I said, ' Yes '. . . .

This general of the Englishmen is a nephew of John Hawkins, and is the same who, about five years back, took the port of Nombre de Dios. He is called Francisco Drac, and is a man of about 35 years of age, low of stature, with a fair beard, and is one of the greatest mariners that sail the seas, both as a navigator and as a commander. His vessel is a galleon of nearly four hundred tons, and is a perfect sailer. She is manned with a hundred men, all of service, and of an age for warfare, and all are as practised therein as old soldiers from Italy could be. Each one takes particular pains to keep his arquebuse clean. He treats them with affection, and they treat him with respect. He carries with him nine or ten cavaliers, cadets of English noblemen. These form a part of his council, which he calls together for even the most trivial matter, although he takes advice from no one. But he enjoys hearing what they say and afterwards issues his orders. He has no favourite.

The aforesaid gentleman sits at his table, as well as a Portuguese pilot, whom he brought from England, who spoke not a word during all the time I was on board. He is served on silver dishes with gold borders and gilded garlands, in which are his arms. He carries all possible dainties and perfumed waters. He said that many of these had been given to him by the Queen.

None of these gentlemen took a seat or covered his head before him, until he repeatedly urged him to do so. This galleon of his carries about thirty heavy pieces of artillery and a great quantity of firearms with the requisite ammunition and lead. He dines and sups to the music of viols. He carries trained carpenters and artisans, so as to be able to careen the ship at any time. Beside being new, the ship has a double lining. I understood that all the men he carries with him receive wages, because, when our ship was sacked, no man dared take anything without his orders. He shows them great favour, but punishes the least fault. He also carries painters who paint for him pictures of the coast in its exact colours. . . .

This corsair, like a pioneer, arrived two months before he intended to pass through and during that time for many days there were great storms. So it was that one of the gentlemen,[1] whom he had with him, said to him : ' We have been a long while in this strait and you have placed all of us, who follow or serve you, in danger of death. It would therefore be prudent for you to give order that we return to the North Sea, where we have the certainty of capturing prizes, and that we give up seeking to make new discoveries. You see how fraught with difficulties these are.'

This gentleman must have sustained this opinion with more vigour than appeared proper to the General. His answer was that he had the gentleman carried below deck and put in irons. On another day, at the same hour, he ordered him to be taken out, and to be beheaded in presence of all.

The term of his imprisonment was no more than was necessary to substantiate the lawsuit that was conducted against him. All this he told me, speaking much good about the dead man, but adding that he had not been able to act otherwise, because

[1] July 1578 in Port St. Julian Drake with his own hand executed Thomas Doughty for mutiny and treachery.

this was what the Queen's service demanded. He showed me the commissions that he had received from her and carried.[1] I tried to ascertain whether any relatives of the dead man had remained on board. They told me that there was only one, who was one of those who ate at his table. During all this time that I was on board, which was fifty-five hours, this youth never left the ship, although all the others did so, in turn. It was not that he was left to guard me. I think that they guarded him.

I managed to ascertain whether the General was well liked, and all said that they adored him.

This is what I was able to find out during the time I spent with him. . . .

AN ENGLISHMAN AND THE SPANISH INQUISITION IN THE CANARIES

1586

In 1504 the Inquisition was set up in the Canary Islands, whither came many merchants from the northern and Protestant European countries. For the most part Englishmen did not give much trouble, except between 1586 and 1596, when a fair number of English sailors found their way into the secret cells, a period when the relations between England and Spain were at their worst. The following account shows the routine questions which were put to the accused. Sentences of perpetual imprisonment were frequent, but they were seldom enforced, and escapes were common and perhaps connived at. John Ware escaped twice. It was this sort of treatment which roused the wrath of Drake.

Source : *English Merchants and the Spanish Inquisition in the Canaries.* extracted from the archives in the possession of the Most Hon. The Marquess of Bute, edited by Alberti and Wallis Chapman, for the R.H.S. 1912, pp. 7 sqq.

[1] This sentence seems to dispose of the accusation that Drake had no commission from the Queen and that the execution was thus illegal.

1st Audience.

In Canary the 13th day of the month of September . . . the Inquisitor Francisco Madaleno commanded a man to be brought in from the cells. . . .

Said, that his name is John Ware, native of Swanage in England, that he is seventeen years of age and a fisherman, and that six days since he was brought to the cells. . . .

Questioned what religion is observed by his said parents.

Said, that they live alone and no other person lives in their house, in which there are images which they told him were of God and Holy Mary, but that these images are kept secret as, if it were known, his parents would be burnt, because the Queen is a Lutheran. . . .

2nd Audience.

Questioned, whether this confessant in abstaining from meat on Wednesdays thought he was serving God, and what he thought to gain thereby.

Said, that meat was prohibited by the Queen's order, and for this reason he abstained from it, because had he been seen eating it he would have been thrown into prison, but that he did not think that he was doing any good work, because his mother had told him that according to the old faith one might very well eat meat on Wednesdays. . . .

In Canary 18th day of September . . . the Inquisitor . . . said that as the cells were occupied, and as there were other persons to be sent there, and as the said John was being fed at the expense of the fiscal who has not the wherewithal to provide for him, he commanded, and commands, that the said John be placed in the Dominican monastery . . . until his case should be concluded, the friars being charged to instruct him in Christian doctrine. . . .

Publication.

Questioned, whether this confessant knows what it is to be a Lutheran

Said, that he understands that to be a Lutheran means not to attend Mass and to steal, and he could give no other explication whatever. . . .

Canary 14th day of March 1586 . . . the Inquisitor . . . commanded that the said John Ware be brought in, who, being present, was asked whether he has remembered anything further. . . .

Said, that he has nothing further to add. . . .

He was reminded that he has been many times admonished to speak the entire truth as to all that he himself has said or done, or that he knows others have said or done . . . but that he has not wished to do so, as by the said process it appears that he conceals many things . . . and he is admonished in the name of God, Our Lord, and of his glorious and blessed Mother, Our Lady the Virgin Mary, to speak and confess the entire truth as to what has been testified. . . .   But if not, he is notified that this process has been examined by persons of learning and of upright conscience, who are of opinion that he should be put to the torture, that therein he may speak the truth.

Said, that he has nothing further to say, as he has spoken the truth.

And then the said Inquisitor and Ordinary seeing that the said John Ware was ' negative ' pronounced the following sentence : . . . Christi nomine invocato.   We find having considered the proceedings, and merits of the case, from signs and suspicions resulting therefrom against the said John Ware, that we must condemn him to be put to torture, which we command shall be continued during such time as we think fit, that therein he may speak the truth. . . .

And we protest unto him, that if in the said torture he should die, or be maimed, or if any effusion of blood or mutilation of any member should ensue, the fault must lie with him, and not with us, because he has not willed to speak the truth. . . .

And upon this order was given to proceed to the torture chamber . . . and arriving there order was given for the arms of the said John Ware to be tied, and being thus tied :

He was admonished by the love of God to speak the truth, and not to bring this great trouble on himself.

[Under torture John Ware hereupon confessed that he had prevaricated in many of his answers.]

Questioned, why he has not spoken the truth before.

Replied, that the devil deceived him, in order to prevent him from speaking it until now.

Questioned, whether the devil has also misled him into persevering in the new religion, which he has believed up to the present, which may be inferred from his not speaking the truth till now.

Replied, that he has spoken the truth, and that when he was arrested by the Holy Office, he abandoned belief in the said religion of England, and returned to the Holy Catholic Faith.

He is notified it is not credible that he was entirely converted to our Catholic Faith, since he denied the truth of the charges brought against him by the witnesses, and has not confessed until now.

Says that he asks God's pardon for this and could give no other explication whatever, and thus it appearing to the Inquisitor and Ordinary that the said John Ware had given satisfaction, they suspended the torture, and so he was untied and found to all appearance sound in all his limbs, and thus this matter ended after ten in the morning. . . .

Votes. In Canary 21st day of the month of March 1586 . . . were of opinion and voted unanimously that he should be reconciled as a penitent in a public *auto-da-fé*, with confiscation of property, habit, and three years imprisonment, to be accomplished by rowing in his Majesty's galleys without pay. . . .

[John Ware in company with three other Englishmen escaped from the island of La Palma. Their effigies were carried in an *auto-da-fé* upon Wednesday 1st of May, 1586 and were then handed over to the secular autnorities, with instructions that they were to be burned.]

THE SPANISH ARMADA

1588

The Spanish Armada set sail for the invasion of England on Saturday, May 18th, 1588, from Lisbon. It was driven into Corunna by winds and shortage of water, whence it sailed again on Friday, July 12th, was sighted off the Lizard on July 19th. A running fight took place up the Channel from the 21st to the 27th. On the 28th was begun the battle of Gravelines, with the sending of eight fire-ships among the Spaniards. The Armada was driven out of the Channel into the North Sea, but the English had to abandon the pursuit on August 1st because of a shortage of powder. A general account of the whole campaign is given by Hawkins in the first letter: the second letter describes an episode which took place on Monday, July 29th.

(1) *Source*: A letter from Sir John Hawkins to Walsingham, dated July 31st, 1588. State Papers Dom. Eliz. ccxiii 71 printed in Laughton, *Defeat of the Spanish Armada*, vol. i, pp. 358 sqq.

Further Reading: Corbett, *Drake and the Tudor Navy*, vol. ii.

My bounden duty humbly remembered unto your good Lordship :—I have not busied myself to write often to your Lordship in this great cause, for that my Lord Admiral doth continually advertise the manner of all things that doth pass. So do others that understand the state of all things as well as myself. We met with this fleet somewhat to the westward of Plymouth upon Sunday in the morning, being the 21st of July, where we had small fight with them in the afternoon. By the coming aboard one of the other of the Spaniards, a great ship, a Biscayan, spent her foremast and bowsprit; which was left by the fleet in the sea, and so taken up by Sir Francis Drake the next morning. The same Sunday there was, by a fire chancing by a barrel of powder, a great Biscayan spoiled and abandoned, which my Lord took up and sent away.

The Tuesday following, athwart of Portland, we had a sharp fight with them, wherein we spent a great part of our powder and shot ; so as it was not thought good to deal with them any more till that was relieved.

The Thursday following, by the occasion of the scattering of one of the great ships from the fleet, which we hoped to have cut off, there grew a hot fray, wherein some store of powder was spent; and after that, little done till we came near to Calais, where the fleet of Spain anchored, and our fleet by them; and because they should not be in peace there, to refresh their water or to have conference with those of the Duke of Parma's party, my Lord Admiral, with firing of ships, determined to remove them; as he did, and put them to the seas; in which broil the chief galleass spoiled her rudder, and so rode ashore near the town of Calais,[1] where she was possessed of our men, but so aground as she could not be brought away.

That morning, being Monday, the 29th of July, we followed the Spaniards, and all that day had with them a long and great fight, wherein there was great valour showed generally of our company. In this battle there was spent very much of our powder and shot; and so the wind began to blow westerly, a fresh gale, and the Spaniards put themselves somewhat to the northward, where we follow and keep company with them. In this fight there was some hurt done among the Spaniards. A great ship of the galleons of Portugal, her rudder spoiled, and so the fleet left her in the sea. I doubt not but all these things are written more at large to your Lordship than I can do; but this is the substance and material of matter that hath passed.

Our ships, God be thanked, have received little hurt, and are of great force to accompany them, and of such advantage that with some continuance at the seas, and sufficiently provided of shot and powder, we shall be able, with God's favour, to weary them out of the sea and confound them. . . .

(2) *Source* : A letter from Richard Tomson to Walsyngham. State Papers Dom. Eliz : ccxiii 67, printed in Laughton, *Defeat of the Spanish Armada*, vol. i, pp. 344 sqq.

At the break of day upon Monday morning, my Lord and all the fleet setting sail after our enemies, we espied riding within shot of the town of Calais the greatest of the King's galleasses, the rest of the Spanish fleet being two leagues to leeward of her.

[1] See next letter.

My Lord Admiral began to go toward the galleass with his ship, the *Ark*, but finding the water to be shallow, other ships of less draught bare in with her and shot at her ; whereupon she let slip and run the galleass aground hard before the town.

In our ship, which was the *Margaret and John of London*, we approached so near that we came on ground also ; but afterwards came safely off again with the flood, being damaged by nothing but by the town of Calais, who, off the bulwarks, shot very much at us, and shot our ship twice through. And the like powder and shot did Monsieur Gourdan[1] bestow upon sundry of our countrymen, and make us relinquish the galleass which otherwise we had brought away, being master of her above two hours, and gotten by hard assault, to the great credit of our country, if Monsieur Gourdan herein had not showed his affection to the Spaniards to be greater than our nation, or seemed by force to wrest from us that which we had gotten with bloody heads.

My Lord Admiral, seeing he could not approach the galleass with his ship, sent off his long boat unto her with 50 or 60 men, amongst whom were many gentlemen as valiant in courage as gentle in birth, as they well showed. The like did our ship send off her pinnace, with certain musketeers, amongst whom myself went. These two boards came hard under the galleass sides, being aground ; where we continued a pretty skirmish with our small shot against theirs, they being ensconced within their ship and very high over us, we in our open pinnaces and far under them, having nothing to shroud and cover us ; they being 300 soldiers, besides 450 slaves, and we not, at the instant, 100 persons. Within one half hour it pleased God, by killing the captain with a musket shot, to give us victory above all hope or expectation ; for the soldiers leaped overboard by heaps on the other side, and fled with the shore, swimming and wading. Some escaped with being wet ; some, and that very many, were drowned. The captain of her was called Don Hugo de Moncada. son to the viceroy of Valencia. He being slain, and the most part of their soldiers fled, some few soldiers remaining in her,

---

[1] The Governor of Calais.

seeing our English boats under her sides and more of ours coming rowing towards her, some with 10 and some with 8 men in them, for all the smallest shipping were the nearest the shore, put up two handkerchiefs upon two rapiers, signifying that they desired a truce. Hereupon we entered, with much difficulty, by reason of her height over us, and possessed us of her by the space of an hour and a half as I judge ; each man seeking his benefit of pillage until the flood came, that we might haul her off the ground and bring her away. . . .

HANS BUTTBER'S ACCOUNT OF THE ARMADA

(3) The Fugger family was the great German banking concern which financed many of the sixteenth century rulers in Europe. They had many trading concerns and agents all over Europe who kept the headquarters at Augsburg well informed on current affairs. Hans Buttber was skipper of one of the Fugger trading ships. On July 21st, 1588, there took place the first engagement between the British ships and the Spanish Armada. That night Drake was ordered to lead the English fleet, which was to follow his light. Suddenly his light went out and Drake went off on some ploy of his own. He maintained that he had seen some strange ships and went to investigate. In the morning he was far in the rear of the fleet in possession of a rich prize he had captured. Many, including Frobisher, refused to accept Drake's explanation and accused him of going off to capture a Spanish ship for his own advantage. This letter of Hans Buttber would seem to prove that Drake's explanation was in fact true, that he found the strange ships to be German and invited Buttber on board his own ship, *Revenge*.

Source : *The Fugger News-Letters*, Second Series, ed. by Victor von Klarwill : translated by L. S. R. Byrne. Bodley Head. 1926. p. 168.

Further Reading : Corbett, *Drake and the Tudor Navy* vol. ii. Williamson, *The Age of Drake*.

Hamburg, August 3 and 4, 1588.

Hans Buttber has arrived off the town in a big ship. He comes through the Channel from San Lucar. He was with Captain Drake for four or five days and joined the Englishman on the 21st O.S. of last month, just after the latter had had an engagement with the Spanish Armada. From the 21st to the 26th they had skirmished and fired heavily at each other, but they could not board, and the English with their little ships[1] sailed so well and manoeuvred so skilfully, firing meanwhile, that the galleasses could not get at them. Drake captured Don Pedro de Valdez, Admiral of fourteen vessels, and had him and ten other nobles brought on to his own ship. He gave them a banquet and treated them very handsomely and entertained them besides with trumpets and music. On this ship he took sixty guns and made four hundred and fifty prisoners. Moreover, he got yet another ship which caught fire of itself. All this happened in the presence of the skipper. On the 26th he received a pass, but only on condition of carrying a letter to another English port. There 28 Queen's ships were lying. As soon as their Admiral had read the document he got ready for sea to join Drake, but sent two yachts to Holland and Zeeland to tell them to keep a sharp look-out there and to prevent the Dunkirk people from coming out.

This noon there comes from Holland a vessel which was at Enkhuizen actually on the last day of July. It brings news that eighteen ships of the Spanish Armada were sunk by gunfire, and eight taken and brought to England. The rest of the Spanish Armada has fled to the French coast. If this is true it will somewhat abate Spanish insolence and give the English fresh courage, though they have no lack of insolence either.

[1] How early was begun the legend that the English ships were small! They were in fact of much the same size as the Spanish, but their streamlined appearance, introduced by Hawkins, made them look much smaller. The Spanish method of reckoning tonnage gave a higher result than the English method.

THE DISCOVERY OF TOBACCO

On April 9th, 1585, Sir Ralph Lane (d. 1603) sailed in the expedition led by Sir Richard Grenville to establish a plantation in North America. The colony was established in what is now North Carolina, and was then named Virginia. After Grenville had sailed for home, the colony was moved to Roanoke, where much exploration of the country took place. But in the end the colony was a failure and Francis Drake brought the survivors home in 1586. Among the members of the expedition was Thomas Heriot, 'servant to Sir Walter Ralegh, a member of the colony and there imployed in discovering a full twelvemonth'.

(1) *Source*: *A briefe and true report of the new-found land of Virginia*, by Thomas Heriot. From Hakluyt's *Principal Voyages*, taken from the 2nd (and first complete) edition, 1600, p. 254.

Further Reading: Rowse, *Sir Richard Grenville,*

There is an herbe which is sowed apart by itselfe, and is called by the inhabitants Uppowoc; in the West Indies it hath divers names, according to the severall places and countreys where it groweth and is used; the Spanyards generally call it Tabacco. The leaves thereof being dried and brought into pouder, they use to take the fume or smoake thereof, by sucking it thorow pipes made of clay, into their stomacke and head; from whence it purgeth superfluous fleame and other grosse humours, and openeth all the pores and passages of the body: by which meanes the use thereof not onely preserveth the body from obstructions, but also (if any be, so that they have not bene of too long continuance) in short time breaketh them; whereby their bodies are notably preserved in health, and know not many grievous diseases, wherewithall we in England are often times afflicted.

This Uppowoc is of so precious estimation amongst them, that they thinke their gods are marvellously delighted therewith: whereupon sometime they make hallowed fires, and cast some of the pouder therin for a sacrifice: being in a storme upon the waters, to pacifie their gods, they cast some up into the aire and into the water: so a weare for fish being newly set up, they cast some therein and into the aire: after an escape from danger, they cast some into the aire likewise : but all done with strange gestures, stamping, sometime dancing, clapping of hands, holding up of hands, and staring up into the heavens, uttering therewith-all, and chattering strange words and noises.

We ourselves, during the time we were there, used to sucke it after their manner, as also since our return, and have found many rare and woonderfull experiments of the vertues thereof : of which the relation would require a volume by it selfe : the use of it by so many of late, men and women of great calling, as els, and some learned Physicians also, is of sufficient witnesse.

(2) *Source* : *A Journey into England in the Year M.D.XCVIII*, by Paul Hentzner, translated by Horace Walpole for the Aungervylle Society, 1757. Evidently fifteen years after Heriot's description smoking had become a habit in England, as the following extract shows. Hentzner described a visit he made to a theatre to see the baiting of bulls and bears, and he concludes his account thus :

At these spectacles, and everywhere else, the English are constantly smoking tobacco, and in this manner : they have pipes on purpose made of clay, into the farther end of which they put the Herb, so dry that it may be rubbed into powder, and putting fire to it, they draw the smoke into their mouths, which they puff out again through their nostrils, like funnels, along with plenty of plegm and defluxion from the head.

SIR WALTER RALEGH

Sir Walter Ralegh was, perhaps, the most brilliant of all the Elizabethan figures. Born probably in 1552, he was half-brother to Sir Humphrey Gilbert, with whom he collaborated in plans of dis-covery, and for the plantation of colonies. His most famous attempt —a failure— was the plantation of Virginia. After taking part in the fight against the Armada in 1588, in 1595 he set out on a voyage to discover El Dorado : what he did find was the country of Guiana. Sentenced to death for alleged complicity in the plot to put Lady

Arabella Stuart on the throne, he remained a prisoner in the Tower for twelve years, during which time he wrote his *History of the World*. In 1617 he was set free to take an expedition to Guiana to search for gold. If he failed, he pledged himself to return. He failed, came back and was executed, 1618.

Source : *The Discovery of the Large Rich, and Bewtiful Empire of Guiana, performed in the year 1595 by Sir W. Ralegh, Kt.* (from the first edition in Eton College Library).

Spelling has been modernized.

Further Reading : Quinn, *Raleigh and the Empire.*

The next day we arrived at the port of *Morequito*, and anchored there, sending away one of our Pilots to seek the king of *Aromaia*, uncle to *Morequito*, slaine by *Berreo*, as aforesaid. The next day following, before noon, he came to us on foot from his house, which was 14 English miles (himself being 110 years old) and returned on foot the same day, and with him many of the borderers, with many women and children, that came to wonder at our nation, and to bring us down victual, which they did in great plenty, as venison, pork, hens, chickens, fowl, fish, with divers sorts of excellent fruits, and roots, and great abundance of *Pinas*, the princess of fruits, that grow under the *Sun*, especially those of *Guiana*. They brought us also store of bread, and of their wine, and a sort of *Paraquitos*, no bigger than wrens, and of all other sorts both small and great : one of them gave me a beast called by the Spaniards *Armadilla*, which they call *Cassacam*, which seemeth to be barred over with small plates somewhat like to a *Renocero*, with a white horn growing in his hinder parts, as big as a great hunting horn, which they use to wind instead of a trumpet. *Monardus*, writeth that a little of the powder of that horn put into the ear, cureth deafness.

After this old king had rested a while in a little tent, that I caused to be set up, I began by my interpreter to discourse with him of the death of *Morequito* his predecessor, and afterward of the Spaniards, and ere I went any farther I made him know the cause of my coming thither, whose servant I was, and that the Queen's pleasure was, I should undertake the voyage for their defence, and to deliver them from the tyranny of the Spaniards, dilating at large (as I had done before to those of *Trinedado*) her

Majesty's greatness, her justice, her charity to all oppressed nations, with as many of the rest of her beauties and virtues, as either I could express, or they conceive, all which being with great admiration attentively heard, and marvellously admired, I began to sound the old man as touching *Guiana*, and the state thereof, what sort of common wealth it was, how governed, of what strength and policy, how far it extended, and what nations were friends or enemies adjoining, and finally of the distance, and way to enter the same : he told me that himself and his people with all those down the river towards the sea, as far as *Emeria*, the Province of *Carapana*, were of *Guiana*, but that they called themselves *Orenoqueponi*, because they bordered the great river *Orenoque*, and that all the nations between the river and those mountains in sight called *Wacarima*, were of the same cast and appellation : and that on the other side of those mountains of *Wacarima* there was a large plain (which after I discovered on my return) called the valley of *Amariocapana*, in all that valley the people were also of the ancient *Guianians*. I asked what nations those were which inhabited on the further side of those mountains, beyond the valley of *Amariocapana*, he answered with a great sigh (as a man which had inward feeling of the loss of his country and liberty, especially for that his eldest son was slain in a battle on that side of the mountains, whom he most entirely loved) that he remembered in his father's life time when he was very old, and himself a young man that there came down into that large valley of *Guiana*, a nation from so far off as the *Sun* slept (for such were his own words), with so great a multitude as they could not be numbered nor resisted, and that they wore large coats, and hats of crimson colour, which colour he expressed, by shewing a piece of red wood, wherewith my tent was supported, and that they were called *Oreiones*, and *Epuremei*, those that had slain and rooted out so many of the ancient people as there were leaves in the wood upon all the trees, and had now made themselves Lords of all, even to that mountain foot called *Curaa*, saving only of two nations, the one called *Iwarawaqueri* and the other *Cassipagotos*, and that in the last battle fought between the *Epuremei* and the *Iwarawaqueri*, his eldest son was chosen to carry to the aid of the *Iwarawaqueri*, a great troup of *Orenoqueponi*, and was there slain, with all his people and friends, and that he had now remaining but one son. . . .

After he had answered thus far, he desired leave to depart, saying that he had far to go, that he was old and weak, and was every day called for by death, which was also his own phrase : I desired him to rest with us that night, but I could not intreat him. . . . The same night he returned to *Orocotona* his own town, so as he went that day 28 miles, the weather being very hot, the country being situate between 4 and 5 degrees of the *Equinoctial*. This *Topiawari* is held for the proudest, and wisest of all the *Orenoqueponi*, and so he behaved himself towards me in all his answers at my return, as I marvelled to find a man of that gravity and judgement, and of so good discourse, that had no help of learning nor breed.

A GERMAN TRAVELLER IN ENGLAND IN 1602

Philip Julius, Duke of Pomerania-Wolgast, Duke of Stettin (born 1584) set out on the Grand Tour and in 1602 visited England.

Source : *The Diary of the Duke of Stettin*, compiled by Frederic Gerschow (died 1635) by the command of Philip Julius. The MS. is lost, but a copy was found in the library of Count von der Osten of Plathe. Printed by the Royal Historical Society, Transactions vol. vi, 1892.

1602, September 10th—On the 10th at half-past twelve we went on board [at Boulogne] for the third time,[1] commending ourselves to God ; and with a pretty good wind we reached Dover at half-past five in the evening.

. . . 19th—The 19th. As it was Sunday we did not go out much, and did not notice the great splendour of the dresses, because the

---

[1] Three times the travellers had been delayed from sailing by contrary winds. Duke suspected the sailors to be acting in agreement with the innkeeper.

English show themselves very well dressed every day, having splendid silken stuffs, such as we always found in Italy. Nothing is too expensive for them, and the ladies especially look very clean with their linen and frills all starched in blue.

All wear shawls of silk and velvet, and graceful and stately gowns ; are of polite manners and gestures, and are esteemed to be, as I have often heard it said, the most beautiful people, men as well as women, of good proportion and of a healthy, natural colour. . . .

23rd—On the 23rd as far as Bicester, 23 miles. Mr. Joachim Tribsees, the Duke's governor [steward] and Fredericus Gerscho rode about six miles out of their way, for our postilion did not know the road himself, and I must at this opportunity praise the kindly spirit of the English, for a gentleman noticing us from afar, and easily recognising us to be foreigners who had got off the right road, rode up to us and asked us in Latin where we wished to get to, and left his wife and ladies to show us the right way.

When at last we reached an inn, we could not, for want of an interpreter, get anything to eat or drink, until Frederick Gerscho found a learned parson in the village, who procured everything we wanted, and even for a short time left some of his own guests whom he had invited on that evening to settle accounts with the landlord, and thus showed us great honour and kindness. That day I would not have missed knowing Latin for a thaler. . . .

24th—When his Highness was on his way back the Governor [of Woodstock] sent his chaplain and a nobleman after him, respectfully requesting that his Highness, whose rank he had just learned, would do him the honour to return and to attend the hunt that was to take place the following day. His Highness, however, politely declined.

The English hold the chase in high esteem ; there is scarcely any royal residence, or even a nobleman's house, which has not at least one deer park—sometimes two, or even three, may be found.

Good level ground is left between them for following the deer and wounding them in the chase, there being no other large game.

If a man finds strange dogs in his deer park, he hangs them, however valuable they may be, as an insult to the huntsman.

This is also done with game killed by a strange huntsman, it being believed that the arrows, still frequently used, are poisoned.

The hunting parties are, however, generally arranged in honour of the ladies. As soon as a stag or other animal is killed, the lady is expected to give it the first cut with the hunting-knife on the shoulder, the rest of the work being left to the hunts-man.

Coursing hares is practised very often in England, and affords great sport, and as there is coppice and thickets in plenty, they are rarely baited by dogs, but only followed by them until they get fatigued or fall down. We were told that, after having followed a hare for pleasure's sake a whole day, the hunter would often leave the animal to his dogs, taking a rabbit instead.

The reason is that the game is thought less of than the amusement. This is the case even with the peasants, who also are permitted to hunt; they keep fine big dogs, at little expense, for with a little money they can procure the heads, entrails and feet of lambs and calves, which in England are always thrown away, with the exception of the tongue. . . .

26th—On the 26th his princely Grace arrived at Oeteland [Oatlands], where the servants of the court had set up their tents like a military camp, there not being enough lodgings. It was a cheerful hunting-box. The Queen[1] gave orders to lead us by her furrier to the garden close to the Palace, and her Royal Majesty passed us several times, walking as freely as if she had been only eighteen years old, always taking off her mascara and bowing deeply to his princely Grace, who, however, not willing to make himself known, stood almost behind.

Her Majesty also gave him to understand that she would like to see his princely Grace, according to English fashion, kiss her

[1] Elizabeth I.

hands, which, however, his Grace for various weighty reasons politely declined to do.

At last the Queen, to show her royal rank, ordered some of the noble lords and counsellors to approach, and they, in their stately dress, were obliged to remain on their knees all the time the Queen addressed them.

Meanwhile the Queen uncovered herself down to the breasts, showing her snow-white skin.

To judge from the portraits showing her Majesty in her thirtieth year, there cannot have lived many finer women at the time ; even in her old age she did not look ugly, when seen from a distance.

JAMES THE SIXTH OF SCOTLAND AND FIRST OF ENGLAND 1603–1625

James I was born in 1566, the only son of Mary, Queen of Scots and Lord Darnley. He became king of Scotland in 1567 on the abdication of his mother and succeeded to the English throne in 1603, on the death of his cousin, Elizabeth I.

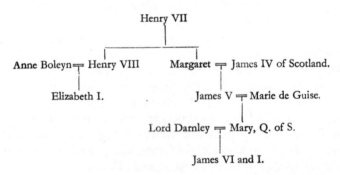

Source : *Court and Character of James I*, by Sir Anthony Weldon. The date of his birth is unknown : he died probably in 1649. He was Clerk of the Kitchen to James I in 1604, and became Clerk of the

Green Cloth in 1609, from which office he was dismissed in 1617 for satirising the Scots. In the Civil War he joined the Parliamentarian side. (Spelling modernized).

Further Reading : Carlyle, *Historical Portraits.*

He was of a middle stature, more corpulent through his clothes than in his body, yet fat enough, his clothes ever being made large and easy, the doublets quilted for stiletto proof, his breeches in great pleats and full stuffed. He was naturally of a timorous disposition, which was the reason for his quilted doublets; his eyes large, ever rolling after any stranger came in his presence, insomuch as many for shame have left the room, as being out of countenance. His beard was very thin, his tongue too large for his mouth, which ever made him speak full in the mouth, and made him drink very uncomely, as if eating his drink, which came out into the cup of each side of his mouth. His skin was as soft as taffeta sarsnet, which felt so because he never washed his hands, only rubbed his finger ends slightly with the wet end of a napkin. His legs were very weak, having had (as was thought) some foul play in his youth, or rather before he was born, that he was not able to stand at seven years of age; that weakness made him ever leaning on other men's shoulders. His walk was ever circular. . . .

He was very temperate in his exercises and in his diet, and not intemperate in his drinking : however, in his old age and Buckingham's jovial suppers, when he had any turn to do with him, made him sometimes overtaken, which he would the very next day remember, and repent with tears. It is true he drank very often, which was rather out of a custom than any delight, and his drinks were of that kind for strength, as Frontiniack, Canary, High Country wine, Tent Wine and Scottish ale, that had he not had a very strong brain, might daily have been overtaken, although he seldom drank at any one time above four spoonfuls, many times not above one or two. . . .

In his diet and apparel and journeys he was very constant; in his apparel so constant as by his good will he would never change his clothes until worn out to very rags : his fashion, never; insomuch as one bringing to him a hat of a Spanish block, he cast it from him, swearing he neither loved them nor their fashions. Another time, bringing him roses on his shoes, he asked if they would make him a ruff-footed Dove; one yard of six-penny ribbon served that turn. His diet and journeys were so constant that the best observing courtier of our time was wont to say, were he asleep seven years and then awakened, he would tell where the King every day had been and every dish he had had at his table. . . .

He was very witty and had as many ready witty jests as any man living, at which he would not smile himself, but deliver them in a grave and a serious manner. He was very liberal, of what he had not in his own gripe, and would rather part with £100 he never had in his keeping than one twenty shillings piece within his own custody. . . .

He would make a great deal too bold with God in his passion, both in cursing and swearing, and one strain higher verging on blasphemy, but would in his better temper say he hoped God would not impute them as sins and lay them to his charge, seeing they proceeded from passion. . . .

In a word, he was (take him altogether and not in pieces) such a King I wish this kingdom have never any worse, on the condition not any better, for he lived in peace, died in peace, and left all his kingdoms in a peaceable condition, with his own motto

Beati Pacifici.

JAMES I AT THE HAMPTON COURT CONFERENCE, 1604

On the accession of James I there was a general feeling that some concessions might be made to the High Church and to Presbyterian groups in England. James had already on his way to England received the Millenary Petition. He arranged for a Conference between the Established Church and the Presbyterians to take place at Hampton Court on Saturday, January 14th, 1604 (N.S.). James himself presided. The only good thing which came out of the Conference was the Authorised Version of the Bible.

Source : *The Summe and Substance of the Conference*, 1604, written by William Barlow, who was present, at the request of Archbishop Whitgift. Barlow was later Bishop of Rochester and then of Lincoln. The account is a good deal prejudiced against the Puritans.

Further Reading : Frere, *History of the Church of England*. Gardiner, *History of England*, vol. 1.

After a while, his excellent Majesty came in, and having passed a few pleasant gratulations with some of the Lords, he sat down in his chair . . . where beginning with a most grave and princely declaration of his general drift in calling this assembly, no novel device, but according to the example of all Christian princes, who in the commencement of their reign usually take the first course for the establishing of the Church, . . . and especially in this land King Henry the 8 toward the end of his reign ; after him, King Edward the 6, who altered more ; after him, Queen Mary, who reversed all ; and last, the Queen of famous memory, so his Highness added (for it is worth noting that his Majesty never remembered her but with some honourable addition) who settled it as it now standeth : wherein he said that he was happier than they in this, because they were fain to alter all things they found established, but he saw yet no cause so much to alter and change anything as to confirm that which he found well settled already ; which state, as it seemed, so affected his royal heart that it pleased him both to enter into a gratulation to Almighty God (at which words he put off his hat) for bringing him into the promised land, where religion was purely professed, where he sat among grave, learned, and reverend men, not as before elsewhere, a King without state, without honour, without order, where beardless boys would brave him to his face, and to assure us that he called not this assembly for any innovation, acknowledging the government eccelesiastical as now it is to have been approved by manifold blessings from God himself. . . .

[Dr. Reynolds referred to] the episcopal synod, where the bishop with his presbytery should determine all such points as before could not be decided. At which speech his Majesty was somewhat stirred, yet, which is admirable in him, without passion or show thereof ; thinking that they aimed at a Scottish presbytery, which, saith he, as well agreeth with a monarchy as God with the Devil. Then Jack and Tom and Will and Dick shall meet, and at their pleasures censure me and my Council and all our proceedings. Then Will shall stand up and say, ' It must be thus ' ; then Dick shall reply and say, ' Nay, marry, but we will have it thus '. And therefore here I must once reiterate my former speech, *Le Roy s'avisera*. Stay, I pray you, for one seven years before you demand of me that, and if then you find me pursy and fat and my wind-pipes stuffed, I will perhaps hearken to you. . . .

And here, because Dr. Reynolds had twice before obtruded the King's Supremacy . . . why, then, saith his majesty, I will tell you a tale. After that the religion restored by King Edward the Sixth was soon overthrown, by the succession of Queen Mary here in England, we in Scotland felt the effect of it. Whereupon Master Knox writes to the queen regent (of whom without flattery, I may say, that she was a virtuous and moderate lady) telling her that she was Supreme Head of the Church, and charged her, as she would answer it before God's tribunal, to take care of Christ His evangel, and of suppressing the popish prelates who withstood the same. But how long trow ye, did this continue? Even so long, till by her authority the popish bishops were repressed. He himself and his adherents were brought in and well settled, and by these means made strong enough to undertake the matters of reformation themselves. Then, lo, they began to make small account of her authority, but took the cause into their own hand, and, according to that more light wherewith they were illuminated, made a further reformation of religion. How they used that poor lady my mother is not unknown and with grief I may remember it. . . . How they dealt with me in my minority you all know ; it was not done secretly, and, though I would, I can not conceal it. I will apply it thus. And then, putting his hand to his hat, his majesty said : My lords the bishops . . . if once you were out, and they in place, I know what would become of my supremacy. No bishop, no king, as before I said. . . . If this be all, quoth he, that they have to say, I shall make them conform themselves, or I will harry them out of the land, or else do worse.

GUNPOWDER PLOT

TUESDAY, NOVEMBER 5TH, 1605 (O.S.)

The story is too well known to need any explanation, but one or two points may be noted. The name which Guy Fawkes first gave when he was arrested was John Johnson. Two diametrically opposed views have been expressed on the whole episode. What may be called the Catholic point of view, which holds that no plot ever existed but that the Government invented one in order to discredit the Catholics, has been fully expounded by Father Gerard in his *What was Gunpowder Plot ?* What may be called the generally accepted view has been fully set out by S. R. Gardiner in his *What Gunpowder Plot Was*, and most historians agree that he has conclusively demolished Father Gerard's case. Father Gerard's reply *The Gunpowder Plot and the Gunpowder Plotters* and his *Thomas Winter's Confession and the Gunpowder Plot*, carry the controversy very little further. In 1951 Hugh Ross Williamson in

I

his *The Gunpowder Plot* reiterated the Catholic point of view. The very full bibliography and the illustrations are most valuable. The best short account is that by G. M. Trevelyan in his *England under the Stuarts.*

(1) *Source*   The following letter was almost certainly written by by Tresham. It was sent to Lord Monteagle as a warning to his Catholic friends not to attend the opening of Parliament. Monteagle sent the letter on to the government. It is here reproduced exactly as it was sent. (Public Record Office, London).

> my lord out of the loue i beare to some of youer frends i haue a caer of youer preseruacion therefor i would aduyse yowe as yowe tender youer lyf to deuys some excuse to shift of youer attendance at this parleament for god and man hath concurred to punishe the wickednes of this tyme and thinke not slightlye of this aduertisment but retyere youre self into youre contri wheare yowe maye expect the euent in safti for thowghe theare be no apparance of anni stir yet I saye they shall receyue a terrible blowe this parleament and yet they shall not seie who hurts them this councel is not to be contemned because it may do yowe good and can do yowe no harm for the dangere is passed as soon as yowe haue burnt the letter and i hope god will give yowe the grace to mak good use of it to whose holy proteccion i comend yowe.
>
> To the right honorable the lord mowteagle.

(2) *Source:* From a letter written by Sir Edward Hoby, a gentleman of the Bedchamber, to his friend, Sir Thomas Edmondes, the English ambassador at Brussels. It is dated November 19th, 1605 (a Tuesday) and describes the examination of Guy Fawkes (John Johnson), immediately after his arrest, in the presence of James I on November 5th. It is likely that Hoby was present at the examination. Spelling has been modernized. B. M. Stowe MS. *168, f. 230.*

. . . On the 5th of November we began our Parliament, to which the King should have come in person, but refrained, through a practice but that morning discovered. The plot was to have blown up the King at such time as he should have been set in his royal throne, accompanied by his children, Nobility and Commons and[1] . . . with all Bishops, Judges and Doctors,

[1] One word in the original MS. has been damaged.

at one instant and blast to have ruined the whole estate and kingdom of England. And for the effecting of this there was placed under the Parliament house, where the king should sit, some 30 barrels of gunpowder, with great store of wood, faggots and bars of iron. . . .

. . . In a vault under the parliament chamber before spoken of one Johnson was found with one of these close lanterns preparing the train against the next morrow, who, being after brought into the galleries of the court, and there demanded if he were not sorry for his so foul and heinous a treason, answered that he was sorry for nothing but that the act was not performed. Being replied unto him that no doubt there had been a number in that place of his own religion, how in conscience he could do them hurt, he answered a few might well perish to have the rest taken away. Others telling him that he should die a worse death than he that killed the Prince of Orange, he answered that he could bear it as well; and oftentimes repeated that he should have merited pardon if he had performed it. . . .

When he was brought into the King's presence, the King asked him how he could conspire so hideous a treason against his children and so many innocent souls which never offended him? He answered that it was true, but a dangerous disease required a desperate remedy. He told some of the Scots that his intent was to have blown them back into Scotland.

(3) *Source: The True Copy of the Declaration of Guido Fawkes of Nov. 17th taken in the presence of the Councillors whose names are underwritten.* This is part of the so-called *King's Book* published in 1605 under the title of *His Majesty's Speech in this last Session of Parliament. . . .* (Brit. Museum Press Mark E 1940, No. 10). The Catholic point of view rejects the authenticity of this account, but there seems no good reason for doubting its genuineness. It will be found reprinted in the Harleian Miscellany 1809 edition, vol. iii.

I confesse, that a practise in generall was first broken unto me, against his Maiestie for reliefe of the Catholic cause, and not invented or propounded by my selfe. And this was first propounded unto mee about Easter Last was twelve moneth beyond the seas, in the Lowe Countreys of the *Archdukes* obeissance, by *Thomas Winter*, who came thereupon with mee into England, and there we imparted our purpose to three other Gentlemen more, namely, *Robert Catesby*, *Thomas Percy* and *Iohn Wright*, who all five consulting together of the means how to execute the same, and taking a vow among our selves for secrecie, *Catesby* propounded to have it performed by Gunpowder, and by making a Myne under the upper House of Parliament : which place wee made a choice of the rather because Religion having been unjustly suppressed there, it was fittest that Iustice and punishment should be executed there.

This being resolved amongst us, *Thomas Percy* hired an House at Westminster for that purpose, neere adioyning to the Parliament House, and there we begun to make our Myne about the 11 of December 1604.

The five that first entred into the worke were *Thomas Percy*, *Thomas Catesby*, *Thomas Winter*, *Iohn Wright* and myselfe : and soone after wee tooke another unto us, *Christopher Wright* having Sworne him also, and taken the Sacrament for secrecie.

When we came to the very foundation of the Wall of the House, which was about three yards thicke, and found it a matter of great difficultie, wee tooke unto us another Gentleman *Robert Winter*, in like maner with oath and sacrament as afore said.

It was about Christmas when we brought our myne unto the Wall, and about Candlemas we had wrought the wall halfe through : and whilst they were in working, I stood as Sentinell to descrie any man that came neere, whereof I gave them warning, and so they ceased untill I gave notice againe to proceede.

All we seven lay in the House, and had Shot and Powder, being resolved to die in that place before we should yield or be taken. As they were working upon the wall they heard a rushing in the Cellar of remooving of Coales, whereupon we feared we had been discovered : and they sent me to go to the Cellar, who finding that the Coales were a-selling and that the

Cellar was to bee let, viewing the commoditie thereof for our purpose, *Percy* went and hired the same for yeerely rent.

We had before this provided and brought into the House twentie Barrels of Powder, which we remooved into the Cellar, and covered the same with Billets and Faggots, which were provided for that purpose.

About Easter, the Parliament being prorogued till October next, we dispersed ourselves and I retired into the Low countreys by advice and direction of the rest, as well to aquaint *Owen* with the particulars of the Plot, as also lest by my longer stay I might have growen suspicious, and so have come in question.

In the meantime *Percy* having the key of the Cellar, laide in more Powder and wood into it. I returned about the beginning of September next, and then receiving the key againe of Percy, we brought in more Powder and Billets to cover the same againe, and so I went for a time into the Countrey till the 30 of October.

It was a further resolve amongst us that the same day that this act should have been performed, some other of our Confederates should have surprised the person of Lady Elizabeth the King's eldest daughter, who was kept in Warwickshire at Lo. *Harrington's* house, and presently have her proclaimed as Queen, having a proiect of a Proclamation ready for that purpose, wherein we made no mention of altering of Religion, nor would have avowed the deede to be ours, untill we should have had power enough to make our partie good and then we would have avowed both.

Concerning Duke Charles, the King's second sonne, wee had sundry consultations how to seise on his Person. But because we found no means how to to compasse it (the Duke being kept neere London, where we had not Forces y-nough) we resolved to serve our turn with the Lady Elizabeth.

THE NAMES OF OTHER PRINCIPALL
persons, that were made privy
afterwards to this horrible
conspiracie

Everard Digby, Knight
Ambrose Rookwood
Francis Tresham
John Grant
Robert Keyes

————————

Commiss :
Notingham   Worcester
Suffolke   Devonshire
Northampton   Salisbury
Marre   Dunbar
Popham (*The Lord Chief Justice*)

Edw. Coke

W. Waad (*The Lieutenant
of the Tower*)

THE FIRST TURKISH AMBASSADOR TO
ENGLAND

The invasion of Europe by the Turks in the sixteenth century had so frightened everybody that it was a century before any European country sent a minister to Turkey, and a century and a half before any Turkish minister was received in Europe.

Source : Ellis, *Original Letters*, 1st series, vol. iii, pp. 85 sqq. From the Cotton MSS. Nero B. fol. 245. An anonymous letter to Sir Edward Hoby. Spelling modernized.

Strand, this Tuesday Morning, August, 1607.

Honourable Knight,

The letter enclosed containeth, as you see, a recommendation of the Turk lately arrived, both from his quality and his errand, by that famous Murat-Rey admiral of Algier, being now

a man of seventy years old, who heretofore was as much re-
nowned for his exploits in the Levant seas as ever Drake was for
his attempts upon the Ocean.

For the person of this Mustapha, he seems to me and others
that have visited him, a man of a goodly presence and a gallant
spirit, sociable, affable, and full of entertainment to all comers,
and one who to give the better content to those that come to
see him, is content to dispense with some of his Turkish fashions,
and to accustom himself to ours. For being invited to accompany
Sir Thomas Low governor of the Company[1] to dinner, I saw
Mustapha sit in a chair at the board's end, and drink a solemn
health to the King of Great Britain and the Grand Signor. . . .
He is come but slenderly attended, with some dozen of Turks,
whereof three only are civilly apparelled, the rest looking like
the ambassadors that came to Joshua with old shoes and thread-
bare apparel. For his own person he hath many changes of
garments very rich, and several turbans, and hath brought with
him either for presents or for a pledge in time of necessity,
twenty-one pieces of cloth of gold and silver, valued at 1000
marks. . . . He was some eight years ago, treasurer of the wars
to Sinan Bassa, when Raab alias Saverin was won from the
Christians, and when Mr. Barton our Ambassador was in the
army. He had the charge there (believe him who list) of 3600
camels laden with gold coins, 40,000 upon a camel, which being
cast up do amount to 144 millions of gold coins, which is about
50 millions of pounds sterling. . . .

Mustapha desires to be dispatched and to return home not
by the way of France, but by sea ; but he will hardly get his
audience till the King come to Salisbury. His table stands the
Merchants[1] in some £4 a day.

Yours a centro cordis.

[1] Of the Turkey Company, the English trading company with the Levant.

THE ARRIVAL OF FREDERICK, ELECTOR PALATINE

FRIDAY, OCTOBER 16TH, 1612

James I's daughter, Princess Elizabeth, known as the Queen of Hearts because of her beauty and popularity with the young gallants in London, was betrothed to the Protestant Frederick V, Elector Palatine, who later accepted the throne of Bohemia, thus contributing to the outbreak of the Thirty Years War. After the defeat at the battle of the White Hill (1620), Frederick lost his throne and Elizabeth came to be known as the Winter Queen.

Source : This account of the Elector's arrival in England for his marriage to Elizabeth is taken from a letter written by Mr. John Fynnet to Mr. Trumbull, October 23rd, 1612, printed in the *Winwood Memorials*, vol. iii, p. 403, pub. in 1725.

Further Reading : Oman, *Elizabeth of Bohemia*.

The Count Palatine landed at Gravesend on Friday night last, the 16th of this present. . . . His Approach, Gesture and Countenance, were seasoned with a well-becoming Confidence ; and bending himself with a due Reverence before the King, he told him among other Compliments, that in his Sight and Presence he enjoyed a great part (reserving it should seem the greatest to his Mistress) of the End and Happiness of his Journey. After turning to the Queen she entertained him with a fixed Countenance : and though her Posture might have seemed (as was judged) to promise him the Honour of a Kiss for his Welcome, his Humility carried him no further than her Hand. From which, after some few Words of Compliment, he made to the Prince, and exchanging with him after a more familiar Straine certain Passages of Courtesy, he ended (where his Desires could not but begin) with the Princess (who was noted till then not to turn so much as a corner of an Eye towards him), and stooping low to take up the lowest part of her Garment to kiss it, shee most gracefully courtesying lower than accustomed, and with her Hand staying him from that humblest Reverence, gave him at his rising a fair Advantage (which he took) of kissing her. This was the årst Day. The next was spent in re-visiting the King and Queen, find twice the Lady Elizabeth ; once in the afternoon at her own Lodging in State, and after Supper with somewhat less Ceremony. . . .

THE MARRIAGE OF PRINCESS ELIZABETH AND FREDERICK, ELECTOR PALATINE

SUNDAY, FEBRUARY 14TH, 1613 (N.S.)

See the last letter.

Source : a letter from Mr. Chamberlaine to Sir Ralph Winwood, the English agent to the States-General of Holland. *Winwood Memorials,* vol. iii, pp. 434–5.

Further Reading : Oman, *Elizabeth of Bohemia.*

London, 23rd February, 1612 (o.s.)

My very good Lord,

Since my last of the 10th of this present here hath ben little to advertise but the Consummation of the Lady Elizabeth's Marriage with the Count Palatine, together with the Triumphs and Shewes both before and after. I need not tell you how much this Match is to the Contentment of all well-affected People, and what Joy they take in it ; as being a firm Foundation for the stabilising of Religion, which (upon what Conceipt I know not) was before suspected to be in branslé.[1] But the Roman Catholicks malign it as much, and do what they can to disgrace yt, as being the Ruine of their Hopes. The Queen who seemed not to taste it so well at first, is since so come about, that she doth all she can to grace it, and takes speciall Comfort in him. The Solemnities were performed in the Chappell ; whither the Bride was con-

---

[1] in agitation, unstable.

veyed on a Scaffold or open Gallery all along the Court-yard
arrayed in white, with her Hair hanging down along and a rich
Coronet on her Head, led by the young Prince and the Earl of
Northampton her Bridemen; and her Traine carried up by
thirteen young Ladies (or Lords Daughters at least) besides five
or six more that could not come near it, all suited in the same
Livery of white and embroiderie. The Bishop of Bath and Wells
preached, and the Archbishop performed the other Rites and
Ceremonies upon a Stage raised in the Middle of the Chappell.
On the right Side thereof sate the King, with the Prince, Palsgrave
and Count Henry; on the other the Queen, with the Bride, the
Lady Harrington and one or two more. The Chappell was kept
very straight, and none admitted under the Degree of a Baron,
saving the three Lords Chief Justices. The Contract and Marriage
was celebrated all in English, and the Prince Palatine had learned
as much as concerned his Part reasonably perfect. It were no
end to write of the Curiositie and Excess of Bravery both of
Men and Women, with the extream daubing on of Cost and
Riches, only a Touch shall serve in a few for a Pattern of the
Rest. The Lady Wotton was said to have a Gown that cost
fifty Pound a Yard the embroidering; and the Lord Montague
(that hath paid reasonably well for Recusancie) bestowed fifteen
hundred Pound in Apparell upon his two Daughters. The
Bridegroom and the Bride, with the Prince, French, Venetian,
Count Henry, and States Ambassadors, dined in a Room built
on purpose for this Marriage. The Spaniard was, or would be,
sick; and the Archdukes Ambassador being invited for the
next Day made his Excuse; and the Ambassadors that were
present were not altogether pleased (as I hear), but every one
found some Punctilio of Disgust. There was a matter happened
the same Day, which tho' it were not then so much noted, hath
since bred much Speech, Lion, the Scottish King of Heralds
being expressly sent for, wore a rich Coat of Arms (provided
here) with the Arms of Scotland before England; which is
reckoned to be a great Affront offered at such a Time, in such
a Place, to such a People. Now for the Fireworks and Fight
upon the Water (the one performed on Thursday Night, the

other on Saturday in the Afternoon before the Marriage), there was nothing in either answerable to the great Expectation conceived or the Cost bestowed, which amounted to more than 9000 l. . . .

THE VOYAGE OF THE MAYFLOWER

After the Hampton Court Conference the policy of the government became more and more hostile to the Puritans. Gradually the Puritan congregations began to break away from the Anglican church. In 1608 over 100 Puritans emigrated to Holland, where they remained for twelve years. They were never happy there and in 1620 they went overseas to America. These were the Pilgrim Fathers, who sailed from Plymouth in the *Mayflower* on Wednesday, September 6th, 1620 (O.S.). They landed at the harbour formed by Cape Cod, which John Smith had named Plymouth in 1614.

Source : The Bradford MS. *folios 109 sqq.* William Bradford (1590–1657) was one of the emigrants. He became the second governor of the colony of Plymouth in 1621 and was re-elected every year, except on one or two occasions at his own request. The following extracts are taken from *The Story of the Pilgrim Fathers*, ed. from the original texts by E. Arber, 1897, ch. xl.

And I may not omit here a special work of GOD's Providence. There was a proud and very profane young man, one of the seamen ; of a lusty able body, which made him the more haughty. He would always be contemning the poor people in their sickness, and cursing them daily with grievous execrations, and he did not let to tell them, That he hoped to help to cast half of them overboard before they came to their journey's end ; and to make merry with what property they had. And if he were by any gently reproved, he would curse and swear most bitterly.

But it pleased GOD, before they came half the seas over, to smite this young man with a grievous disease ; of which he died in a desperate manner. And so he was himself the first that was thrown overboard. Thus his curses lighted on his own head ; and it was an astonishment to all his fellows ; for they noted it to be the just hand of GOD upon him.

After they had enjoyed fair winds and weather for a season, they were incountered many times with cross winds ; and met with many fierce storms ; with which the ship was shrewdly shaken, and her upper works made very leaky. . . . In sundry of these storms, the winds were so fierce and the seas so high, as they could not bear a knot of sail : but were forced to hull for divers days together.

And in one of them, as they thus lay at hull, in a mighty storm, a lusty young man, called JOHN HOWLAND,[1] coming upon some occasion above the gratings, was with the seel[2] of the ship thrown into the sea : but it pleased GOD that he caught hold of the top sail halliards, which hung overboard and ran out at length ; yet he held his hold, though he was sundry fathoms under water, till he was hauled up, by the same rope, to the brim of the water ; and then, with a boathook and other means, was got into the ship again, and his life saved. And though he was something ill with it, yet he lived many years after ; and became a profitable member, both in Church and Common Wealth.

[1] Howland was a manservant. He married Elizabeth Tilley, ' and they are both now living in 1650 ; and have 10 children now, all living. And their eldest daughter hath 4 children ; and their second daughter 1 ; all living. So 15 are come of them.' He died at Plymouth, N.E. 1673. Plymouth remained a separate colony until 1691, when it was absorbed into Massachusetts.

[2] sudden heeling over.

CHARLES I.   1625—1649

No introduction is needed to the most unfortunate of English kings who was born in 1600, the son of James I and Anne of Denmark, and who was executed on Monday, January 30th, 1649. (O.S.)

(1) *Source*: *Memoirs of the Reign of Charles I*, pp. 64 sqq. by Sir Philip Warwick (1609–1683). From 1647 he was one of Charles I's secretaries. Spelling and punctuation modernized.

Further Reading: Clarendon, *History of the Great Rebellion*.

His deportment was very majestic, for he would not let fall his dignity, no, not to the greatest foreigners that came to visit him at his court; for though he was far from pride, yet he was careful of majesty and would be approached with respect and reverence.   His conversation was free, and the subject matter of it (on his own side of the court), was most commonly rational, or if facetious, not light.   With any artist or good mechanic, traveller or scholar he would discourse freely, and as he was commonly improved by them, so he often gave light to them in their own art or knowledge.   For there were few gentlemen in the world that knew more of useful or necessary learning than this prince did; and yet his proportion of books was but small, having like Francis the first of France learnt more by the ear than by study.   His way of arguing was very civil and patient, for he seldom contradicted another by his authority, but by his reason; nor did he by any petulant dislike quash another's arguments, and he offered his exception by this civil introduction, *By your favour, Sir, I think otherwise on this or that ground*: yet he would discountenance any bold or forward address unto him. . . .

His exercises were manly, for he rode the great horse very well, and on the little saddle he was not only adroit, but a laborious hunter or field-man: and they were wont to say of him that he failed not to do any of his exercises artificially, but not very gracefully, like some well-proportioned faces which yet want a pleasant air of countenance. . . .

His exercises of religion were most exemplary, for every morning early, and evening not very late, singly and alone, in his own bed-chamber or closet he spent some time in private meditation—(for he durst reflect and be alone)—and through the whole week, even when he went a hunting, he never failed before he sat down to dinner, to have part of the Liturgy read unto him and his menial servants, came he never so hungry or so late in. And on Sundays and Tuesdays he came (commonly at the beginning of Service) to the Chapel, well attended by his Court-Lords and chief attendants, and most usually waited on by many of the nobility in town, who found those observances acceptably entertained by him. . . .

And though he was of as slow a pen as of speech, yet both were very significant; and he had that modest esteem of his own parts that he would usually say, *He would willingly make his own despatches, but that he found it better to be a cobbler than a shoemaker.* I have been in company with very learned men, when I have brought them their own papers back from him with his alterations, who ever confessed his amendments to have been very material. And I once by his commandment brought him a paper of my own to read, to see whether it was suitable unto his directions, and he disallowed it slightingly. I desired him I call Doctor Sanderson to aid me, and that the Doctor might understand his own meaning from himself; and with his Majesty's leave I brought him, whilst he was walking and taking the air; whereupon we two went back, but pleased him as little, when we returned with it, for smilingly he said, *A man might have as good ware out of a chandler's shop*: but afterwards he set it down with his own pen very plainly and suitable unto his own intentions.

(2) *Source*: *The History of the Great Rebellion,* by Edward Hyde, Earl of Clarendon (1609–1674), 1819 ed. vol. iii Bk. XI, O.U.P.

There were so many miraculous circumstances contributed to his ruin, that men might well think that heaven and earth and the stars designed it. Though he was, from the first declension of his power, so much betrayed by his own servants, that there were very few who remained faithful to him, yet that treachery proceeded not from any treasonable purpose to do him any harm, but from particular and personal animosities against other men. And, afterwards, the terror all men were under of the Parliament, and the guilt they were conscious of themselves, made them watch all opportunities to make themselves gracious to those who could do them good ; and so they became spies upon their master, and from one piece of knavery were hardened and confirmed to undertake another ; till at last they had no hope of preservation but by the destruction of their master. And after all this, when a man might reasonably believe that less than a universal defection of three nations could not have reduced a great King to so ugly a fate, it is most certain, that, in that very hour when he was thus wickedly murdered in the sight of the sun, he had as great a share in the hearts and affections of his subjects in general, was as much beloved, esteemed, and longed for by the people in general of the three nations, as any of his predecessors had ever been. To conclude, he was the worthiest gentleman, the best master, the best friend, the best husband, the best father, and the best Christian, that the age in which he lived produced. And if he were not the best King, if he were without some parts and qualities which have made some kings great and happy, no other prince was ever unhappy who was possessed of half his virtues and endowments, and so much without any kind of vice.

THE MURDER OF THE DUKE OF BUCKINGHAM

SATURDAY, 23RD OF AUGUST, 1628

George Villiers, 1st Duke of Buckingham, the favourite of James I and the intimate friend and companion of Charles I, was a brilliant but erratic man, a failure both as a statesman and as a soldier. Detested by Parliament, he was saved from impeachment by Charles I's dissolving Parliament. He was assassinated at Portsmouth by John Felton on August 23rd, 1628. Buckingham had refused Felton's application for a captain's commission.

Source : A letter from Dudley Lord Carleton to Queen Henrietta Maria. Ellis, *Original Letters*, 1st series vol. iii, letter CCCXI.

Further Reading : Gardiner, *History of England*, vol. vi.

Maddam,
          I am to trouble your Grace, with a most Lamentable Relation ; This day betwixt nine and ten of the clocke in the morning, the Duke of Buckingham, then coming out of a Parlor, into a Hall, to go to his coach and soe to the King (who was four miles of), having about him diverse Lords, Colonells, and Captains, & many of his own Servants, was by one Felton (once a Lieutenant of this our Army) slain at one blow, with a dagger-knife. In his staggering he turn'd about, uttering onely this word, ' Villaine! ' & never spake a word more, but presently plucking out the knife from himself, before he fell to the ground, he made towards the Traytor, two or three paces, and then fell against a Table although he were upheld by diverse that were neare him, that (through the villain's close carriage in the act) could not perceive him hurt at all, but guessed him to be suddenly over-sway'd with some apoplexie, till they saw the blood come gushing from his mouth and the wound, soe fast, that life, and breath, at once left his begored body.
          Maddam, you may easily guess what outcries were then made, by us that were Commanders and Officers there present, when once we saw him thus dead in a moment, and slaine by an

unknowne hand; for it seems that the Duke himself onely knew who it was that had murdered him, and by meanes of the confused presse at the instant about his person, wee neither did nor could. . . . In the meane time Felton pass'd the throng, which was confusedly great, not so much as mark'd or followed, in soe much that not knowing where, nor who he was that had done that fact, some came to keepe guard at the gates, and others went to the Ramports of the Towne; in all which time the villaine was standing in the kitchin of the same house, and after inquiry made by a multitude of captaines and gentlemen then pressing into the house and court, and crying out a maine ' Where is the villain? Where is the butcher? ' he most audaciously and resolutely drawing forth his sword, came out and went amongst them, saying boldly, ' I am the Man, here I am '; upon which diverse drew upon him, with the intent to have dispatcht him; but Sir Thomas Morton, myself, and some others, us'd such means (though with much trouble and difficulty) that we drew him out of their hands, and by order of my Lord High Chamberlaine, wee had the charge of keeping him from any comming to him untill a guard of muskateers were brought, to convey him to the Governor's House, where wee were discharg'd.

My Lord High Chamberlaine and Mr. Secretary Cooke that were then at the Governor's House, did there take his examination of which as yet there is nothing knowne, onely whilst he was in our custody I asked him several questions, to which he answer'd; vizt. He sayd, he was a Protestant in Religion; he also express'd himself that he was partly discontented for want of eighty pounds pay which was due unto him; and for that he being Lieutenant of a company of foot, the company was given over his head unto another, and yett, he sayd, that that did not move him to this resolution, but that he reading the Remonstrance of the house of Parliament it came into his mind, that in committing the Act of killing the Duke, hee should do his Country great good service. And he sayd that to-morrow he was to be prayd for in London. I then asked him att what Church, and to what purpose; he told me at a Church by Fleet-Street-Conduit, and, as for a man much discontented in mind. . . .

K

But to returne to the screeches made att the fatall blow given, the Duchesse of Buckingham and the Countesse of Anglesey came forth into a Gallery which look'd into a Hall where they might behold the blood of their dearest Lord gushing from him ; ah, poor Ladies, such was their screechings, teares, and distractions, that I never in my Life heard the like before, and hope never to heare the like againe. His M^aties griefe for the losse of him, was express'd to be more then great, by the many teares hee shed for him, with which I will conclude this sad and untimely News.

Felton had sowed a writing in the crowne of his hatt, half within the lyning, to shew the cause why he putt this cruell act in excution ; thinking hee should have beene slaine in the place : and it was thus : ' If I bee slaine, letno man condemne me, but rather condemne himself ; it is for our sinns that our harts are hardned, and become sencelesse, or else hee had not gone soe long unpunished.'

' John Felton.'

' He is unworthy of the name of a Gentleman, or Soldier, in my opinion, that is afraid to sacrifice his life for the honor of God, his King and Country.'

' John Felton.'

RUBENS, ON ENGLAND

In 1629 Peter Paul Rubens, the painter, came on a diplomatic mission to England. The following extracts from his letters show the kind of art world in which he moved. Charles I was the most enthusiastic and discerning collector of pictures in England at the time. Cotton was the founder of the Cottonian Library. (See Introduction).

(1) *Source* : Letter from Rubens to his French correspondent, Pierre Dupuy, dated August 8th, 1629. Quoted in *Rubens, Painter and Diplomat*, by Emile Cammaerts, Faber and Faber, 1932, p. 209.

This island seems to me worthy the consideration of a man of taste, not only because of the charm of the countryside and the beauty of the people, not only because of the outward show, which appears to me most choice and to announce a people rich and happy in the bosom of peace, but also by the incredible quantity of excellent pictures, statues and ancient inscriptions which are in this Court.

(2) *Source* : ib. from Rubens to Peiresc : p. 210.

If I were allowed to dispose of my affairs according to my wishes and to arrange my occupations as I like, I should have come to you long ago, or I should be with you now, but I do not know what spirit, whether good or bad, is always disturbing my projects and drawing me in opposite directions. My only pleasure is to see, during my pilgrimages, so many various countries, so many cities, so many peoples following different customs. I am far from finding in this island the barbarous ways which its climate might warrant, since it is so different from gracious Italy, and I must even confess that, from the point of view of painting, I have never seen such a quantity of pictures by great masters as in the Palace of the King of England and in the gallery of the late Duke of Buckingham. The Earl of Arundel possesses an enormous number of antique statutes and of Greek and Latin inscriptions, which you have seen since they have been published by John Selden, with the learned commentaries which one might have expected from that talented and cultivated author. You have no doubt seen his treatise *De Diis Syris*, which has just been reprinted in a revised and enlarged edition. But I wish that he would confine himself to the bounds of science without mixing in political disorders, which have made him lose his liberty, with several other members of Parliament, who are accused of offending the King during the last session.

There are also here the ' Cavalier ' Cotton, a great anti-quarian, very remarkable for the variety of his knowledge, and the secretary Boswell, and other people whom you must know perfectly and with whom you are no doubt in correspondence, as you are with all the distinguished men of the world.

THE FIRST BISHOPS' WAR, 1639

Episcopacy had ceased in Scotland when the Reformation took place there. Puritanism was much stronger in Scotland than in England. Therefore when Charles I and Laud, the Archbishop of Canterbury, decided to force episcopacy and a new Prayer Book on the Scots, the First Bishops' War broke out. Charles led an army of some 21,000 men, but he had no money, the army was badly fed, badly equipped and its heart was not in its work. Charles knew that he must agree to peace, which he did on Wednesday, June 24th, 1640.

Source : *Memoirs of the Verney Family*, vol. 1, by F. P. Verney, 1892. These extracts are from the letters of Sir Edmund Verney, Standard-bearer to Charles I, who accompanied him with the army to Scotland on March 21st, 1639 He was killed at the battle of Edgehill, 1642. Spelling has been modernized.

Further Reading : Gardiner, *History of England*, vol. ix.

March 31st. The King has been basely betrayed ; all the party that he hoped upon all this while has basely left him ; as we are this day informed : the two castles of Edinburgh and Dunbarton are yielded up without one blow ; and yet they were both provided so well as they were impregnable so long as they had victual, which they wanted not.

Dalkeeth, a place of great strength, where the Crown and Sceptre lay is yielded too ; and the Covenanters have taken them away and a great deal of arms and ammunition too ; yet my lord Treasurer of Scotland undertook to the King to keep all that safe ; and all these are given up without one blow. Aberdeen we hear is yielded up and no blow given ; and the King sent 4,000 of the choicest arms he had thither ; so that now I am confident the show of making a party there for the King has been only to get arms from us, and to feed us with hopes till they were fully provided.

April 25th. Yesterday the King received a letter from the Lords of the Covenant ; I think there were 20 of their hands to it. . . . First they express great civility to my Lord ; and they seem to wonder that a man so well affected to the peace & welfare of his country will appear in such a way, as he does in this business; and they wonder that there are such unusual preparations for war in England . . . protesting that they never had a thought of offering the least injury to this kingdom, that they have often represented their grievances to his Majesty & by reason of some ill-minded men of their nation can obtain no answer. . . . They have done nothing but what is warranted by their laws & they conclude with a great desire of Amity & peace with this kingdom, adding that if they be invaded they must & will defend themselves & their liberties as long as there is a man living amongst them. All these heads are in the letter : but in my opinion they are expressed with a great deal of modesty, yet my lord General (who is tender of the honour of the King) thinks it full of insolence & braving the King; in briefe, I fear it will rather exasperate than mollify, and add fuel to that fire that raged enough before; truly I think it will come to blows, but you must not say so to your mother.

About April 29th. Our Army is but weak; our purse is weaker; and if we fight with these forces & early in the year we shall have our throats cut; and to delay fighting long we can not for want of money to keep our Army together. My lord Marshall puts on the King to fight by all the ways & means he can possibly devise; daily urging the King how nearly it concerns him in honour to punish the rebels, telling him that they are weak; . . . then the King is persuaded to it from Whitehall[1] with all the industry that can be imagined. The Catholics make a large contribution as they pretend and indeed use all the means and ways they can to set us by the ears; and I think they will not fail of their plot. I dare say there was never so raw, so unskilful and so unwilling an Army brought to fight. My lord Marshall himself will, I dare say, be safe, & then he cares not what becomes of the rest; truly here are many brave Gentlemen that for point of honour must run such a hazard as truly would grieve any heart but his that does it purposely to ruin them. For my own part I have lived till pain and trouble has made me weary to do so; and the worst that can come shall not be unwelcome to me; but it is a pity to see what men are like to be

[1] Queen Henrietta Maria.

slaughtered here unless it shall please God to put it in the King's heart to increase his Army or stay till these may know what they do; for as yet they are as like to kill their fellows as the enemy.

June 9th. The Lords of the Covenant have petitioned the King that they may represent their complaints and grievances by some of the English nobility (for they say their own countrymen have been false to them and have misreported them and their actions to the King). His Msty has assented to their petition and has assigned six of our lords to meet with as many of theirs at our lord General's Tent in our camp; they have petitioned for an assurance under the King's hand, for their safe return, but he refuses it and says they shall trust to his word; this difficulty lies yet in the way, but I assure myself there will be a way found to satisfy them in that, and I doubt not we shall have a treaty. . . . I hope it will be a good one. Upon their petition to the King I was sent by his Msty with a message to them wherein though I had a hard part to play yet I dare boldly say I handled the business so that I begot this treaty; otherwise we had I doubt been at blows by this time.

SIR THOMAS WENTWORTH, EARL OF STRAFFORD

Thomas Wentworth was born in 1593 and was executed in 1641. He took a leading part in the stand made by the Commons against Charles I in 1628, which resulted in the Petition of Right. When he saw that an accommodation between the Crown and Parliament was not possible, and that while the quarrel went on government was breaking down, he gave his services to Charles I to provide the efficiency which was lacking to the executive. He was made Baron Wentworth, and thus occurred the so-called 'apostasy'. In 1632 he went as Lord Deputy to Ireland and he began to carry out that efficient form of government which came to be known as Thorough, and which earned for him the name of Black Tom Tyrant. In 1640 he advocated the use of Irish troops to defeat the Scottish rebels. In 1640 he was impeached by the Commons, but his vigorous defence made an acquittal too probable to be accepted by the Commons. The impeachment was dropped and an Act of Attainder substituted, which was signed by the King only under the pressure of mob violence. Strafford was beheaded on Tower Hill on Tuesday, May 11th, 1641.

Source: *Memoirs of the Reign of Charles I*, pp. 109 sqq., 162, by Sir Philip Warwick, who was M.P. for Radnor in the Long Parliament. Spelling and punctuation modernised.

Further Reading: Wedgwood, *Strafford*: Lady Burghclere, *Strafford*.

(1) He was every way qualified for business, his natural faculties being very strong and pregnant, his understanding, aided by a good fancy, made him quick in discerning the nature of any business ; and through a cold brain he became deliberate and of a sound judgement. His memory was great, and he made it greater by confiding in it. His elocution was very fluent, and it was a great part of his talent readily to reply or freely harangue upon any subject. And all this was lodged in a sour and haughty temper, so as it may probably be believed, he expected to have more observance paid to him than he was willing to pay to others, though they were of his own quality ; and then he was not like to conciliate the good will of men of lesser station.

His acquired parts, both in the University and Inns-of-Court learning, as likewise his foreign travels, made him an eminent man before he was a conspicuous ; so as when he came to show himself first in public affairs, which was in the House of Commons, he was soon a bell-wether in that flock. As he had these parts, he knew how to set a price on them, if not overvalue them, and he too soon discovered a roughness in his nature, which a man no more obliged by him than I was would have called an injustice ; though many of his confidants (who were my good friends, when I like a little worm, being trod on, would turn and laugh, and under that disguise say as piquant words as my little wit would help me with) were wont to swear to me that he endeavoured to be just to all, but was resolved to be gracious to none but to those whom he thought inwardly affected him : which never bowed me till his broken fortune and, as I thought, very unjustifiable prosecution, made me one of the fifty-six who gave a negative to that fatal bill which cut the thread of his life. . . . In person he was of a tall stature, but stooped much in the neck. His countenance was cloudy whilst he moved or sat thinking, but when he spake, either seriously or facetiously, he had a lightsom and a very pleasant air ; and indeed, whatever he then did, he performed very gracefully. The greatness of the envy that attended him made many in their prognosticks to bode him an ill end. . . . Sure I am that his station was like those turfs of earth or sea-banks which, by the storm swept away, left all the inland to be drowned by popular tumult.

After the Execution

(2) And to show how mad this whole people were, especially in and about this then bloody and brutish city [London], in the evening of the next day wherein he was executed, the greatest demonstrations of joy that possibly could be expressed, ran through the whole town and countries hereabout ; and many that came up to Town on purpose to see the execution, rode in triumph back, waving their hats, and with all expressions of joy, through every town they went crying, *His head is off, his head is off!*, and in many places committing insolences upon, and breaking the windows of those persons who would not solemnize this festival with a bonfire. So ignorant and brutish is a multitude.

THE PASSING OF THE GRAND REMONSTRANCE

MONDAY, NOVEMBER 22ND, 1641

While the King was in Scotland, Parliament got news of the Irish Rebellion (Nov. 1st) : rumour connected with it the name of the Queen. Fearing a plot to suppress Protestantism in all three kingdoms, Pym and his followers became more revolutionary in their policy. They now split the House of Commons over the Grand Remonstrance. This document rehearsed the evils from which the country had suffered, listed the reforms which the Long Parliament had already carried, and set out the grievances still to be remedied. It made no mention of the concessions already made by the King. It also contained a statement of religious policy which was almost that of Root and Branch—the destruction of Episcopacy—and it made proposals that the Crown should only employ ministers in whom Parliament could have confidence. As the following extract shows, the Grand Remonstrance was hotly debated : the division was not taken until after midnight, an unheard of thing in those days : the Remonstrance was carried by only eleven votes—159 to 148.

Source : *Memoirs of the Reign of Charles I*, p. 201, by Sir Philip Warwick, M.P. for Radnor.

Upon the King's return out of Scotland, the City of London's splendid entertainment of him and the discourses that flew in all parts of the ample satisfaction the King had given (both which they foresaw before it was put in execution), made them prepare so foul a Remonstrance to give the King his first entertainment amongst them, that a blacker libel could not be framed either against his person or government ; and it passed so tumultuously two or three nights before the King came to Town, that at three of the clock in the morning, when they voted it, I thought we had all sat in the valley of the shadow of death ; for we, like Joab's and Abner's young men, had catched at each other's locks, and sheathed our swords in each other's bowels, had not the sagacity and great calmness of Mr. Hampden by a short speech prevented it, and led us to defer our angry debate until the next morning.

CHARLES I'S ATTEMPT TO ARREST THE FIVE MEMBERS

TUESDAY, JANUARY 4TH, 1642 (N.S.)

While the King was in Scotland, on Nov. 1st, 1641, news reached England of the Irish insurrection and of the massacre of English Protestants. This led to the House of Commons' carrying the Grand Remonstrance, which was a vote of want of confidence in the King. On Nov. 25th the King returned to London. He resented the Grand Remonstrance, especially the decision of the House to have it printed and circulated. He discovered that during the autumn five M.P.s, leaders of the opposition to the Crown, had been communicating with the Scots. Legally they were guilty of treason. On Jan. 3rd, Charles sent the Attorney General to impeach Pym, Hampden, Hazlerigg, Holles and Strode before the House of Lords. The House of Commons made an evasive answer to the demand that these five members should be surrendered. On Tuesday, Jan. 4th the King went down in person to arrest them, but found ' the birds were flown '.

Source : During the episode of Charles I's visit to the House of Commons the young assistant clerk, John Rushworth (1612?–1690), took down ' in cypher ' everything which occurred and was said. Later he was sent for by the King and was compelled to give the King a copy of what he had said to the House of Commons. Rushworth then and there translated the King's speech from his ' cypher ' (shorthand notes) into a full report. That report was years later printed in his *Historical Collections*, from which the following extract is taken. At the same time Sir Ralph Verney, one of the members of the Long Parliament, was hurriedly making notes, writing on his knee, and these confirm Rushworth's account. See *Memoirs of the Verney Family*, vol. ii, pp. 36–38, where is also a facsimile of one of Verney's pages of notes.

Further Reading : Gardiner *History of England*, vol. x.

They were no sooner in their places but the House was informed by one Captain Langrish, lately an officer in arms in France, that he came from among the officers and soldiers at Whitehall, and understanding by them that His Majesty was coming with a guard of military men, commanders and soldiers, to the House of Commons, he passed by them with some difficulty to get to the House before them, and sent in word how near the said officers and soldiers were come : whereupon a certain member of the House having also private information from the Countess of Carlisle, sister to the Earl of Northumberland, that endeavours would be used this day to apprehend the five Members, the House required the five Members to depart the House forthwith, to the end to avoid combustion in the House, if the said soldiers should use violence to pull any of them out. To which command of the House four of the said Members yielded ready obedience, but Mr. Stroud was obdurate, till Sir Walter Earle (his ancient acquaintance) pulled him out by force, the King being at that time entering into the New-Palace-Yard in Westminster ; and as His Majesty came through Westminster Hall, the Commanders, Reformadoes, &c that attended him made a lane on both sides the Hall, (through which His Majesty passed and came up the stairs to the House of Commons) and stood before the guard of Pensioners and Halberdiers (who also attended the King's person), and the door of the H.o.C. being thrown open, His Majesty entered the House, and as he passed up towards the Chair, he cast his eye on the right hand near the Bar of the House, where Mr. Pim used to sit ; but His Majesty not seeing him there (knowing him well) went up to the Chair and said, ' By your leave, (Mr. Speaker) I must borrow your chair a little ' ; whereupon the Speaker came out of the Chair and His Majesty stepped up into it ; after he had stood in the Chair a while, casting his eye upon the Members as they stood up un-covered, but could not discern any of the five Members to be there, nor indeed were they easy to be discerned (had they been there) among so many bare faces all standing up together.

Then His Majesty made this speech,

Gentlemen,

I am sorry for this occasion of coming unto you. Yesterday I sent a Sergeant at Arms upon a very important occasion, to apprehend some that by my command were accused of High Treason ; whereunto I did expect obedience and not a message. And I must declare unto you here, that albeit no King that ever was in England shall be more careful of your privileges, to maintain them to the uttermost of his power, than I shall be ; yet you must know that in cases of treason no person hath a privilege. And therefore I am come to know if any of these persons that were accused are here. For I must tell you, gentlemen, that so long as these persons whom I have accused (for no light crime but for treason) are here, I cannot expect that this House will be in the right way that I do heartily wish for it. Therefore I am come to tell you that I must have them wheresoever I find them. Well, since I see all the birds are flown, I do expect from you that you shall send them unto me as soon as they return hither. But I assure you, on the word of a King, I never did intend any force, but shall proceed against them in a legal and fair way, for I never meant any other.

And now, since I see I cannot do what I came for, I think this no unfit occasion to repeat what I have said formerly, that whatsoever I have done in favour and to the good of my subjects, I do mean to maintain it.

I will trouble you no more, but tell you I expect as soon as they come to the House, you will send them to me ; otherwise I must take my own course to find them.'

When the King was looking about the House, the Speaker standing below by the Chair, His Majesty asked him whether any of these persons were in the House, whether he saw any of them? And where were they? To which the Speaker, falling on his knee, thus answered : ' May it please your Majesty I have neither eyes to see, nor tongue to speak in this place, but as the House is pleased to direct me, whose servant I am here : and humbly beg your Majesty's pardon that I cannot give any other answer than this to what your Majesty is pleased to demand of me.'

The King having concluded his speech went out of the House again, which was in great disorder, and many members cried out aloud, so as he might hear them, Privilege! Privilege! and forthwith adjourned till the next day at one of the clock.

ON THE BRINK OF CIVIL WAR. 1642

The attempt to arrest the Five Members led to great unpopularity for the King. On January 10th, 1642 (N.S.) Charles left the City, went to Hampton Court, then to Windsor, and early in March he went north and settled at York. He issued Commissions of Array and began to recruit an army. The following extract describes the tension which existed in the Midlands and the North.

Source : *Truths from Leicester and Nottingham, August* 1, *Anno. Dom.* 1642. The following undated and anonymous letter is no. 48 in the collection of Proclamations, Petitions, etc., of Charles I in Eton College Library. Spelling modernized.

I do hereby give you some short notion how things stand in these Northern parts. I met his Majesty at Nottingham this day seven night (where his Majesty was) to make observation. The Mayor was expected to have been committed for refusing to go to York to his Majesty, being twice sent for, not publishing Proclamations sent to him, and other things. The King accepted his mace and delivered it to him again, but gave him no hand to kiss. The town presented the Prince with a purse and 50 pieces. From thence I went to Leicester with the court on Friday, where the King was earnestly put upon it to have, by force of blowing up or battering down the Magazine House, recovered it ; for which end 3 great ordnance was brought to the town ; but upon a petition from the Grand Jury to the King that the powder, match and bullets therein might be distributed to every town in the county, it was approved of by the King. . . . I was in the Magazine every day, which was a place of that strength that those 40 men that were in it (all Round-heads as they call them) would have kept out 500. . . .

The Lord Ruthven and Sir Arthur Hazlerigg (who are knights of Leicestershire and Deputy Lieutenants) did train a good part of the Trained bands two days last week ; and hearing that the King was coming with a good force to bring in Hastings to the Assizes, the High Sheriff that he hath lately made, they departed towards London for avoiding blood shedding, which would have followed (as was conceived) had they stayed. . . .

The gentry of the county are most of them for the King only and were very active with him. His Majesty did on Tuesday morning last return from Leicester to Beverley, 5 miles from Hull . . . it is thought he will presently set upon Hull and so march to London, &c. Hull is very strong and fears no opposition, yet the Cavaliers give out it will be fired in 4 days space. I believe it not. The Bishop of York rides about with His Majesty. The women of Leicester petitioned the King against Hastings.

ANOTHER LETTER

The following letter from Mr. Henry Wilmot was written from York, dated June 22nd, 1642 (a Wednesday) to Mr. William Crofts, who was in attendance on the Queen at the Hague. The letter was intercepted at sea ' by one of the ships in his Majesty's service '—but the Navy had declared for Parliament. At this point of time the fiction was kept up by the Parliament that their forces were being maintained in defence of King and Parliament. The letter was sent to the House of Commons and was printed as propaganda for Parliament.

Source : A collection of Proclamations, Petitions, etc., no. 48a, of Charles I, in Eton College Library.

Deare Will,

By these last letters to the Queene, you will finde a great alteration of businesse here ; the King, that very lately appeared almost abandoned by all his Subjects, is now become the Favourite of the Kingdome ; yet I beleeve His Enemies are not so neglected as not to be able to raise an Army to oppose Him ; and indeed here lies the jest, for they will be followed just enough to forfeit their estates, which I have heard you often say, were better bestowed on some of us. Yesterday there came a Messenger from the House, who had an Order (and did raise the power of the County) to entreat *Bartley Ashburnham*, and myself, to come to speake to the House ; but the King gave the Messenger a short Answer, and an Officer or two gave him a short Cudgell, so he is returned to *London* (a fine Gentleman) with his Arme in a Scarfe. Deare Will, preserve me in your good opinion, for I assure you I am

June 22. Yorke 1642.   your most affectionate humble servant,

Pray if M. *Jermin* be with you, present   H. WILMOT.
 my most humble service to him.

THE OPENING OF THE CIVIL WAR. 1642

THE REACTION IN FAVOUR OF THE KING, CHARLES I

Down to the end of August, 1641, the Long Parliament was unanimous in its desire to carry out the necessary reforms in order to prevent a return of the arbitrary government which Charles I had imposed during the ' Eleven Years' Tyranny ', 1629–1640. But when those reforms had been carried and the more extreme members went on to revolutionary measures, such as the Militia Bill, a split began in the opposition to the Crown and a reaction in favour of the King set in.

Source : *The Copie of a Letter sent from the Right Honourable The Lord Paget, unto the Honourable House of Parliament, declaring the Reasons for his departure from the Parliament unto the King's Most Excellent Majesty at York. Printed for Hugh Perry,* 1642. A copy, no. 46 (undated), is preserved in a collection of Proclamations, Petitions, etc., of Charles I in Eton College Library.

It may seem strange that I, who with all zeal and earnestness have prosecuted in the beginning of this Parliament, a Reformation of all disorders in the Church, and Common-wealth, should now in a time of such great distractions, desert the cause. Most true it is, that my ends were the common good; And whilst that was prosecuted, I was ready to lay downe both my life and fortune : But when I found a Preparation of Armes against the KING, under the shadow of Loyaltie, I rather resolved, to obey a good conscience, then[1] particular ends, and am now on my way to His Majesty, where I will throw myselfe downe at his feet, and die a loyall Subject.   PAGET.

[1] than

THE OPENING OF THE CIVIL WAR. THE SKIRMISH AT POWICK BRIDGE

THURSDAY, SEPTEMBER 22ND, 1642

The King set up his standard at Nottingham on Monday, 22nd of August. He then marched westwards to the counties which were most Royalist and in which he could recruit his army. The first engagement took place at Powick Bridge, close to Worcester. The Parliamentarian army under Essex was moving towards Worcester.

Source: *The Autobiography* of Richard Baxter. Everyman edition, p. 40. Richard Baxter was a Puritan minister, born 1615, died 1691.

Further Reading: Gardiner, *Hist. of the Great Civil War*, vol. i.

All this time the king, having marched from Nottingham to Shrewsbury, had there very successfully made up his army, especially out of Shropshire, Worcestershire, Herefordshire and Wales, though many also came out of other parts. And the Earl of Essex's army was filled up, and was marching down towards Worcester.

The fury of the rabble was so hot at home that I was fain to withdraw again, and being with one Mr. Hunt near Inkberrow, there came a party of the Earl of Essex's army before the rest to block up the Lord Byron in Worcester till the Earl of Essex came to take him there. This party lay in a meadow near Powick, above a mile from Worcester, Mr. Hunt, with other countrymen, bringing them in provision. I had a great mind to go see them, having never seen any part of an army. As soon as I came, a messenger came out of Worcester secretly to tell them that the Lord Byron was mounted and ready to be gone. Hereupon the commanders (Colonel Brown, a Scot, Colonel Edwin Sands of Kent, and Colonel Nath. Fienes, Captain Joh. Fienes and Captain Wingate) consulted what was to be done. Brown and Sands were hot for the leaving of their ground (where they were secure by a river) and presently[1] to pursue the enemy. The rest said, ' This message may be a deceit to draw us into a snare ; let us first send scouts and see how it is.' But the other prevailed, and over the

[1] i.e. immediately.

bridge they went (being all horse and dragoons); and by that time they had passed a narrow lane, and half of them entered a field beyond it. They found the king's horse, under the command of Prince Rupert, drawn up ready to charge them (when they knew not whom they fought with, nor knew that Prince Rupert was within twenty miles of them); so he charged them before the rest came in, and Colonel Sands was wounded and taken prisoner, and died of his wounds; and Major Douglas slain and the rest fled. And though the enemy pursued them no farther than the bridge, yet fled they in grievous terror to Pershore and the Earl of Essex's lifeguard lying there took the alarm that the enemy was following them, and away they went. This sight quickly told me the vanity of armies, and how little confidence is to be placed in them.

THE BATTLE OF EDGEHILL

SUNDAY, OCTOBER 23RD, 1642

After the successful skirmish at Powick Bridge, the King moved south, intending to keep Christmas at Whitehall. He was forced to turn and meet the pursuing army of the Parliament under the Earl of Essex at Edgehill. This was a battle with ' reversed fronts ', since the King had his back to his objective—London. This, the first real battle of the Civil War, was indecisive, but the King was able to continue south.

Source : A letter from C. H. to Sancroft of Emmanuel College, Cambridge, later Archbishop of Canterbury. Ellis, *Original Letters*, 2nd series, vol. iii, Letter CCLXXXVIII. Harleian MSS. 3784, fol. 141.

Further Reading : Gardiner, *Hist. of the Great Civil War*, vol. i.

On Sunday last I saw the Battle which was the bloudiest I believe the oldest soldiers in the field ever saw. We have routed

L

utterly their horse and slain & chased away so considerable a party of their foot, that the Enemy is very weak. Though we have lost some, yet few of eminency, save some prisoners. The Earl of Lindsey, Willoughby, and Colonel Lunston, the Lord St. John, with the Lord Fielding are slain, with many others. My Lord of Essex escaped us by being in an alehouse. We have his coach and much money in it. There needs no more to assure any understanding man we had the day, than to tell them (which is true) we had all their ordnances in the field and fetcht them out next morning in their sight. They are so weak they have entrenched themselves, and we are now going on our intended march to Oxford, having only gone backward on Sunday to bestow this breathing on them. We have taken about five colours and cornetts, and lost about five or six colours, but never a cornett. The King hath five hundred of their horse alive, and of eighteen hundred not one horse is left them. At the beginning of the fight, two double troops came over to the King's party commanded by Sir Faithfeill Fortescue and Mr. Gervase Pain, & fought on that side. It is commonly reported the Earl of Essex his soldiers ran away dayly Three hundred prisoners are taken, among which is Sergeant Major Barrey, a recusant of the Irish. My Lord Albany is slain on the King's side, and Dr. Lake. The King gave fire to the first piece, the Lord General having first demanded the word, which was ' *Go in the name of God and I'll lay my bones with yours.*' Marquis Hartford is now on the march with ten thousand men armed out of Wales, and intends to meet the King at Oxford. Sir R. Hopton and Mr. Rogers bring as many from the West Country.

C.H.

THE BATTLE OF MARSTON MOOR

Tuesday, July 2nd, 1644

In September 1643 Parliament made an alliance with the Scots—
the Solemn League and Covenant. 1644 the Scots crossed the Border
and joined Manchester and Fairfax in the siege of York. Prince
Rupert hurried to the help of York and the Parliamentarians were
forced to raise the siege, thus letting out Newcastle's army. Rupert
persuaded Newcastle to bring about a decisive battle with the Parliamentarian Army. The Battle of Marston Moor was fought and the
Royalists were heavily defeated.

Source : A Scotsman, David Buchanan, had written some slander-
ous criticisms of the Parliamentarian leaders, especially of Cromwell,
and of their conduct of the battle. The following extract is taken from
a rare pamphlet written almost certainly by Lord Saye in answer to
Buchanan. It is entitled, *The Scots Design Discovered*, and has been
reprinted in the Eng. Hist. Rev. vol. v, p. 351. Punctuation has been
simplified.

Further Reading : Buchan, *Oliver Cromwell*, ch. iv.

. . . it is well know to all that were present, and by their report
to all other who are not willing to believe lyes rather than receive
what is true, that both the General of the *Scots* Armie and also
Lord *Fairfax* gave the day for lost : and so lost, that the one
stayed not till he came to Hull, and the other, as is said, went
further from the place where the Battle was fought, before he
made a stay. And as it is reported by those that were present,
at least 10,000 ran away, most of the *Scotch* Armie, if not all. But
those I formerly mentioned were run out of the Field, and the
day theirs in the Enemies' opinion that were on that side of the
Field, as also in the opinion of ours, both Generals and Soldiers,
who thereupon left the Field : When things were brought into
this condition, it pleased God to use, as instrumens under Him,
Cromwell, who Commanded them, and the Regiments of Horse
that were in my Lord of *Manchesters* Armie, to give the turn,
win the day, and take the Victorie out of the enemies hands.
This was the Lord's doing, to whom belong the issues of War,

and it was indeed a mervailous mercy. . . . Now, as for that which concerneth *Cromwell* himself, *that he did not appear at all in the heat of the business*, but *for a little skar kept himself off, till the worst was past* ; what man is there, *English* or *Scot*, that hath either worth or honestie in him, who was present, that will not abhor such an envious, malicious falsehood as this, fit to be fathered by none but the father of lyes himself? for it is known, that *Cromwell* charged in the Head of those Regiments of Horse in my Lord *Manchesters* Army, which Horse he commanded, and with those Regiments brake all the Regiments of the Enemies Army, first the Horse, and after that the Foot ; and that he continued with them, untill the victory was fully obtained (yea, and the Psalm of praise for it sung to God, to whom alone the Glory is due) ; commanding all the while they charged, and taking special care to see it observed, that the Regiments of Horse, when they had broken a Regiment of the Enemies, should not divide, and, in pursuit of the Enemie, break their order, but keep themselves still together in bodies, to charge the other Regiments of the Enemie, which stood firm, and were in bodies both of Horse and Foot. By this wise direction and order which himself was present to see observed, his Regiments at last brake the Enemies Regiments, all, first the Horse, then the Foot ; and herein indeed was the good service which *David Lesley* did that day, with his little light *Scotch* Nags (for such they were then, and not such as afterwards they made them out of Sr. *John Fennicks* breed, and our best Northern Horse, for which they at their pleasure would exchange their *Scotch* little Coursers when they came into those parts) I say, in this he did very good service, that when a Regiment of the Enemies was broken, he then fell in, and followed the chase, doing execution upon them, and keeping them from rallying again, and getting into Bodies ; whereby *Cromwell* with his Regiments had the better means and opportunity, keeping firm together in Bodies, to fall upon the other Regiments which remained, untill they were, one after another, all broken and routed both Horse and Foot. The Enemies Horse, being many of them, if not the greatest part, Gentlemen, stood firm a very long time, coming to a close fight with the

Sword, and standing like an Iron Wall, so that they were not easily broken. If the *Scots* light, but weak nags had undertaken that work, they had never been able to stand a charge, or indure the shock of the Enemies Horse, both Horse and men being very good and fighting desperately enough. . . .

THE CIVIL WAR DAY BY DAY

The Civil War never was a war ' of classes nor of districts, but of ideas '. It split families, so that father and son, brother and brother-in-law were on opposite sides. At the beginning, for some time, and always at its best, it was a chivalrous war. But from the start there were scoundrels on both sides, and after a time tempers became frayed and animosities hardened. The war was largely a war of skirmishes, minor clashes, chance engagements, and sieges of country houses. The following extracts illustrate these various phases and aspects.

(1) *Source* : *The Memoirs of Edmund Ludlow*, ed. by C. H. Firth. Ludlow was born in ?1617 and died in 1692. He was one of the most prominent of the Parliamentarians, both as a soldier and as a politician. A man of courage and of wrath (' solid ' is the word Carlyle uses of him), he is one of the less attractive personalities of the times. His memory was excellent, and where he is writing of events in which he took part he may be relied on. But his passions were great; he became a violent and unreasoning opponent of Cromwell. He was one of the regicides. His accounts of events in which he was not concerned are usually a good deal warped. The following extracts illustrate the gentler and the crueller sides of the war.

(*a*)   THE SIEGE OF WARDOUR CASTLE
                    SEPTEMBER 1644

Between these two garrisons of Southampton and Pool lay my troop of horse, to do what service they could against the enemy and to favour our relief : where my cornet, afterwards known by the name of Major William Ludlow, was shot through

the body, and into the thigh and his horse in two places, by some
of the enemy from an ambuscade ; being brought to Southampton, and his wounds searched, the bullet that went in at his belly
was found at the chine of his back, with a piece of the wastband
of his breeches, which being cut out, he wonderfully recovered
to be in some measure serviceable to the publick.

(*b*)   A CHANCE ENCOUNTER
                         July 1644

Two days after my coming to Southampton Col. Norton
received advice, that the enemy was preparing to send some
forces, in order to beat off those of ours that blocked up Basing
House. He being then before Winchester, and resolving to
march with his troop to reinforce the beseigers, desired me with
my troop to supply his place at Winchester till his return. Being
unwilling to refuse any public service, tho my men were very
much harassed, I marched thither ; and that those in the castle
might see they were not at liberty to ravage the country, I drew
out my troop and faced them ; upon which they sent out what
horse they had to skirmish with us ; amongst whom observing
one Mr. William Neale, who was of my acquaintance, and
formerly my schoolfellow, I called to him telling him, that I
was sorry to see him there ; but since it was so, I offered to
exchange a shot with him, and riding up to that purpose, he
retreated towards his party, where making a stand, he called to
me to come on, which I did ; but he retreated again till he came
within the shelter of their foot, and one with him dismounting,
fired a musquet at me loaded with a brace of bullets, of which
one went into the belly of my horse, the other struck upon my
breast-plate, within half an inch of the bottom of it : my horse
carried me off, but died that night.

(*c*)   THE HORRORS OF WAR
                         July 1644

Sir Francis Doddington being informed by one Bacon, who
was parson of the parish, that one of the prisoners had threatened

to stick in his skirts, as he called it, for reading the Common-Prayer, struck the man so many blows upon the head, and with such force, that he broke his skull, and caused him to fall into a swound; from which he was no sooner recovered, but he was picked out to be one of the twelve which Sir Francis had granted to Sir William St. Leger to be hanged, in lieu of six Irish rebels who had been executed at Warum by Col. Sydenham, in pursuance of an order from Parliament to give them no quarter. These twelve being most of them clothiers, were hanged upon the same tree; but one of them breaking his halter, desired that what he had suffered might be accepted, or else that he might fight against any two for his life; notwithstanding which they caused him to be hanged up again, and had proceeded much farther, had not Sir Ralp Hopton sent orders to put a stop to their butcheries.

(2)   THE GARRISON AT RUSHALL

Rushall was garrisoned by the Royalists. It was captured in May 1644 by the Earl of Denbigh for the Parliamentarians, who left a garrison of Roundheads in it. Here are two descriptions of that garrison.

Source: Quoted in *The Great Civil War in Midland Parishes*, by D. R. Guttery, Cornish, Birmingham, 1950. p. 83.

(1)   Francis Pitt, a Wednesbury farmer's opinion:

I never heard more swearing nor saw more drunkennesse and prophanenesse than I saw in the garrison at Rushall. I'le mention one: The Martial (I have forgotten his name) he did swear and blaspheme as if he would cause the stones to flie out of the Walls and after I fell into his hands he stript me and abused me more like a Jew than a Christian.

(2)   A Parliamentarian officer's opinion:

To my apprehension I never observed braver spirits and civiller men in any place where I have served.

(3)   THE FALL OF DUDLEY CASTLE

WEDNESDAY, MAY 13TH, 1646

Sir William Brereton (1604–1661) was one of the Parliamentarian commanders and a fervid Puritan. Clarendon records that he ' was most considerable for a known averseness to the government of the church '. A pamphlet of the times records that he was ' a notable man at a thanksgiving dinner, having terrible long teeth and a prodigious stomach, to turn the archbishop's chapel at Croydon into a kitchen ; also to swallow up that palace and lands at a morsel.' All the same, it was he who secured the surrender of Dudley Castle and who wrote the following letter :—

Source : *The Great Civil War in Midland Parishes*, by D. R. Guttery, p. 114.

To Mr. Ashurst and Mr. Swinfen touching the Surrender of Dudley Castle.   May 13, 1646.

Srs, This day the strong Castle of Dudley was delivered unto me, whereunto wee entered about one of the Clocke. The Condicions for the surrender whereof were sent unto you by the last which I shall not now Repeate but shall give you this further Accompt touching this place.

There marched out of the Castle neere 300 Foote of the Common Soldyers besides Horse and neere 40 Reformade Officers marched out with their Horses and Armes. They were well furnished with Beare and plentifully with Water Soe as if that God (which by the sounding of Rammes Hornes and seaven tyme Compassinge the Walles of Jericho brought down those stronge Walles) had not alsoe taken away their Courage and divided them against themselves this might have been a teadious and expensive Worke and one of the last Reduced Garrisons in the kingdome. I desire the whole honour and glory may be ascribed to God with whom it is easie to deliver upp the strongest as the weakest Houlds. . . .

THE EXECUTION OF KING CHARLES THE FIRST, 1649

TUESDAY, JANUARY 30TH, 1649 (N.S.)

Source : This account is taken from the diary of Philip Henry, a Nonconformist divine, who was born at Whitehall in 1631 and died in 1696. It was while he was an undergraduate at Christ Church, Oxford, that he had leave to go to London and there saw, when he was just over 17 years old, the execution of Charles I.

At the later end of the year 1648 I had leave to goe to london to see my Father, & during my stay there at that time at Whitehal it was that I saw the Beheading of King Charles the first ; He went by our door on Foot each day that hee was carry'd by water to Westminster, for he took Barge at Gardenstayres where we liv'd & once he spake to my Father & sayd Art thou alive yet! On the day of his execution, which was Tuesday, Jan. 30, I stood amongst the crowd in the street before Whitehal gate, where the scaffold was erected, and saw what was done, but was not so near as to hear any thing. The Blow I saw given, & can truly say with a sad heart ; at the instant whereof, I remember well, there was such a Grone by the Thousands then present, as I never heard before & desire I may never hear again. There was according to Order one Troop immediately marching from-wards charing-cross to Westmr & another from-wards Westmr to charing-cross purposely to masker the people, & to disperse & scatter them, so that I had much adoe amongst the rest to escape home without hurt.

POVERTY IN EXILE

THE DUKE OF NEWCASTLE

William Cavendish, Duke of Newcastle (1592–1676) had been commander of the Royalist armies in the north of England. After the defeat of the Royalists at Marston Moor, 1644, he retired to the Continent and lived in great financial difficulties at Paris, Rotterdam, and finally until the Restoration in 1660 at Antwerp. He pawned his wife's jewels, he borrowed money right and left, obtained an allowance out of his confiscated estates in England, but in the end he only recovered a part of those estates, although he had expended nearly one million pounds in the service of the Royalist cause. He was a great lover of horses and the best horseman of his time. In spite of his shortage of money and his large debts, somehow he managed to keep as many as eight horses while in exile. He wrote a book on a sumptuous scale on the art of training horses, which he had published at a cost of £1,300 with the help of two friends. This extract illustrates the difficulties which faced the Royalist exiles, whose estates had been sequestrated by Parliament.

Source : *The Life of The Thrice Noble, High and Puissant Prince, William Cavendish, Duke of Newcastle*, by his wife, Margaret, Duchess of Newcastle, Everyman edition.

Further Reading : The article in the *Dictionary of National Biography* is the only other biography.

Not long after, when My Lord had begun to settle himself in his mentioned new house, his gracious master the prince, having taken a resolution to go into Holland upon some designs, Her Majesty the Queen[1] desired my Lord to follow him, promising to engage for his debts which hitherto he had contracted at Paris, and commanding her controller and treasurer to be bound for them in her behalf ; which they did, although the creditors would not content themselves, until My Lord had joined his word to theirs ; so great and generous was the bounty and favour of Her Majesty to My Lord! considering she had already given him heretofore near upon £2000 sterling, even at that time when Her Majesty stood most in need of it. . . .

[1] Queen Henrietta Maria, wife of Charles I.

That day when we left Paris, the creditors coming to take their farewell of My Lord, expressed so great a love and kindness for him, accompanied with so many heart prayers and wishes, that he could not but prosper on his journey. . . .

My Lord having now lived in Rotterdam almost six months, at a great charge, keeping an open and noble table for all comers, and being pleased especially to entertain such as were excellent soldiers, and noted commanders of war, whose kindness he took as a great obligation, still hoping that some occasion would happen to invite those worthy persons into England to serve His Majesty ; but seeing no probability of either returning into England, or doing His Majesty any service in that kind, he resolved to retire to some place where he might live privately ; and having chosen the city of Antwerp for that purpose, went to the Hague to take leave of His Highness the Prince, now our gracious sovereign. My Lord had then but a small stock of money left ; for though the then Marquess of Hereford (after Duke of Somerset), and his cousin-german, once removed, the now Earl of Devonshire had lent him £2000 between them ; yet all that was spent, and above £1000 more, which My Lord borrowed during the time he lived in Rotterdam, his expence being the more, by reason (as I have mentioned) he lived freely and nobly. . . .

— About this time My Lord was much necessitated for money, which forced him to try several ways for to obtain so much as would relieve his present wants. At last Mr. Alesbury, the onely son to Sir Th. Alesbury, Knight and Baronet, and brother to the now Countess of Clarendon, a very worthy gentleman, and great friend to My Lord, having some moneys that belonged to the now Duke of Buckingham, and seeing My Lord in so great distress, did him the favour to lend him £200 (which money My Lord, since his return, hath honestly and justly repai'd). This relief came so seasonably, that it got My Lord credit in the city of Antwerp, whereas otherwise he would have lost himself to his great disadvantage ; for My Lord, having hired the house aforementioned, and wanting furniture for it, was credited by the citizens for as many goods as he was pleased to have, as also for meat and drink, and all kind of necessaries and provisions, which certainly was a special blessing of God, he being onely a stranger in that nation, but to all appearance, a ruined man. . . .

My Lord continued to live there with as much content as a man of his condition could do, and his chief pastime and divertisement consisted in the mannage of the two afore-mentioned horses ; which he had not enjoyed long, but the Barbary-horse for which he paid 200 pistols in Paris, died, and soon after the horse which he had from the Lord Crofts ; and though he wanted present means to repair these his losses, yet he endeavoured and obtained so much credit at last that he was able to buy two others, and by degrees so many as amounted in all to the number of 8. In which he took so much delight and pleasure, that though he was then in distress for money, yet he would have sooner tried all other ways, then (*than*) parted with any of them ; for I have heard him say, that good horses are so rare, as not to be valued for money, and that he who would buy him out of his pleasure (meaning his horses) must pay dear for it.

THE EXECUTION OF MONTROSE

TUESDAY, 21ST MAY, 1650

James Graham, 1st Marquis of Montrose, born 1612, was made Lieutenant-General of Charles I's forces in Scotland in 1644. Between 1644 and 1645 he won six victories with an army of mixed Scottish and Irish troops, but was defeated at Philiphaugh in 1645. He escaped to the Continent, returned to Scotland in 1650, was defeated at Invercarron, and was betrayed by Macleod of Assynt. He was hanged in the Grassmarket at Edinburgh, May 21st, 1650.

Source : *The Relation of the Death of Montrose, Written from Edinburgh to London by an Eyewitness*, 21st May, 1650. The Eyewitness is said by Buchan in his life of Montrose, p. 376, to be an Englishman and a

Commonwealth agent. Part of the letter here printed was clearly written while the execution was being carried out. From the Nicolas Vansittart Paper in the B.M. Printed by Napier in *The Memorials of Montrose*, vol. ii. pp. 447–9.

Further Reading : Buchan, *Montrose.*

What with the early going away of the Post, and with the *hubaub* wee are in, *Montrose being now on the Scaffold*, I must cut short.

Satterday hee was brought into the towne, sitting tyed with a rope upon a highe chayre, upon a cart ; the hangman having beefore taken off his hatt, and riding beefore him with his bonnet on. Sen I have beene with him, he saith, for personall offences he hath deserved all this, but justifies his cause. Hee caused a new suit to bee made for himselfe, and came yesterday into the Parliament House with a scarlet rocket,[1] and suit of pure cloath, all laid with rich lace, a beaver and rich hatt-band, and scarlett silk stockings. The Chancellour made a large speech to him, discovering how much formerly he was for the Covenant, and how he hath since broake it. Hee desired to know wheather hee might be free to answer ; and being admitted, he told them his cause was good, and that hee hade not only a *commission*, but *particular orders*, for what hee hadd done, from his Majestie, which hee was engaged to bee servant to : and they also hadd professed to comply : and upon that accompte, however they dealt with him, yet hee would owne them to bee a true Parliament. And hee further told them, that if they would take away his life, the world knew hee regarded it not ; that it was a debt that must once bee payd ; and that he was willing and did much rejoice that hee must goe the same way as his Master did ; and it was the joy of his heart, not only to doe but to suffer for him.

His sentence was to bee hanged upon a galhouse thirty foote high, three houres, at Edinburgh Crosse, to have his head strucken off, and hanged upon Edinburgh Towleboothe, and his armes and legges to be hanged upp in other publique townes in the

[1] i.e. mantle.

Kingdome, as Glescoe, etc., and his body to bee buried at the common burying-place, in case excommunication from the Kirke was taken off, or else to bee buryed where those are buried that were hanged.

All the tyme, while the sentence was given, and also when hee was executed, he seemed noe way to be altered, or his spirit moved; but his speech was full of composure, and his carriage as sweete as I saw a man in all my dayes. When they bidd him kneele, he told them he was willing to observe any posture that might manifest his obedience, especially to them whoe were soe neere conjunction with his master. It is absolutely beleeved that hee hath overcome more men, by his death, in Scotland, then hee would have done if he had lived. For I never saw a more sweeter carriage in a man in all my life. I should wryte more largely if I hadd tyme, *but he is just now a turning of from the lather*[1] : but his countenance changes not. But the rest, that came with him a Satterday, are in great feares. The King is expected dayly.

. . .

But I shall say noe more, but rests

Really yours.

JAMES GRAHAM, FIRST MARQUIS OF MONTROSE

Source: *A Relation of the True Funerals of the great Lord Marquis of Montrose*. Printed in the year 1661. Reprinted in the *Harleian Miscellany*, vol. vii, pp. 236 sqq. 1810. Authorship anonymous.

Further Reading : Buchan, *Montrose*.

I shall acquaint you with what I know myself (having followed him several years in his expeditions) and what I have learned from others of good name and credit. He was of a middle stature,

[1] i.e. ladder.

and most exquisitely proportioned limbs; his hair of a light chestnut, his complexion betwixt pale and ruddy, his eye most penetrating, though inclining to grey; his nose rather aquiline than otherwise: As he was strong of body and limbs, so was he most agile, which made him excel most others in those exercises where these two are required: In riding the great horse, and making use of his arms, he came short of none; I never heard much of his delight in dancing, though his countenance, and other his bodily endowments, were equally fitting the court as the camp: In his younger days he travelled France and Italy, where he made his work to pick up the best of their qualities necessary for a person of honour, having rendered himself perfect in the academies . . . though he had never been bred a soldier, yet he shewed admirable knowledge in the art of war; and though he never confined himself to the practice of other nations, yet he never did anything but with strong reason, his strategems seldom missing of being successful; his vigilance and toil were so wonderful, that the enemy knew not where he was, till he was on them, and he again never ignorant of their place, strength, and condition. His fight was still on the plains, though the hills were advantageous to him, his cavalry not being the fourth part of the enemies, but all of gentlemen, particularly of the noble families of Gordon and Ogilvy. He shewed greatest chearfulness in his greatest extremities: If his infantry at any time scrupled the wading of little rivers, he was the first who dismounted to shew others the way, and this banished all re-pining: He accustomed himself to coarse feeding, and constant drinking of water; he knew they were still to be found, so that the want of delicacies should be no temptation to him to be weary of the service. . . . It was wonderful with what dexterity he kept his army intire, without pay or plunder. . . . His vast knowledge in military and state affairs was admirable: He was pleasant and witty in conversation, with an affability in private becoming a comrade; scandalous and obscene wit durst not appear before him. In this sort he made war in Scotland against his majesty's enemies, for the space of eighteen months, bearing the trophies of six battles, with the defeat of six armies: And, no doubt, he had continued victorious, if the art of trepanning[1] had not been prevalent : However, the slur he received at Philipshaugh was not the cut-throat of his majesty's army ; for, through his enemy, he made his way to his friends in the north, though far off, where his presence gave life to drooping spirits, and in a short time made up so considerable forces, as could give check to the insulting enemy : But his majesty, coming to Newcastle, put a period to that war. . . . I shall not speak of his barbarous usage, whilst he was prisoner, because they were countrymen and pretended to be christians ; but as to himself, never martyr for the cause of Christ went with greater chearfulness to the fire, than he did embrace all the indignities put on him, and all without vanity or pageantry, as many are used to do on such occasions. . . . When he was reviled, and the lye put upon him . . . he returned no other answer, than that he had heard him speak to better purpose at other times. He was frequent in his devotions and heavenly meditations ; and, having reconciled himself with a true contrition to his gracious God, he advanced to finish his course with a courageous gravity, and pious modesty, as his glorious martyred master had done before ; which carriage turned the hearts of his enemies, who came to insult at the butchery, and generally the barbarity of his usuage was condemned by all. . . . I shall say no more of this great martyr, than was said of the reverend Archbishop of Canterbury, martyred on the same account, when a worthy knight was, in a contemptible, jeering way, demanded, what his epitaph should be, he answered, that, so long as St. Paul's church stood, and his book was preserved, he could want neither monument nor epitaph ; so, I say, so long as his history is in being, and the heaps of stones which covered his enemies carcases in Tipper-moor, Aberdeen, Ennerlochy, Aldern, Alford, and Kilsyth, are lasting, he can neither want the one nor the other ; and that is so long as there is a summer to succeed the spring, and the celestial bodies to terminate their usual course.

[1] Entrapping.

OLIVER CROMWELL

As with Charles I, no introduction is needed for one of the greatest of Englishmen. He was born in 1599, became Commander-in-Chief 1650, Protector 1653, refused the title of King in 1657, became Protector the second time, 1657, given the right to nominate his successor, died on Friday, September 3rd, 1658, the anniversary of his victories at Dunbar (1650) and Worcester (1651).

(1) *Source* : *Memoirs of the Reign of Charles I,* by Sir Philip Warwick, p. 247.

I have no mind to give an ill character of Cromwell, for in his conversation towards me he was ever friendly, though at the latter end of the day, finding me ever incorrigible and having some inducements to suspect me a tamperer, he was sufficiently rigid. The first time that ever I took notice of him was in the very beginning of the Parliament held in November 1640, when I vainly thought myself a courtly young gentleman (for we courtiers valued ourselves much upon our good clothes). I came one morning into the House well clad, and perceived a gentleman speaking (whom I knew not) very ordinarily apparelled, for it was a plain-cloth suit, which seemed to have been made by an ill country tailor : his linen was plain and not very clean, and I remember a speck or two of blood upon his little band, which was not much larger than his collar. His hat was without a hat-band. His stature was of good size, his sword stuck close to his side, his countenance swollen and reddish, his voice sharp and untunable, and his eloquence full of fervour, for the subject matter would not bear much of reason, it being in behalf of a servant of Mr. Prynne's, who had dispersed libels against the Queen for her dancing and such like innocent and courtly sports : and he aggravated the imprisonment of this man by the Council-Table unto that height that one would have believed the very government itself had been in great danger by it. I sincerely profess it lessened much my reverence unto that great council, for he was very much hearkened unto. And yet I lived to see this very gentleman, whom out of no ill will to him I thus describe, by multiplied good successes and by real

M

(but usurped) power (having had a better tailor and more converse among good company) in my own eye, when for six weeks together I was a prisoner in his sergeant's hands and daily waited at Whitehall, appear of a great and majestic deportment and comely presence. Of him therefore I will say no more, but that verily I believe he was extraordinarily designed for those extraordinary things which one while most wickedly and facinorously he acted, and at another as successfully and greatly performed.

(2) *Source* A letter from John Maidston, a steward in Cromwell's Household and an M.P., to Governor Winthrop of Connecticut 1659. Thurloe, S. P., 1. 763–8.

His body was well compact and strong, his stature under 6 foot (I believe about two inches), his head so shaped as you might see it a storehouse and shop both of a vast treasury of natural parts. His temper exceeding fiery, as I have known, but the flame of it kept down, for the most part, or soon allayed with those moral endowments he had. He was naturally compassionate towards objects in distress, even to an effeminate measure : though God made him a heart wherein was left little room for any fear but what was due to himself, of which there was a large proportion, yet did he exceed in tenderness towards sufferers. A larger soul, I think, hath seldom dwelt in a house of clay than his was. I do believe, if his story were impartially transmitted and the unprejudiced world possessed with it, she would add him to her nine worthies, and make up that number to a decemviri. He lived and died in comfortable communion with God, as judicious persons near him well observed. He was that Mordecai that sought the welfare of his people, and spake peace unto his seed, yet were his temptations such, as it appeared frequently, that he, that hath grace enough for many men, may have too little for himself, the treasure he had being but in an earthen vessel, and that equally defiled with original sin, as any other man's nature is.

CROMWELL AT THE STORMING OF DROGHEDA

September 10th–11th, 1649

After the execution of the King, fearing that Ireland might become the jumping-off point for a Royalist invasion of England, Cromwell crossed thither on August 15th, 1649 and began the conquest of that island. On Monday and Tuesday, September 10th and 11th, took place the storming of Drogheda, where frightful scenes of massacre took place, perhaps the least justifiable of Cromwell's actions.

Source : Carlyle's *Letters and Speeches of Cromwell*: letters civ and cv.

Further Reading : Buchan, *Oliver Cromwell*, pp. 337 sqq.

Wood, *Athenae Oxonienses*, the Preface, for an account by his brother, Tom Wood, who served there.

(1)   LETTER CIV

To the Hon. John Bradshaw, Esquire, President of the Council
        of State.   These.   Dublin, 16th September, 1649.

Sir,

It hath pleased God to bless our endeavours at Tredah.[1] After battery, we stormed it. The enemy were about 3,000 strong in the Town. They made a stout resistance ; and near 1000 of our men being entered, the Enemy forced them out again. But God giving a new courage to our men, they attempted again, and entered ; beating the enemy from their defences.

The Enemy had made three retrenchments, both to the right and left of where we entered ; all which they were forced to quit. Being thus entered, we refused them quarter ; having, the day before, summoned the Town. I believe we put to the sword the whole number of the defendants. I do not think Thirty of the whole number escaped with their lives. Those that did, are in safe custody for the Barbadoes. Since that time, the Enemy quitted to us Trim and Dundalk. In Trim they were in such haste that they left their guns behind them.

This hath been a marvellous great mercy. The Enemy, being

[1] i.e. Drogheda

not willing to put an issue upon a field of battle, had put into this Garrison almost all their prime soldiers, being about 3000 horse and foot, under the command of their best officers; Sir Arthur Ashton[1] being made Governor. There were some seven or eight regiments, Ormond's being one, under the command of Sir Edmund Varney.[2]   I do not believe, neither do I hear, that any officer escaped with his life, save only one Lieutenant, who, I hear, going to the Enemy said, That he was the only man that escaped of all the garrison. The Enemy upon this were filled with much terror. And truly I believe this bitterness will save much effusion of blood, through the goodness of God.

I wish that all honest hearts may give the glory of this to God alone, to whom indeed the praise of this mercy belongs. As for instruments, they were very inconsiderable the work throughout. . . .

Captain Brandly did with forty or fifty of his men very gallantly storm the Tenalia[3]; for which he deserves the thanks of the State. I rest,

Your most humble servant,
OLIVER CROMWELL.

LETTER CV

For the Honourable William Lenthall Esquire, Speaker of the Parliament of England : These.

Dublin, 17th September, 1649.

Sir,

. . . Upon Tuesday the 10th instant, about five o'clock in the evening, we began the Storm; and after some hot dispute we entered, about seven or eight hundred men; the enemy disputing it very stiffly with us. And indeed, through the advantages of the place, and the courage God was pleased to give the defenders, our men were forced to retreat quite out of the breach,

---

[1] Sir Arthur Ashton had a wooden leg which the soldiers were very eager for, understanding it to be full of gold coin : but it proved to be mere timber : all his gold, 200 broad pieces, was sewed in his belt, and scrambled for when that came to light.

[2] The Sir Edmund Varney mentioned here was the son of the Sir Edmund Verney, the King's Standard-bearer, who was killed at Edgehill.

[3] Tenalia = a kind of advanced work which takes its name from its resemblance, real or imaginary, to the lip of a pair of pincers. Carlyle's footnote.

not without some considerable loss ; Colonel Castle being there shot in the head, whereof he presently died ; and divers officers and soldiers doing their duty killed and wounded. There was a Tenalia to flanker the south Wall of the Town, between Duleek Gate and the corner Tower before mentioned ;—which our men entered, wherein they found some forty or fifty of the Enemy, which they put to the sword. And this ' Tenalia ' they held : but it being without the Wall, and the sally-port through the Wall into that Tenalia being choked up with some of the Enemy which were killed in it, it proved of no use for an entrance into the Town that way.

Although our men that stormed the breaches were forced to recoil, as is before expressed ; yet, being encouraged to recover their loss, they made a second attempt ; wherein God was pleased so to animate them that they got ground of the enemy, and by the goodness of God, forced him to quit his entrenchments. And after a very hot dispute, the Enemy having both horse and foot, and we only foot, within the Wall—they gave ground, and our men became masters both of their retrenchments and of the Church ; which, indeed, although they made our entrance the more difficult, yet they proved of excellent use to us ; so that the Enemy could not now annoy us with their horse, but thereby we had the advantage to make good the ground, that so we might let in our own horse ; which accordingly was done, though with much difficulty.

Divers of the Enemy retreated into the Mill-Mount : a place very strong and difficult of access ; being exceedingly high, having a good graft, and strong palisadoed. The Governor, Sir Arthur Ashton, and divers considerable Officers being there, our men getting up to them, were ordered by me to put them all to the sword. And indeed, being in the heat of action, I forbade them to spare any that were in arms in the Town : and, I think, that night they put to the sword about 2000 men ;—divers of the officers and soldiers being fled over the Bridge into the other part of the Town, where about 100 of them possessed St. Peter's Church-steeple, some the west Gate, and others a strong Round Tower next the Gate called St. Sunday's. These being summoned to yield to mercy, refused. Whereupon I ordered the steeple of St. Peter's Church to be fired, when one of them was heard to say in the midst of the flames : ' God damn me, God confound me ; I burn, I burn.'

The next day, the other two Towers were summoned ; in one of which was about six or seven score ; but they refused to yield themselves : and we knowing that hunger must compel them, set only good guards to secure them from running away until their stomachs were come down. From one of the said Towers, notwithstanding their condition, they killed and wounded some of our men. When they submitted, their officers were knocked on the head ; and every tenth man of the soldiers killed ; and the rest shipped for the Barbadoes. The soldiers in the other Tower were all spared, as to their lives only ; and shipped likewise for the Barbadoes.

I am persuaded that this is a righteous judgement of God upon these barbarous wretches, who have imbrued their hands in so much innocent blood ; and that it will tend to prevent the effusion of blood for the future. Which are the satisfactory grounds to such actions, which otherwise cannot but work remorse and regret. The officers and soldiers of this Garrison were the flower of their army. And their great expectation was, that our attempting this place would put fair to ruin us. . . . And now give me leave to say how it comes to pass that this work is wrought. It was set upon some of our hearts, That a great thing should be done, not by power or might, but by the Spirit of God. And is it not so, clearly? That which caused your men to storm so courageously, it was the Spirit of God, who gave your men courage, and took it away again ; and gave the Enemy courage, and took it away again ; and gave your men courage again, and therewith this happy success. And therefore it is good that God alone have all the glory. . . .

Your most obedient servant,

OLIVER CROMWELL.

CROMWELL IN SCOTLAND. THE BATTLE OF DUNBAR

Tuesday, September 3rd, 1650

In the spring of 1650 Cromwell returned to England from Ireland. Things were going wrong in Scotland. The exiled Montrose had landed there, but he found little support, was taken and hanged. But the Scots proclaimed Prince Charles king as Charles II and Charles landed on June 24. Royalism was strong in England: the danger to the newly established Commonwealth in England was great. Cromwell took an army north: on July 28th he was in front of Edinburgh, but he had to retreat to save his men from starvation. On August 31st he was back at Dunbar, but the Scottish army had seized the pass which led to England. Cromwell found himself and his army hemmed in between the sea and the Scots on the top of a low hill. The Scots grew tired of waiting and on September 2nd they began to move down from the hill.

Source : Carlyle's *Letters and Speeches of Cromwell.* Letter cxl.

Further Reading : Buchan, *Oliver Cromwell,* pp. 358 sqq.

Letter CXL

For the Honourable William Lenthall, Esquire, Speaker of the Parliament of England : These.

Dunbar, 4th September, 1650.

Sir,

... The Enemy lying in the posture before mentioned, having those advantages ; we lay very near him, being sensible of our disadvantages, having some weakness of the flesh, but yet consolation and support from the Lord himself to our poor weak faith, wherein I believe not a few amongst us stand : That because of their numbers, because of their advantages, because of their confidence, because of our weakness, because of our strait, we were in the Mount, and in the Mount the Lord would be seen ; and that He would find a way of deliverance and salvation for us :—and indeed we had our consolations and our hopes.

Upon Monday evening,—the Enemy's whole numbers were very great ; about Six-thousand horse, as we heard, and Sixteen-thousand foot at least ; ours drawn down, as to sound men, to about Seven-thousand five-hundred foot, and Three-thousand five-hundred horse—upon Monday evening, the Enemy drew down to the right wing about two-thirds of their left wing of horse. To the right wing ; shogging also their foot and train much to the right ; causing their right wing of horse to edge down towards the sea. We could not well imagine but that the Enemy intended to attempt upon us, or to place themselves in a more exact condition of interposition. The Major-General and myself coming to the Earl Roxburgh's House, and observing this posture, I told him I thought it did give us an opportunity and advantage to attempt upon the Enemy. To which he immediately replied, That he had thought to have said the same thing to me. So that it pleased the Lord to set this apprehension upon both of our hearts, at the same instant. We called for Colonel Monk and showed him the thing : and coming to our quarters at night, and demonstrating our apprehensions to some of the Colonels, they also cheerfully concurred.

We resolved therefore to put our business into this posture : That six regiments of horse, and three regiments and a half of foot should march in the van ; and that the Major-General, the Lieutenant-General of the horse, and the Commissary-General and Colonel Monk to command the brigade of foot, should lead on the business ; and that Colonel Pride's brigade, and the remaining two regiments of horse should bring up the cannon and rear. The time of falling-on to be by break of day :—but through some delays it proved not to be so ; not till six o'clock in the morning.

The Enemy's word was, *The Covenant* ; which it had been for divers days. Ours, *The Lord of Hosts*. The Major-General, Lieutenant-General Fleetwood, and Commissary-General Whalley, and Colonel Twistleton, gave the onset ; the Enemy being in a very good posture to receive them, having the advantage of their cannon and foot against our horse. Before our foot could come up, the Enemy made a gallant resistance, and there was a very hot dispute at sword's point between our horse and theirs. Our first foot, after they had discharged their duty (being overpowered with the Enemy) received some repulse, which they soon recovered. For my own regiment, under the command of Lieutenant-Colonel Goffe and my Major, White, did come seasonably in; and, at the push of pike, did repel the stoutest regiment the Enemy had there, merely with the courage the Lord was pleased to give. Which proved a great amazement to the residue of their foot; this being the first action between the foot. The horse in the meantime did, with a great deal of courage and spirit, beat back all oppositions; charging through the bodies of the Enemy's horse, and of their foot; who were, after the first repulse given, made by the Lord of Hosts as stubble to their swords. . . .

The best of the Enemy's horse being broken through and through in less than an hour's dispute, it became a total rout; our men having the chase and execution of them near eight miles. We believe that upon the place and near it were about Three-thousand slain. . . .

Thus you have the prospect of one of the most signal mercies God hath done for England and His people, this war. . . .

Beseeching you to pardon this length, I humbly take leave; and rest,

Sir,

Your most obedient servant,

OLIVER CROMWELL.

CROMWELL AFTER THE BATTLE OF WORCESTER

WEDNESDAY, SEPTEMBER 3RD, 1651

After Dunbar, the Scots still had an army in the field. Hoping that a rising would take place in their favour in England, they invaded England, Charles II being in their army. Cromwell pursued them as far as Worcester. No rising in England took place.

Source : Carlyle's *Letters and Speeches of Cromwell.* Letter clxxxiii.

Further Reading : Buchan, *Oliver Cromwell*, pp. 380 sqq.

LETTER CLXXXIII

For the Honourable William Lenthall, Esquire, Speaker of The Parliament of England : These.

Sir,   Worcester, 4th September, 1651.

I am not able yet to give you an exact account of the great things the Lord hath wrought for this Commonwealth and for His People : and yet I am unwilling to be silent ; but, according to my duty, shall represent it to you as it comes to hand.

This Battle was fought with various successes for some hours, but still hopeful on your part ; and in the end became an absolute victory,—and so full an one as proved a total defeat and ruin of the Enemy's Army ; and a possession of the Town, our men entering at the Enemy's heels, and fighting with them in the streets with very great courage. We took all their baggage and artillery. What the slain are, I can give you no account, because we have not taken an exact view ; but they are very many :—and must needs be so ; because the dispute was long and very near at hand ; and often at push of pike, and from one defence to another. There are about Six or Seven thousand prisoners taken here ; and many Officers and Noblemen of very great quality : Duke Hamilton, the Earl of Rothes, and divers other Noblemen,—I hear the Earl of Lauderdale ; many Officers of great quality ; and some that will be fit subjects for your justice.

We have sent very considerable parties after the flying Enemy ; I hear they have taken considerable numbers of prisoners, and are very close in pursuit. Indeed, I hear the Country riseth upon them everywhere ;   and I believe the forces that lay, through Providence, at Bewdley, and in Shropshire and Staffordshire, and those with Colonel Lilburn, were in a condition, as if this had been foreseen, to intercept what should return.

A more particular account than this will be prepared for you as we are able. I hear that they had not many more than a Thousand horse in their body that fled : and I believe you have near Four-Thousand forces following, and interposing between them and home ;—what fish they will catch, Time will declare.[1] Their Army was about Sixteen-thousand strong ; and fought ours on the Worcester side of Severn almost with their whole, whilst we had engaged about half our Army on the other side but with parties of theirs. Indeed, it was a stiff business ; yet I do not think we have lost Two-hundred men. Your new-raised forces did perform singular good service ; for which they deserve a very high estimation and acknowledgement ; as also for their willingness thereunto,—forasmuch as the same hath added so much to the reputation of your affairs. They are all despatched home again ; which I hope will be much for the ease and satisfaction of the Country ; which is a great fruit of these successes.

The dimensions of this mercy are above my thoughts. It is, for aught I know, a crowning mercy. . . .

Sir,

Your most humble and obedient servant,

OLIVER CROMWELL.

---

[1] This phrase was omitted when the letter was published in the Newspaper. In the margin of the original an official hand has written ' omit this '. Carlyle's note.

KING CHARLES II

Charles II was the eldest son of Charles I and Henrietta Maria. He was born in 1630. During the Civil War he withdrew to the Continent, first to France and then to Holland. He returned to Scotland in 1650 and was crowned King at Scone, 1651. After the defeat at Worcester by Cromwell, 1651, he escaped to the Spanish Netherlands. He was restored to the English throne, 1660, and died in 1685.

Source : *A History of His Own Time*, by Gilbert Burnet (1643–1715), Bishop of Salisbury, vol. I Bk. ii, pp. 158 sqq. 1823 ed. O.U.P.

Further Reading. Bryant, *Charles II* : Airey, *Charles II* : especially the character of Charles II by George Savile, Marquis of Halifax.

The King was then thirty years of age and, as might have been supposed, past the levities of youth and the extravagance of pleasure. He had a very good understanding. He knew well the state of affairs both at home and abroad. He had a softness of temper that charmed all who came near him, till they found out how little they could depend on good looks, kind words and fair promises, in which he was liberal to excess, because he intended nothing by them but to get rid of importunities and to silence all farther pressing upon him. He seemed to have no sense of religion : both at prayers and sacrament he, as it were, took care to satisfy people that he was in no sort concerned in that about which he was employed. So that he was very far from being a hypocrite, unless his assisting at those performances was a sort of hypocrisy (as no doubt it was). But he was sure not to increase that by any the least appearance of religion. He said once to myself he was no atheist, but he could not think God would make a man miserable only for taking a little pleasure out of the way. He disguised his Popery to the last. . . .

He was affable and easy, and loved to be made so by all about him. The great art of keeping him long was the being easy, and the making everything easy to him. He had made such observations on the French government that he thought a King who might be checked or have his ministers called to an account by a Parliament, was but a King in name. He had a great compass of knowledge, though he was never capable of much application or study. He understood the mechanics and physics, and was a good chemist, and much set on several preparations of mercury, chiefly the fixing it. He understood navigation well, but above all he knew the architecture of ships so perfectly that in that respect he was exact rather more than became a Prince. His apprehension was quick and his memory good. He was an everlasting talker. He told his stories with a good grace, but they came in his way too often. . . . He thought nobody did serve him out of love, and so he was quits with all the world and loved others as little as he thought they loved him. He hated business and could not be easily brought to mind any. But when it was necessary and he was set to it, he would stay as long as his ministers had work for him. The ruin of his reign and of all his affairs was occasioned chiefly by his delivering himself up at his first coming over to a mad range of pleasure.

THE RESTORATION : THE ARRIVAL OF CHARLES II IN ENGLAND

FRIDAY, MAY 25TH, 1660

After the execution of Charles I the government of England passed through a series of experiments, all of which were a failure. It became clear that the Parliamentary system would not work without the Monarchy. In order, therefore, to restore proper Parliamentary government, it was decided to restore the Monarchy in the person of Charles II, the eldest son of Charles I. Charles was at the time in exile in Holland. His recall was largely engineered by Monk.

Source : *England's Joy*, an anonymous account published in 1660 From the Harleian Miscellany, vol. vii, 1810 edition, pp. 111 sqq.

Further Reading : Bryant, *Charles II* : Ogg, *Reign of Charles II*.

Being come aboard one of the fairest of those ships, which attended at Sluys, for wafting him over from the Hague in Holland; and, therein having taken leave of his sister, the princess royal, he set sail for England on Wednesday evening, May 23, 1660. And having, during his abode at sea, given new names to that whole navy (consisting of twenty-six goodly vessels) he arrived at Dover on the Friday following (viz. May the 25th) about two of the clock in the afternoon. Ready on the shore to receive him, stood the Lord General Monk, as also the Earl of Winchelsea, constable of Dover castle, with divers persons of quality on the one hand, and the mayor of Dover, accompanied by his brethren of that corporation on the other, with a rich canopy.

As soon as he had set foot on the shore, the lord general, presenting himself before him on his knee, and kissing his royal hand, was embraced by his majesty, and received divers gracious expressions of the great sense he had of his loyalty, and in being so instrumental in this his restoration. . . .

From thence taking coach immediately, with his royal brothers, the Dukes of York and Gloucester, he passed to Barham-down . . . where multitudes of the country people stood, making loud shouts, he rode to the head of each troop (they being placed on his left hand, three deep) who, bowing to him, kissed the hilts of their swords, and then flourished them above their heads, with no less acclamations; the trumpets, in the mean time, also echoing the like to them.

In the suburb at Canterbury stood the mayor and aldermen of that ancient city, who received him with loud musick, and presented him with a cup of gold, of two-hundred and fifty pounds value. Whence after a speech made to him by the recorder, he passed to the Lord Camden's house, the mayor carrying the sword before him. . . .

From Canterbury he came, on Monday, to Rochester, where the people had hung up, over the midst of the streets, as he rode, many beautiful garlands, curiously made up with costly scarfs and ribbands, decked with spoons and bodkins of silver, and small plate of several sorts ; and some with gold chains, in like sort as at Canterbury ; each striving to outdoe others in all expressions of joy.

On Tuesday, May the 29th (which happily fell out to be the anniversary of his majesty's birth-day) he set forth of Rochester in his coach ; but afterwards took horse on the farther side of Black-heath, on which spacious plain he found divers great and eminent troops of horse, a most splendid and glorious equipage ; and a kind of rural triumph, expressed by the country swains, in a Morrice-dance, with the old musick of taber and pipe, which was performed with all agility and chearfulness imaginable.

. . .

In this order proceeding towards London, there were placed in Deptford, on his right hand (as he passed through the town) above an hundred proper maids, clad all alike, in white garments, with scarfs about them ; who, having prepared many flaskets covered with fine linnen, and adorned with rich scarfs and ribbands, which flaskets were full of flowers and sweet herbs, strowed the way before him as he rode.

From thence passing on, he came to St. George's Fields in Southwark, where the lord mayor and aldermen of London, in their scarlet, with the recorder, and other city council, waited for him in a large tent, hung with tapestry ; in which they had placed a chair of state, with a rich canopy over it. When he came thither, the lord mayor presented him with the city sword, and the recorder made a speech to him ; which being done, he alighted, and went into the tent, where a noble banquet was prepared for him. . . .

In . . . magnificent fashion his majesty entered the borough of Southwark, about half an hour past three of the clock in the afternoon ; and, within an hour after, the city of London at the Bridge ; where he found the windows and streets exceedingly thronged with people to behold him ; and the walls adorned with hangings and carpets of tapestry and other costly stuff ; and in many places sets of loud musick ; all the conduits, as he passed, running claret wine ; and the several companies in their liveries, with the ensigns belonging to them ; as also the trained bands of the city standing along the streets as he passed, welcoming him with joyful acclamations.

And within the rails where Charing-cross formerly was, a stand of six-hundred pikes, consisting of knights and gentlemen, as had been officers of the armies of his majesty of blessed memory; the truly noble and valiant Sir John Stowell, Knight of the honourable Order of the Bath, a person famous for his eminent actions and sufferings, being in the head of them.

From which place, the citizens, in velvet coats and gold chains, being drawn up on each hand, and divers companies of foot soldiers ; his majesty passed betwixt them, and entered White-hall at seven of the clock, the people making loud shouts, and the horse and foot several vollies of shot, at this his happy arrival. Where the house of lords and commons of parliament received him, and kissed his royal hand. At the same time likewise the Reverend Bishops of Ely, Salisbury, Rochester, and Chichester, in their episcopal habits, with divers of the long oppressed orthodox clergy, met in that royal chapel of king Henry the Seventh, at Westminster ; there also sung *Te Deum*, *&c.* in praise and thanks to Almighty God, for this his unspeakable mercy, in the deliverance of his majesty from many dangers, and so happily restoring him to rule these kingdoms, according to his just and undoubted right.

THE GREAT PLAGUE, 1665

Source : A letter from a Cambridge undergraduate, who visited London in July, 1665, and sent a description to his Tutor. Printed by Mr. J. R. Wardale, Fellow of Clare College, Cambridge, in his *Clare College—Letters and Documents*, Cambridge, 1903. Quoted by W. G. Bell in his *The Great Plague in London*, p. 80 : Bodley Head, 1951.

Further Reading : Bell, *The Great Plague in London*.

Honoured Sir, London, July 18th, 1665.

Blessed be the Lord I got to London safe on wensday by eleven of the clock : and there is but very little notice tooke of the sicknesses here in London though the bills are very great there dyd threescore and 18 in st. giles in the feilds since the bill ; and 5 in one hour, in our parish since, it spreads very much ; I went by many houses in London that were shut up ; all over the city almost ; nobody that is in London feares to go anywhere but in st. giles's : they have a bellman there with a cart ; there dye so many that the bell would hardly ever leave ringing and so they ring not at all : the citizens begin to shut up apace ; nothing hinders them from it for fear of the houses breaking open : my fathers has been shut up about a week ; but theyr is hardly an house ope in the strand : nor the exchange : the sicknesse is at Tottenham high crosse but Mr. Moyse would not have you let his son know. it is much at hogsden[1] ; so I saw them as I went in the road, ly in a small thackt house, and I beleeve all most starved so great a dread it strikes into the people: I taryd in london till thursday in the afternoon, because the tide would not serve. but then went to Wandsor. . . . It is very credibly reported that de Ryter is beat and taken or sunke. one wensday night such news came from hampton Court. the sickness is at Richmond and we beleeve the King will reside not there long.

thus with my humble service to you and Mr. Blith Jun

I rest your Obedient pupill

SAM: HERNE.

For his Honoured Tutour
   Mr Samuel Blithe fellow of
   Clarehall In Cambridge.

[1] Hoddesdon.

N

THE GREAT FIRE OF LONDON. 1666

(1) *Source* : *A short but Truthful Account of the Terrifying Fire which on the 12th, 13th, 14th, 15th and 16th of September destroyed the City of London.* Written from London on September 20th, 1666, by an anonymous German.   In Lincoln's Inn Library, quoted by W. G. Bell in his *The Great Fire of London,* p. 329. Bodley Head, ed. 1951.

Further Reading : Bell, *The Great Fire of London.*   Evelyn's *Diary, Sept. 2nd,* 1666.

With the pen alone it is hardly possible to set down an adequate account of the pitiful state of things brought about by the most destructive fire England has ever seen.   The fire lasted five days and nights, and raged with such fury that all human means of combating it were unavailing.   It began on the night of September 12th (*N.S.*), about one o'clock, in a baker's shop in Pudding Lane, a narrow passage close by New Fish Street, which leads to the Bridge.   This was a closely built district, and most of the houses were of wood, some being coated with pitch and others with plaster.   As there was a very strong north-east wind blowing, the flames got the upper hand before daybreak, to such an extent that all attempts made to control them were futile. It might, perhaps, have been possible to confine the fire to smaller dimensions if the houses at first affected could have been isolated ; but the flames obtained complete mastery and raged the whole day, spreading to Grace-church Street and thence to Cannon Street, and along the Thames side as far as the Three Cranes in Vintry.

The King and the Duke of York and many other notables were on the spot on the first day of the Fire and the following days, and helped to maintain order ; but they could do nothing to stay its progress.   As the inhabitants of the district realized that the flames could not be checked, they seized as much of their property as they could carry, and made off to wherever they could find safety.

On Monday the fire raged even more fiercely, and defied all efforts of the people to limit its ravages.   By seven o'clock in the evening, the whole neighbourhood by the River Thames as far as Baynard's Castle was burnt out. On the north the fire spread as far as Gracechurch Street, Lombard Street, Cornhill. and Bucklersbury, and so caught the houses built about the Exchange.

Before Tuesday's dawn the Exchange and other buildings in the neighbourhood were burnt. By that night the flames had spread to Fleet Street, and had burnt all the houses as far as St. Dunstan's Church, together with all the buildings lying between the Exchange and the Temple, Crown Court, etc., the whole sweep of which was consumed by the fire, which then deviated from its straight course and turned up Fetter Lane about half-way towards Holborn.

Thus it lasted until Wednesday night. Then a fresh fire broke out in the Temple, and was got under control by about two o'clock Thursday morning, when it had destroyed the buildings about the cloisters and ignited a portion of the church and the hall.

By Thursday the fire had, for the most part, been overcome— at Temple Church, near Holborn Bridge, at Pie Corner, Aldersgate, Cripplegate, the lower end of Coleman Street, the end of Basinghall Street, the gates at Bishopsgate Street and Fall Street, the Standard in Cornhill, the church in Fenchurch Street, Clothworkers' Hall in Mincing Lane, the middle of Mark Lane, and the Tower Dock. And here the destruction came to an end, after the fire had burnt out and destroyed the largest and best part of the city, where most of the merchants lived. In an hours walk from the Temple to the Tower there is, within the walls, hardly anything left standing ; and without the walls, in Fleet Street and from Holborn to Fleet Bridge, all is in ruins.

In all there were burnt about 12,000 houses and 80 churches, including St. Paul's.

As one may easily imagine, most of the people had to camp out under the blue sky ; and they presented such an abject appearance, deprived of all means of subsistence, that the cry rose that they should make for the Royal Naval stores, and there provide themselves with what they needed.

The Tower remained standing, after all the houses around it were burnt out, but the flames came up to the very gates.

The fire has wrought so much destruction that a proposal is made that an entirely new city be built on a new plan.

May God Almighty protect all cities and places from such damage and misfortune.

(2) *Source* : Pepys's *Diary*. 1666.

September 2nd (Lord's day). Some of our maids sitting up late last night to get things ready against our feast to-day, Jane called us up about three in the morning, to tell us of a great fire they saw in the City. So I rose, and slipped on my night-gown, and went to her window ; and thought it to be on the back-side of Marke-lane at the farthest, but being unused to such fires as followed, I thought it far enough off ; and so went to bed again, and to sleep. About seven rose again to dress myself, and there looked out at the window, and saw the fire not so much as it was, and further off. So to my closet to set things to rights, after yesterday's cleaning. By and by Jane comes and tells me that she hears that above 300 houses have been burned down to-night by the fire we saw, and that it is now burning all down Fish-street, by London Bridge. So I made myself ready presently, and walked to the Tower, and there got up on one of the high places, Sir J. Robinson's little son going up with me ; and there I did see the houses at that end of the bridge all on fire, and an infinite great fire on this and the other side the end of the bridge ; which, among other people, did trouble me for poor little Michell and our Sarah on the bridge. So down with my heart full of trouble to the Lieutenant of the Tower, who tells me that it begun this morning in the King's baker's house in Pudding Lane, and that it hath burned down St. Magnes Church and most part of Fish-street already. So I down to the water-side, and there got a boat, and through bridge, and there saw a lamentable fire. Poor Michell's house, as far as the Old Swan, already burned that way, and the fire running further, that in a very little time it got as far as the Steele-yard, while I was there. Everybody endeavouring to remove their goods, and flinging into the river, or bringing them into lighters that lay off ; poor people staying in their houses as long as till the very fire touched them, and then running into boats, or clambering from one pair of stairs to another. And among other things, the poor pigeons, I perceive, were loth to leave their houses, but hovered about the windows and balconys, till they burned their wings, and fell down. . . .

. . . Having seen as much as I could now, I away to White Hall by appointment, and there walked to St. James's Park, and there met my wife and Creed and Wood and his wife, and walked to my boat; and there upon the water again, and to the fire up and down, it still encreasing, and the wind great. So near the fire as we could for smoke; and all over the Thames, with one's faces in the wind, you were almost burned with a shower of fire-drops. . . . When we could endure no more upon the water, we to a little ale-house on the Bankside, over against the Three Cranes, and there staid until it was almost dark, and saw the fire grow, and as it grew darker, appeared more and more, and in corners and upon steeples, and between churches and houses, as far as we could see up the hill of the City, in a most horrid malicious bloody flame, not like the fine flame of an ordinary fire. Barbary and her husband away before us. We staid still, it being darkish, we saw the fire as only one entire arch of fire from this to the other side the bridge, and in a bow up the hill for an arch of above a mile long : it made me weep to see it. The churches, houses, and all on fire, and flaming at once ; and a horrid noise the flames made, and the cracking of houses at their ruine. So home with a sad heart. . . .

WILLIAM HARVEY

William Harvey (1578–1657) was an anatomist and a physiologist. His theory of the circulation of the blood was delivered to the College of Physicians in 1616, but his treatise on the subject was not published until 1628.

Source : Aubrey's *Brief Lives*; edited from the original MSS. by O. L. Dick, Theodore Brun, London, 1949, from which the above explanatory note is also taken, Aubrey (1626–1697) left the material for these lives in note form.

Further Reading : for the non-medical reader, probably the best approach to Harvey is by way of the Dictionary of National Biography.

. . . I first saw him at Oxford, 1642, after Edgehill fight, but was then too young to be acquainted with so great a Doctor. I remember he came severall times to Trinity College to George Bathurst, B.D., who had a Hen to hatch Egges in his chamber, which they dayly opened to discern the progress and way of Generation. I had not the honour to be acquainted with him till 1651, being my she cousen Montague's physitian and friend. I was at that time bound for Italy (but to my great grief disswaded by my mother's importunity). He was very communicative, and willing to instruct any that were modest and respectfull to him. And in order to my Journey, gave me, i.e. dictated to me, what to see, what company to keepe, what Bookes to read, how to manage my Studies : in short, he bid me goe to the Fountain head and read Aristotle, Cicero, Avicenna, . . .

He wrote a very bad hand, which (with use) I could pretty well read. He understood Greek and Latin pretty well, but was no Critique, and he wrote very bad Latin. The *Circuitis Sanguinis* was, as I take it, donne into Latin by Sir George Ent. . . .

After Oxford was surrendered, which was 24 July 1646, he came to London, and lived with his brother Eliab a rich Merchant in London, who bought, about 1654, Cockaine-house . . . where the Doctor was wont to contemplate on the leads of the house, and had his severall stations, in regard of the sun, or wind.

He did delight to be in the darke, and told me he could then best contemplate. He had a house heretofore at Combe, in Surrey a good aire and prospect, where he had Caves made in the Earth, in which in Summer time he delighted to meditate.

Ah! my old Friend Dr. Harvey—I knew him right well. He made me sitt by him 2 or 3 hours together in his meditating apartment discoursing. Why, had he been stiffe, starcht, and retired, as other formall Doctors are, he had known no more than they. From the meanest person, in some way, or other, the learnedst man may learn something. Pride has been one of the greatest stoppers of the Advancement of Learning.

He was far from Bigotry.

He was wont to say that man was but a great, mischievous Baboon. . . He would say that we Europeans knew not how to order or governe our Woemen, and that the Turks were the only people who used them wisely. . . . He was very Cholerique ; and in young days wore a dagger (as the fashion then was) but this Dr. would be to apt to draw-out his dagger upon every slight occasion.

I have heard him say, that after his Booke of the *Circulation of the Blood* came out, that he fell mightily in his Practize, and that 'twas beleeved by the vulgar that he was crack-brained ; and all the Physitians were against his Opinion, and envyed him ; many wrote against him. With much ado at last, in about 20 or 30 yeares time, it was received in all the Universities in the world ; and Mr. Hobbes says in his book *De Corpore, he is the only man, perhaps, that ever lived to see his owne Doctrine established in his life-time.* . . .

He was much and often troubled with the Gowte, and his way of a Cure was thus ; he would then sitt with his Legges bare, if it were a Frost, on the leads of Cockaine-house, putt them into a payle of water, till he was almost dead with cold, and betake himself to his Stove, and so 'twas gone. . . .

The manner of his dyeing was really, and *bone fide*, thus, viz. the morning of his death about ten a clock, he went to speake, and found he had the dead palsey in his Tongue ; then he sawe what was to become of him, he knew there was then no hopes of his recovery, so presently sends for his brother and young nephewes to come-up to him, to whom he gives one his Watch ('twas a minute watch with which he made his experiments) to another another thing, etc., as remembrances of him; made a signe to Sambroke, his Apothecary, to lett him blood in the Tongue, which did little or no good; and so ended his dayes. The Palsey did give him an easy Passe-port.

He lies buried in a Vault at Hempstead in Essex, which his brother Eliab Harvey built; he is lapt in lead, and on his breast in great letters

DR. WILLIAM HARVEY.

I was at his Funerall, and helpt to carry him into the Vault.

THE FALL OF THE EARL OF CLARENDON

Edward Hyde, first Earl of Clarendon (1609–1674), was one of the most important statesmen in England in the seventeenth century. From the moment when the Civil War broke out he became one of Charles I's chief advisers. He accompanied Charles II in his exile and became his chief minister on the Restoration. By nature a conservative, he may be looked on as the founder of the Tory party. He was dismissed in 1667, impeached, and fled the country to France. He is now best known for his *History of the Great Rebellion*. His name is perpetuated at Oxford in the Clarendon Press.

Source: Evelyn's *Diary*.

Further Reading: Wormald, *Clarendon*: Feiling, *History of the Tory Party*: Firth, *Essays Historical and Literary*.

August 27th, 1667: Visited the Lord Chancellor, to whom his Majesty had sent for the seals a few days before. I found him in his bedchamber very sad. The Parliament had accused him and he had enemies at Court, especially the buffoons and ladies of pleasure, because he thwarted some of them and stood in their way. I could name some of the chief. The truth is, he made few friends during his grandeur among the royal sufferers, but

advanced the old rebels. He was, however, though no consider-
bale lawyer, one who kept up the form and substance of things
in the nation with more solemnity than some would have had.
He was my particular kind friend on all occasions. The Cabal,
however, prevailed and that party in Parliament. Great divisions
at Court concerning him, and divers great persons interceding
for him.

August 28th : I dined with my late Lord Chancellor. . . .
His Lordship pretty well in heart, though now many of his
friends and sycophants abandon him.

October 11th : I went to see Lord Clarendon, late Lord
Chancellor and greatest officer in England, in continual apprehension what the Parliament would determine concerning him.

October 26th : My late Lord Chancellor was accused by Mr.
Seymour in the House of Commons.

December 9th. To visit the late Lord Chancellor. I found
him in his garden at his new-built palace, sitting in his gout wheel-
chair, and seeing the gates setting up towards the north and the
fields. He looked and spake very disconsolately. After some
while deploring his condition to me, I took my leave. Next
morning I heard he was gone, though I am persuaded that had
he gone sooner, though but to Conerbury, and there lain quiet,
it would have satisfied the Parliament. That which exasperated
them was his presuming to stay and contest the accusation as
long as it was possible, and they were on the point of sending him
to the Tower.

THE POPISH PLOT.　1678–1679

The Popish Plot was an imaginary conspiracy alleged to have been hatched by the Catholics in the reign of Charles II. The invention was the work principally of Titus Oates, an English clergyman of bad character, who pretended that he had discovered a Jesuit scheme to kill the King and appoint a Catholic ministry. In building up his story Oates was assisted by a number of informers, including Dr. Israel Tonge, a fanatical clergyman. In order to bring their information to the notice of the King, they got in touch with Christopher Kirkby, a chemist, who was employed at Court.

(1) *Source* : *Complete and True Narrative of the Manner of the Discovery of the Popish Plot to His Majesty by Mr. Christopher Kirkby*, London, 1679. B.M. Tracts of the Popish Plot 193.d.11. no. 13.

Further Reading : Ogg, *England in the Reign of Charles II*. vol. ii, ch. xvi. Dickson Carr, *The Murder of Sir Edmund Godfrey*.

Monday, the 12th of August, 1678, about twelve of the clock, Dr. Tonge acquainted Mr. Christopher Kirkby with the conspiracy of the Papists against the King's sacred person and the Protestant religion, shewing him 43 articles in writing, upon which Mr. Kirkby declared that matters of that concern ought not to be concealed by him, but he would acquaint His Majesty therewith, though he foresaw many dangers and difficulties he should meet with in the discovery, whereupon the Doctor declared his great satisfaction that Mr. Kirkby would make this business known to the King, earnestly requesting him not to acquaint any other person with it, which Mr. Kirkby promised. And about two of the clock in the afternoon went to Whitehall, but could not all that afternoon meet with an opportunity of seeing the King, except in company of His Royal Highness : so he returned to the Dr. and advising what to do and how to proceed, Mr. Kirkby wrote a few lines to present to His Majesty the next morning as he should walk in the Park, signifying that if His Majesty would be pleased to give him a quarter of an hour's audience, he should make known something that, as it was of the greatest importance, so it was only proper for his royal ear, and not to be delayed without imminent danger.

And accordingly upon the 13th of August he waited His Majesty's coming into the Park, and in the outer gallery presented it to His Majesty, which he read as he went down the stairs, and afterward called Mr. Kirkby to him and asked him what he had to say : who answered that His Majesty's enemies had a design against his life, and therefore humbly prayed His Majesty to keep himself within his company, for he did not know but that he might be in danger in that very walk. And His Majesty, asking how that could be, was answered that it might be by being shot at, but that a private place was necessary for a more particular account. Thereupon His Majesty commanded him to wait his return out of the Park, and in the meantime to go to Mr. Chiffins, who would conduct him into his closet. But Mr. Chiffins, not knowing his business, refused to conduct him thither, and therefore he was necessitated to wait His Majesty's return in the gallery ; and His Majesty returning into his bed-chamber and not finding Mr. Kirkby there, was coming out ; when he espied Mr. Kirkby, he called him in, commanding him to tell him what he knew ; whereupon Mr. Kirkby told His Majesty that there were two men, by name Pickering and Grove, that were set to watch an opportunity to shoot His Majesty, and that Sir George Wakeman was employed to poison him ; and being asked how he knew this, he replied he had seen it in writing in the hands of his friends, who the day before had acquainted him therewith, and that he had then waited an opportunity to declare it to His Majesty, that his friend was near at hand and ready with the papers to be brought before him when His Majesty should command, which he pleased should be between eight and nine of the clock in the evening, at which time Mr. Kirkby and Dr. Tonge attended on His Majesty and were commanded into the Red Room, where the 43 articles copied out by the Dr. (who kept the original for his own security) were delivered to His Majesty.

. . .

(2) *Source* : Evelyn's *Diary*, October 1st, 1678.

The Parliament and the whole nation were alarmed about a conspiracy of some eminent Papists for the destruction of the King and introduction of Popery, discovered by one Oates and

Dr. Tongue, *which last I knew, being the translator of the ' Jesuits'
Morals '*. I went to see and converse with him at Whitehall, with
Mr. Oates, one that was lately an apostate to the church of Rome,
and now returned again with this discovery. He seemed to be a
bold man, and in my thoughts furiously indiscreet ; but everybody believed what he said ; and it quite changed the genius and
motions of Parliament, growing now corrupt and interested with
long sitting and court practices ; but withal this popery would
not go down. This discovery turned them all as one man against
it, and nothing was done but to find out the depth of this. Oates
was encouraged and everything he affirmed taken for gospel ;—
the truth is, the Roman Catholics were exceeding bold and busy
everywhere, since the Duke forbore to go any longer to chapel.

(3) *Source* : *An Historical Account of My Own Life*, by Edmund
Calamy D.D. (1671–1731), vol. i, p. 81.

For my own part, I must own, that the first public matter I
can remember I took any distinct notice of, was the discovery
of the Popish Plot. . . . The discovery of this plot put the whole
kingdom into a new fermentation, and filled people universally
with unspeakable terror.

To see the posts and chains put up in all parts of the city,
and a considerable number of the Trained Bands drawn out, night
after night, well armed, watching with as much care as if a considerable insurrection was expected before morning ; and to be
entertained from day to day with the talk of massacres designed,
and a number of bloody assassins ready to serve such purposes,
and recruited from abroad to support and assist them (which
things were the general subjects of all conversation) was very
surprising. The murder of Sir Edmund Bury Godfrey . . . with
the black Sunday that followed soon after it, when it grew so
dark on a sudden, about eleven in the morning, that ministers
could not read their notes in their pulpits without the help of
candles ; together with the frequent execution of traitors that
ensued, and the many dismal stories handed about continually,
made the hearts, not only of the younger, but elder persons to
quake for fear. Not so much as a house was at that time to go
met with, but what was provided with arms ; nor did any be

to rest at night without apprehensions of somewhat that was very tragical might happen before morning. And this was then the case, not for a few weeks or months only, but for a great while together.

Though I was at that time but young, yet can I not forget how much I was affected with seeing several that were condemned for this plot, such as Pickering, Ireland and Grove, etc. go to be executed at Tyburn ; and at the pageantry of the mock processions on the 17th of November [Queen Elizabeth's accession day, in 1679 and 1680]. . . . In one of them . . . there were carried in pageantry upon men's shoulders through the chief streets of the city, the effigies of the Pope, with the representative of the Devil behind him, whispering in his ear and wonderfully soothing and caressing him. (though he afterwards deserted him and left him to shift for himself, before he was committed to the flames), together with the likeness of the dead body of Sir Edmund Bury Godfrey, carried before him by one that rode on horseback, designed to remind people of his execrable murder. And a great number of dignitaries, in their copes, with crosses, monks, friars, and Jesuits, and Popish Bishops in their mitres, and with all their trinkets and appurtenances. Such things as these very discernibly heightened and inflamed the general aversion of the nation from Popery.

(4) Titus Oates had a good run for his, or rather for the nation's money, but vengeance overtook him at last. In May, 1685, he was tried and convicted on a charge of perjury. He was sentenced to stand in the pillory annually and to be flogged and imprisoned for life. The verdict was reversed in 1689 and Oates was released.

Source: An Historical Account of My Own Life, by Edmund Calamy, vol. i, p. 120 ; spelling modernized.

1685. I this year saw Dr. Oates whipped at the cart's tail the second time, while his back, miserably swelled with his first whipping, looked as if it had been flayed. . . . Dr. Oates was a man of invincible courage and resolution, and endured what would have killed a great many others. He occasioned a strange turn in the nation, after a general lethargy that had been of some years continuance. By awakening us out of sleep, he was an instrument in the hand of God for our preservation. Yet, after all, he was but a sorry, foul-mouthed wretch, as I can testify, from what I once heard from him in company.

(5) *Source* : *The Diary of Abraham de la Pryme* (1671–1704), Yorkshire antiquary edited by C. Jackson for the Council of the Surtees Society, Durham. Spelling modernized.

1686. This 25th [*month not given*] Mr. Reading being new come from London, was at my father's. I heard him say that he saw Oates, that discovered the Popish Plot, whipped according to his condemnation, most miserably ; and as he was hailed up the streets the multitude would much pity him and would cry to the hangman or he whose office it was to whip him, ' Enough! Enough! Strike easily! Enough! ' etc. To whom Mr. Oates replied, turning his head cheerfully behind him,' Not enough, good people, for the truth, not enough! '

THE NIGHT BEFORE CHARLES II'S LAST ILLNESS

SUNDAY, FEBRUARY 1ST (O.S.)

1685

Thomas Bruce, later 2nd Earl of Ailesbury (1655?–1741) was in 1685 in attendance on Charles II on the night before the King was taken fatally ill.

Source : *Memoirs of Thomas, Earl of Ailesbury*, printed for the Roxburghe Club, 1896, p. 87.

Further Reading : this passage should be read in conjunction with the next passage, Barillon's letter to Louis XIV. A detailed account is given by Bryant, in his *King Charles II*, pp. 361 sqq.

The King always lying in his own bedchamber, we had a bed placed each night to be near him, and when the page of the back stairs lighted us from the room where we undressed, on his retiring we shut up the door on the inside with a brass knob, and so went to bed. Several circumstances made the lodging very uneasy—the great grate being filled with Scotch coal that burnt all night, a dozen dogs that came to our bed, and several pendulums that struck at the half quarter, and all not going alike, it was a continual chiming. The King constantly being used to it, it was habitual. I sleeping but indifferently, perceived that the King turned himself sometimes, not usual for him ; he always called in the morning of himself; I heard his voice but discovered not any imperfection. We had liberty to go to his bedside in the morning before anybody came in, and might entertain him with discourse at pleasure, and ask of him anything. . . .

Passing by in the next room to the bedchamber, I found there the physicians and chirurgeons that attended to visit his heel. Mr. Robert Howard, a Groom of the bedchamber, came to me and asked me how the King had slept, and if quietly. I told him that he had turned sometimes. ' Lord,' saith he, ' that is an ill mark, and contrary to his custom.'; and then told me that at rising he could not, or would not, say one word, that he was as pale as ashes, and gone to his private closet.

N.B.—The difference of ten days between the date of this passage and the date given by Barillon in the next passage is accounted for by the difference between the Old and the New Styles (see Introduction).

THE DEATH OF CHARLES II

FEBRUARY 16TH, 1685 (N.S.)

Source : An account given by the French Ambassador, Barillon, in a letter to King Louis XIV, dated February 18th, 1685. Printed in Dalrymple's *Memoirs of Great Britain and Ireland*, Appendix, Part I, 94–99.

The letter I do myself the honour to write to your Majesty to-day is only to give you an exact account of what happened, of most importance, at the death of the King of England. His illness, which began on Monday morning the 12th of February, had diverse changes the following days ; sometimes he was thought out of danger, and then something happened that made it judged his disorder was mortal ; in fine, on Thursday, 15 February about noon, I was informed from a good quarter that there were no hopes, and that the physicians believed he could not hold out the night. I went immediately to Whitehall ; the Duke of York had given orders to the officers who guarded the door of the antechamber to let me pass at any hour ; he was continually in the King his brother's room ; from time to time he came out to give orders upon what was passing in the town. The report was more than once spread that the King was dead. As soon as I arrived, the Duke of York said to me, ' The physicians think the King in extreme danger ; I desire you to assure your master, that he shall always have in me a faithful and grateful servant '. I was five hours in the King's antechamber. The Duke of York made me come into the bed-chamber several times, and spoke to me of what was passing without doors, and of the assurances given him from every quarter that all was very quiet in the town, and that he should be proclaimed King the moment the King his brother was dead. I went out for some time to go to the Duchess of Portsmouth's apartment. I found her overwhelmed with grief ; the physicians having taken all hopes from her. However, instead of speaking to me of her affliction, and the loss she was on the point of sustaining, she went into a small closet and said to me : ' Monsieur the Ambassador, I am going to tell you the greatest secret in the world, and my head would be in danger if it was known. The King of England at the bottom of his heart is a Catholic; but he is surrounded with Protestant bishops, and nobody tells him his condition, nor speaks to him of God; I can not with decency enter the room; besides that the Queen is constantly there; the Duke of York thinks of his own affairs, and has too many of them, to take the care he ought of the King's conscience; go and tell him I have conjured you to warn him to think of what can be done to save the King's soul. He commands the room, and can turn out whom he will; lose no time, for if it is deferred ever so little, it will be too late.'

I returned instantly to find the Duke of York, and begged him to make a pretence of going to the Queen, who had left the King's room, and who having fainted was just blooded. The room communicated with both apartments; I followed him to the Queen's, and told him what the Duchess of Portsmouth had said to me. He recovered himself as from a deep lethargy, and said, ' You are in the right; there is no time to lose. I will hazard all rather than not do my duty on this occasion '. An hour after he returned under the same pretence of going to the Queen, and told me he had spoken to his brother, and found him resolved not to take the sacrament which the Protestant bishops had pressed him to receive; that this had surprised them much, but that one or other of them would remain always in the room, if he did not find a pretence to make everybody leave it; in order that he might have an opportunity of speaking to the King his brother with freedom, and disposing him to make a formal renunciation of heresy, and confess himself to a Catholic priest.

We thought of various expedients. The Duke of York proposed that I should ask leave to speak to the King his brother, to tell him something in secret from your Majesty, and that everybody should go out. I offered to do so, but represented to him, that besides the great rumour it would make, there was no likelihood of my being allowed to remain in private with the King of England and himself, long enough for what we had to do. The Duke of York then bethought himself of sending for the Queen, as if it had been to take her last farewell, and ask

o

pardon of the King, if she had ever in anything disobeyed him, who was on his part to return the same ceremony to her. At last the Duke of York resolved to speak to the King his brother in presence of the company, yet so as no person might hear what he said to him; because this would remove all suspicion, and it would be believed, that he spoke only to him of affairs of state, and of what he wished to be done after his death. Thus, without any further precaution, the Duke of York stooped down to the King his brother's ear, after having ordered that no one should approach. I was in the room, and more than twenty persons at the door, which was open. What the Duke of York said was not heard, but the King of England said from time to time very loud, *Yes, with all my heart.* He sometimes made the Duke of York repeat what he said, because he did not easily hear him. This lasted near a quarter of an hour. The Duke of York again went out as if he had gone to the Queen, and said to me, ' The King has consented that I should bring a priest to him : but I dare not bring any of the Duchess's, they are too well known : send and find one quickly.' I told him I would do it with all my heart, but I believed too much time would be lost ; and that I had just seen all the Queen's priests in a closet near the Chamber. He said, You are right ; at the same time he perceived the Earl of Castlemethor, who with warmth embraced the proposal made him, and undertook to speak to the Queen ; he came back in an instant and said, ' Should I hazard my head, in this, I would do it with pleasure ; but I do not know one of the Queen's priests who understands or speaks English.' On this we resolved to send to the Venetian Resident for an English priest, but as the time pressed, the Earl of Castlemethor went where the Queen's priests were, and found amongst them one Hudleston a Scotchman who saved the King of England after the battle of Worcester, and who by act of parliament had been excepted from all the laws made against the catholics, and against the priests ; they put a wig and gown on him to disguise him : and the Earl of Castlemethor conducted him to the door of an apartment that joined by a small step to the King's chamber. The Duke of York, to whom I had given notice that all was ready, sent

Chiffins to receive and bring in Mr. Hudelston; soon after he said aloud: 'The King wills that everybody should retire, except the Earls of Bath and Feversham:' The first was Lord of the bed-chamber, and the other was in waiting. The physicians went into a closet, the door of which was immediately shut, and Chiffins brought Mr. Hudelston in. The Duke of York in presenting him, said: 'Sire, here is a man who saved your life, and is now come to save your soul.' The king answered, 'He is welcome.' He afterwards confessed himself with great sentiments of devotion and repentance. The Earl of Castlemethor had taken care to have Hudelston instructed by a Portuguese Monk of the barefooted Carmelites in what he had to say to the King on such an occasion; for of himself he was no great doctor; but the Duke of York told him he acquitted himself very well in his function, and that he made the King formally promise to declare himself openly a catholic, if he recovered his health. He then received absolution, the communion, and even extreme unction; all this lasted about three quarters of an hour. In the antechamber every one looked at another; but nobody said anything but by their eyes and in whispers: the presence of Lord Bath and Lord Feversham, who are Protestants, has satisfied the bishops a little; but the Queen's women and the other priests saw so much coming and going, that I do not think the secret can be long kept.

After the King of England received the communion, his disorder became a little better; it is certain he spoke more intelligibly, and had more strength; we hoped God was willing to work a miracle by restoring him; but the physicians judged his illness was not abated, and that he could not outlive the night. He nevertheless appeared much more easy, and spoke with more feeling and understanding than he had done from 10 at night to 8 in the morning. He often spoke quite loud to the Duke of York. . . .

The King of England was perfectly sensible the whole night, and spoke upon all things with great calmness. At 6 o'clock in the morning he asked what hour it was, and said: 'Open the curtains, that I may once more see day.' He suffered great pain, and at 7 o'clock they bled him in hopes it might lessen his pain.

At half an hour after 8 he began to speak with great difficulty : at 10 his senses were quite gone ; and he died at noon without any struggle or convulsion. The new king retired to his apartment, was unanimously acknowledged, and then proclaimed.

I thought it my duty to give your Majesty an exact account of what passed on this occasion ; and I esteem myself happy that God granted me the favour to have some part in it. I am etc.

THE GREAT FROST, 1683—1684

Source : Evelyn's *Diary.* 1906 edition, vol. ii, pp. 425 sqq.

[Sunday] Jan. 1st, 1683-4. The weather continuing intolerably severe, streetes of booths were set upon the Thames ; the air was so very cold and thick, as of many yeares there had not ben the like. The small pox was very mortal. . . .

9th. I went crosse the Thames on the ice, now become so thick as to beare not onely streetes of boothes, in which they roasted meate, and had divers shops of wares, quite acrosse as in a towne, but coaches, carts and horses, passed over. So I went from Westminster Stayres to Lambeth, and din'd with the Archbishop. . . .

16th. The Thames was fill'd with people and tents, selling all sorts of wares as in the Citty.

24th. The frost continuing more and more severe, the Thames before London was still planted with boothes in formal streetes, all sortes of trades and shops furnish'd and full of commodities, even to a printing presse, where the people and ladyes tooke a fancy to have their names printed, and the day and yeare set down when printed on the Thames[1] : this humour tooke

[1] By favour of a gentleman possessed of innumerable literary curiosities, I have one of these cards now before me. 'Within a treble border, Monsr. et Madm. Justel. Printed on the river of Thames being frozen. In the 36th year of King Charles II. February the 5th, 1683.' v.s. is added with a pen, probably by Mr. Justell. Editor of the diary.

so universally, that 'twas estimated the printer gain'd £5 a day, for printing a line onely, at sixpence a name, besides what he got by ballads, &c. Coaches plied from Westminster to the Temple, and from several other staires to and fro, as in the streetes, sleds, sliding with skeetes, a bull-baiting, horse and coach races, puppet plays and interludes, cookes, tipling, and other lewd places, so that it seem'd to be a bacchanalian triumph or carnival on the water, whilst it was a severe judgement on the land, the trees not onely splitting as if lightning-struck, but men and cattle perishing in divers places, and the very seas so lock'd up with ice, that no vessels could stir out or come in. The fowles, fish, and birds, and all our exotiq plants and greenes universally perishing. Many parkes of deer were destroied, and all sorts of fuell so deare that there were great contributions to preserve the poore alive. Nor was this severe weather much less intense in most parts of Europe, even as far as Spaine and the most southern tracts. London, by reason of the excessive coldnesse of the aire hindering the ascent of the smoke, was so filled with the fuliginous steame of the sea-coale, that hardly could one see crosse the streets, and this filling the lungs with its grosse particles, exceedingly obstructed the breast, so as one could hardly breath. Here was no water to be had from the pipes and engines, nor could the brewers and divers other tradesmen worke, and every moment was full of disastrous accidents.

Feb. 4th. I went to Says Court to see how the frost had dealt with my garden, where I found many of the greenes and rare plantes utterly destroied. The oranges and mirtalls very sick, the rosemary and laurells dead to all appearance, but yᵉ cypress likely to indure it.

5th. It began to thaw, but froze againe. My coach crossed from Lambeth to the Horseferry at Millbank, Westminster. The booths were almost all taken downe, but there was first a map or landskip cut in copper representing all the manner of the camp, and the several actions, sports, and pastimes thereon, in memory of so signal a frost. . . .

8th. The weather was set in to an absolute thaw and raine, but yᵉ Thames still frozen.

KING JAMES II

James II was the second son of Charles I and Henrietta Maria, brother of Charles II. He was born in 1633, created Duke of York, succeeded his brother in 1685 as King, and fled the country in 1688, after trying to force Roman Catholicism on an unwilling country which called in William of Orange to help. With French help he landed in Ireland in 1690, but he was defeated and returned to France, where he died in 1701.

Source : *History of His Own Time*, by Gilbert Burnet (1643–1715), Bishop of Salisbury.

Further Reading : Ogg, *England in the Reigns of James II and William III* : Macaulay, *History of England*.

I will digress a little to give an account of the Duke's character, whom I knew for some years so particularly, that I can say much upon my own knowledge. He was very brave in his youth, and so much magnified by Monsieur Turenne that, till his marriage lessened him, he really clouded the King, and passed for the superior genius. He was naturally candid and sincere, and a firm friend, till affairs and his religion wore out all his first principles and inclinations. He had a great desire to understand affairs, and in order to that, he kept a constant journal of all that passed, of which he shewed me a great deal. The Duke of Buckingham once gave me a short but severe character of the brothers. It was the more severe because it was true : The King (he said) could see things if he would, and the Duke would see things if he could. He had no true judgement and was soon determined by those whom he trusted, but he was obstinate against all other advices. He was bred with high notions of Kingly authority, and laid it down for a maxim that all who opposed the King were rebels in their hearts. He was perpetually in one amour or other, without being very nice in his choice ; upon which the King said once, he believed his brother had his mistresses given him by his Priests for penance. . . .

He was naturally eager and revengeful, and was against the taking of any that set up in an opposition to the measures of the Court, and who by that means grew popular in the House of

Commons. He was for rougher methods. He continued for many years dissembling his religion and seemed zealous for the Church of England : but it was chiefly on design to hinder all propositions that tended to unite us among ourselves. He was a frugal Prince and brought his Court into method and magnificence, for he had £100,000 a year allowed him. He was made High Admiral, and he came to understand all the concerns of the sea very particularly . . . . The Duke found all the great seamen had a deep tincture from their education—they both hated Popery and loved liberty : they were men of severe tempers and kept good discipline. But in order to the putting the fleet into more confident hands, the Duke began a method of sending pages of honour and other young persons of quality to be bred to the sea ; and these were put in command as soon as they were capable of it, if not sooner. This discouraged many of the old seamen, when they saw in what a channel advancement was like to go, who upon that left the service and went and commanded merchantmen. . . .

He was a Prince who seemed made for greater things than will be found in the course of his life, more particularly of his reign.

MONMOUTH'S REBELLION 1685

James Scott, Duke of Monmouth and Buccleuch, illegitimate son of Charles II and Lucy Walters was born 1649. After a chequered career (see Dict. of Nat. Biog.) he retired to Zeeland 1684. He raised a rebellion against James II, landed at Lyme Regis, June 11th, 1685, was proclaimed King at Taunton, but was defeated by Earl of Feversham at Sedgemoor. He escaped, but was captured, and was executed July 15th, 1685.

Source : *Adam Wheeler, His Account of* 1685. Camden Miscellany, vol. xii, 1910. Adam Wheeler was ' one of the Drums (i.e. Drummers)

of his Honor's owne Company ' (Colonel John Windham Esquire).
The dates given by Wheeler up to July 1st are incorrect: after July
1st they are accurate.

    Further Reading: Macaulay, *History of England*, chapter 5.

    Being Wednesday[1], June 16th I was summoned by a Comand
from his Honor to appeare in the Market-Place of New Sarm in
the County of Wilts by eight of the Clocke in the Morning in his
Regiment compleatly armed according to my place as a *Drum*.
. . .

    June 20. The next day being Sunday[2] on wch day in the
afternoone leaving the Towne of *Wilkton*, we continewed oure
March to Market Lavington.

    June 21. Early the next morning his Honor marched to the
Devizes and there refreshed his Regimt for the Weary and hard
Afternoones March they sustained the day before.

    In the Afternoone by Beate of Drum the Regimt marched as
farre as Chippenham and June 22, being Tuesday,[3] They marched
from Chippenham to the City of Bath, where they Quartered
that night.

    June 23. The Regimt leaving the City of Bath went as farre
as Bradforde *That Night* being very dark there was an *Alarum*.
By reason of which the Regimt could not unite into a Body till
They came to Trowbridge[4]. . . .

    June 25 The Rt Honrble the Ld Lieutenant *Earle* of *Pembrook*
gave Comand for some of the Regimt, and some of the Militia
Horse to goe wth him to Froome, Where he forced the Rebells to
lay downe theire Armes, and brought away with him the Constable of that Towne to Trowbridge who proclaymed the Duke
of Monmouth King, and severall cruell and New invented
murthering Weapons as *Sithes* and ye like. . . .

    July 1st being Wednesday, his Honors Regimt tooke theire
March to Shepton Mallet; Here not farre from the Towne, a
Grounde was shewn which lay within Prospect, where *Monmouth*
and his Army was[5] drawne up and exercised. . . .

    July 4 wee marched to Kings Sedgemoore, marching Eight
Miles in the Moore so farre as Middlesey ; Where being alarumed;

---

[1] The 16th was a Tuesday. [2] was the 21st. [3] Tuesday was the 23rd. [4] i.e., pre-
sumably, the regiment ran away. [5] i.e. had been.

July 6. The R^t Honor^ble The *Earle* of *Pembrooke* Lord Lieutent in great haste came rideing to the house where his Hono^r Colon^ll Windham was quartered, it being betweene Twelve and One of the Clock in the Mornening, calling out *Colon^l Windham Colon^ll Windham the Enemy is Engadged*, and asking for his Drums ; The Colon^lls answer was that he was ready, and soe forthwith prepared himself.

There being then noe Drum in the house but Adam Wheeler, who opened the doors and answered his Lorsh^p that he was ready to obey his Coṁand ; soe his Lor^p immediately coṁanded him to beate an Alarum, wch he presently performed. (Althongh some of the Regim^t did endeavor to have the Credite of that peece of Service ascribed to Themselves ; one saying it was I that did first beate the Alarme ; another in like manner saying the same, soe that *Wheeler* may justly complaine as the Poet Virgil[1] did concerning his, *Sic vos non vobis*, and somewhat after The same manner as he spoke, superscribe, Hos Ego Versiculos feci tulit alter honores.)

When the *Alarum* was beaten by Adam Wheeler in Middlesey according to the Lord Lieutent^s Coṁand : The Regim^t marched through Weston into Weston Moore with as much expedicon as possible could be, where They were drawne up Three deep in order to engadge if Occasion required.

The Aforesaid Sixth of July, the *Fight* began very early in the mornening which Battell was over within the space of Two Howers, and the Enemy received a totall Rowte.

Here Adam Wheeler (being then at his Post) was one of those of the Right Wing of his hono^r Colon^ll Windham's Regim^t who after the Enemy began to run desired Leave of his Hono^r to get such Pillage in the feild as they could finde ; But his Hono^rs Answer and Coṁand was : That uppon Paine of Death not a man of his Regim^t shoul^d move from his Post saying ; That if the Enemy should rally together againe, and the Regim^t be in disorder, every man of them might loose his life.

---

[1] possibly when Wheeler was not a Drum, he was a schoolmaster—in spite of the inconsistent spelling.

The Battell being over the Right Honor^ble the Earle of
Feversham, Generall of his Matie^s Army, came to the Head of
Colon^lls Windhams Regim^t and gave him many thanks for his
readynesse, Saying, his Matie should not hear of it by Letter, but
by Word of Mouth; and that he would certify the *Kinge* himself
of it. . . .

July 9. This is the best account I can give yor Honor of that
successful March: and doe humbly beg yor Honor^s pardon for
this Presumption, and with leave subscribe my Selfe Sir,

Yo^r Honors most dutifull Drum, and most humble and
Obedient Servant,

Adam Wheeler.

THE SECOND DECLARATION OF INDULGENCE
AND THE SEVEN BISHOPS

SUNDAY, APRIL 22ND, 1688

On April 4th, 1687, James II issued his 1st Declaration of Indul-
gence which would suspend all penal laws against Catholics and Nonconformists. This reduced the law to a farce and the Nonconformists
refused to accept toleration on such terms. April 22nd, 1688, James II
tried again by issuing a second Declaration with orders that it was to
be read in all churches on two successive Sundays. This Declaration
was read in only two churches in London. Sancroft, Archbishop of
Canterbury, and Bishops Ken of Bath and Wells, White of Peter-
borough, Lloyd of St. Asaph, Trelawny of Bristol, Lake of Chichester
and Turner of Ely, petitioned the King that they should not be compelled to break the law by publishing an illegal Declaration. James
regarded the petition as a seditious libel and the Seven Bishops were
tried and acquitted, on Saturday, June 30th, 1688.

(1) *Source*: A footnote by the Earl of Dartmouth on p. 218 of
Burnet's *History of England*, vol. iii (1823 ed.), describing the reading
of the 2nd Declaration in Westminster Abbey.

Further Reading: Macaulay, *History of England*, ch. viii.

I was then at Westminster School and heard it read in the Abbey. As soon as Bishop Sprat, who was Dean, gave order for reading it, there was so great a murmur and noise in the church that nobody could hear him : but before he had finished, there was none left but a few prebends in their stalls, the choristers and Westminster scholars. The bishop could hardly hold the proclamation in his hands for trembling, and everybody looked under a strange consternation.

(2) *Source* : *The Memoirs of Sir John Reresby*, pp. 259 sqq. (1735 ed.) Sir John Reresby, Bart. (1634–1689) was a timid and time-serving politician, M.P. for Aldborough and later Governor of York.

Having at two several times obtained leave to repair to London, I there found affairs to stand much in the posture I expected. The Popish party was very urgent with the King to press the repeal of the laws against them, and the others as obstinate and headstrong against it ; and what brought the dispute to a still greater degree of warmth was owing to what follows. His Majesty had lately renewed his proclamation for liberty of conscience, and given order to the bishops to cause it be read in the churches of their respective dioceses. The Archbishop of Canterbury and the rest of the order remonstrated against this, setting forth in a petition they presented to the King that they could not pay His Majesty obedience in what he was pleased to require of them ; that no bishop or minister of the Church of England could assent to the proclamation, which must of course be implied by their reading it or causing it to be read ; that a declaration of the same nature on the part of the King had been in Parliament condemned twice in the late reign ; that therefore they might be liable to be called to an account hereafter for doing what had been adjudged contrary to the law ; that though the King himself could do no wrong, his ministers or agents were responsible for whatever was done infractory of the law . . . at which the King conceived so violent a displeasure that they were commanded to appear in Council before him on the 8th of June. . . .

And now seven of the bishops made their appearance before the King in Council, where they were commanded to enter into recognizances of five hundred pounds a man, to answer to an information to be brought against them the next term for disobedience to the King's orders. This they refused to do, saying they were not to engage themselves under any security of the kind, till the information or indictment was found, and that by so doing they should not only run counter to the law, but betray the liberty of the Peerage ; upon which the Archbishop and his six brethren were committed prisoners to the Tower, a severity most deeply resented by the whole Church. Being then at Whitehall, I saw the bishops going to take water for the Tower. They all looked very cheerfully, and the Bishop of Chichester in particular called to me to ask how I did. The next day the Lord Huntingdon, one of the Privy Council, told me that had the King known how far the thing would have gone, he had never laid the injunction he did, to have the Declaration read in churches. . . .

The imprisonment of the bishops was now uppermost in the minds of most of the people, who flocked to them in such numbers, for their blessing and to condole their hard usage, that great and very extraordinary remarks were made both of persons and behaviour. Among the rest, ten Nonconformist ministers went to pay them a visit, which the King took so heinously that he sent for four of them to reprimand them ; but their answer was that they could not but adhere to the prisoners as men constant and firm to the Protestant faith, or to that purpose. Nay, what is more extraordinary, the very soldiers that kept guard in the Tower would frequently drink good health to the bishops ; which being understood by Sir Edward Hales, Constable of the Tower, he sent orders to the Captain of the Guard to see it was done no more ; but the answer he received was that they were doing it at the very instant, and would drink that and no other health, while the bishops were there. . . .

In the course of the trial, the power of the King to dispense with the laws, that grand point, was most exquisitely discussed by the bishops' counsel, who were so much an overmatch for the King's that at Court it was most heartily wished this business had never been pushed to such a crisis. Westminster and the Palace-yards, and all the streets about, were thronged with an infinite people, whose loud shouts and joyful acclamations upon hearing the bishops were acquitted, were a very rebellion in noise, though very far from so in fact or intention. Bonfires were made, not only in the city of London, but in most towns in England, as soon as the news reached them, though there were strict and general orders given out to prevent such doings, and the clergy preached more loudly and more clearly against the errors of the Latin church. The next day I waited on the King to the camp on Hounslow Heath, where everybody observed him to labour under a very great disturbance of mind; but he spoke very kindly to me as I rode by him on several occasions.

WILLIAM OF ORANGE SETS OUT FOR ENGLAND

Friday, October 19th, 1688

The birth on Sunday, June 10th, 1688, of a son to James II increased the danger of a Catholic dynasty on the throne of England. On June 30th the Seven Bishops were acquitted, and on that day Admiral Herbert, representing all parties and interests in the country, invited William of Orange to come to England with an army in order to ensure the free election of a new Parliament. On October 19th William sailed. For dating, see Introduction.

Source : An anonymous letter to 'A Person of Quality' enclosing *'an account of The Expedition of His Highness the Prince of Orange for England; giving an Account of the most remarkable Passages thereof from the Day of his setting Sail from Holland. . . .'*

Harleian Miscellany 1808 ed. vol. I, pp. 449 sqq.

. . . First you are to take notice that his Highness set sail from Holland with fifty-one men of war, eighteen fire ships, and about three hundred and thirty tenders, being ships hired of merchants, for the carriage of horse and foot, arms, ammunition, &c. The fleet stood out to sea to the northward, which met with horrid storms for two days and two nights together; in which bad weather there were lost above five hundred horse, and a vessel parted from the fleet, wherein were four hundred foot, supposed to be lost, but now known to be arrived at the Texel, though grievously shattered and torn by the storm; two of the Prince's principal men of war were forced to new-rig at Helvetsluce.

The Prince, immediately on his return back, informed the States of the condition of the fleet (which was not so damnified as was presented by the vulgar and ignorant) who, thereupon, to lull a great man[1] asleep, the States, or some one employed by them, ordered that the Haarlem and Amsterdam Courantier should make a dismal story of it, by representing to the world, that the Prince returned with his fleet miserably shattered and torn, having lost nine men of war, and divers others of less concern; a thousand horse ruined; a calenture among the seamen; the loss of Dr. Burnet, and the chief ministers under the Prince; the ill opinion the States had of the expedition; in short, that one hundred thousand pounds would not repair the damage sustained; and, almost next to an impossibility, that the Prince should be in a condition to pursue his design, till the spring. . . .

In eight days' time they were all refitted. The signal being given by the discharge of a gun, all the fleet immediately weighed anchor, and stood out at sea, steering their course northwards, all that night; next day upon tide of ebb, they made a stretch, and made a watch above a league, and then stood westward, and lay all night in the same posture, not making two leagues a watch.

In the middle of the night, an advice-boat brought us an account, that the English fleet, consisting of thirty-three sail, lay to the westward of ours. Upon which the Prince fired a gun, which caused a great consternation in the whole fleet; we, having a brisk easterly wind, concluded ourselves to be all ruined; but the small advice-boats, cruising for a more certain account of the English, brought us back word, that, instead of the English fleet, which the former advice had alarmed us with,

[1] i.e. James II.

it was Admiral Herbert with part of our fleet, which had been separated some hours from the body of our fleet. Upon whose arrival great rejoicing was among us all, and a signal of joy was given for it by the Prince.

In the morning, about eight, the Prince gave a signal, that the Admiral should come a-board him. Immediately after the whole fleet was got into the North Foreland, upon which the Prince gave the usual sign (according to the printed book), and ordered that the fleet should all come up in a body, some fifteen or sixteen deep, his Highness leading the van in the ship the Brill (in English, Spectacles): his flag was English colours, the motto impaled thereon, was, 'The Protestant Religion, and the Liberties of England', and underneath, instead of *Dieu & mon droit*, was, 'And I will maintain it'.

The council of war, from on board the Prince, sent three small frigates into the mouth of the Thames . . . who, on their return, brought us word, that the English fleet lay in the Buoy of the Nore, consisting of thirty-four sail, and three more which lay in the Downs. The wind continuing at E.N.E.

The Prince immediately thereupon gave another signal of stretching the whole fleet in a line, from Dover to Calais, twenty-five deep. This sight would have ravished the most curious eyes of Europe : when our fleet was in its greatest splendour, the trumpets and drums playing various tunes to rejoice our hearts ; this continued for above three hours.

Immediately after, the Prince gave us a sign to close, and sailed that night as far as Beach, and commanded us to follow the signal by lights he had hung out to us, viz. all the small sail should come up to him by morning.

By the morning we espied the Isle of Wight, and then the Prince ordered the fleet to be drawn into the same posture, as before related . . . about five in the morning we made the Start, the wind chopping about to the westward ; upon which we stood fair by Dartmouth, and so made for Torbay, where the Prince again ordered the whole fleet into the same posture as at Dover and Calais.

Upon his arrival at Torbay, the people on land, in great numbers, welcomed his Highness with loud acclamations of joy.

Immediately after the Prince gave two signals, that the Admirals should come aboard him, which they did : and then ordered, that the whole fleet should come to anchor, and immediately land ; and further ordered that the Admirals should stand out at sea, as a guard, as well as the smaller men of war, to attend and guard their landing ; and also ordered six men of war to run in, to guard Torbay.

The Prince then put out a red flag at the mizzen-yard-arm, and provided to land in sixty boats, laid ready for that purpose. Upon which the Prince signified that General Mackay with his six regiments of English and Scotch should first land ; also, that the little Porpus, with eighteen guns, should run aground, to secure their landing ; but there was no opposition ; for the people bid us heartily welcome to England, and gave us all manner of provisions for our refreshment.

The fifth of November (a day never to be blotted out of the Englishman's heart) the Prince caused to be landed about two thousand. On the sixth we landed as many horse and foot as we could possibly, and so it continued the seventh : the country bringing in all manner of provision, both for man and horse, and were paid their price honestly for it.

The Prince the same day commanded Captain M—— to search the Lady Cary's house, at Tor-Abbey, for arms and horses, and so all other houses which were Roman Catholicks. The Lady, entertaining them civilly, said her husband was gone to Plymouth. They brought from thence some horses and a few arms, but gave no further disturbance to the Lady or her house. Nor shall it be forgotten what was faithfully acted at this Lady's house, immediately on our arrival at Torbay : There were a priest and some others with him on a watch-tower, to discover what our fleet was, whether French or Dutch. At last they discovered the white flags on some of our men of war ; the ignorant priest concluded absolutely we were the French fleet, which, with great impatience, they had so long expected ; and having laid up great provisions for their entertainment ; the

priest ordered all to the chapel to sing *Te Deum*, for the arrival of
their supposed forces ; but being soon undeceived on our landing, we found the benefit of their provisions ; and instead of
Vostre Serviteur Monsieur, they were entertained with *Yeen Myn-
heer*, Can you Dutch spraken? Upon which they all ran away
from the house, but the Lady and a few old servants. . . .

November the eighth, the Prince came from Chudleigh
towards Exeter, with the greatest part of his army attending
him ; and about one of the clock entered at the west-gate of the
city, welcomed with loud acclamations by the people.
Wincanton   N.N.
    1st December, 1688.

THE FIRST FLIGHT OF JAMES II
TUESDAY, DECEMBER 11TH, 1688

Once William of Orange had landed in England support steadily
ebbed away from the King to the side of the Prince. James at last lost
his nerve—he suffered greatly from bleeding at the nose—and decided
to leave the country. He only got as far as Faversham, as the following
account makes clear, where he was recognized and returned to London.
But on William's approach to the city, James once again fled and
escaped to France, on Sunday, December 23rd, 1688.

Source : James II's own account, probably extracted from his MS.
Memoirs and translated into French for the use of the nuns in a com-
munity founded at Chaillot, near Paris, by James's mother, Queen
Henrietta Maria. It is printed in French in an appendix to Sir James
Mackintosh's *History of the Revolution*, from which this English version
has been made. The original French version is in the Archives
Générales de France.

Further Reading. Burnet, *History of England*, vol. iii, 1823 ed.

Things were come to that extremity, by the almost universal
defection of the nobility and clergy, by the desertion of the
greater part of the principal officers and others in the army, and

P

by the small confidence the King could place in those Protestants who remained with him, that His Majesty came to the conclusion that there was nothing else for him to do but to withdraw with the Queen and the Prince into safety. . . .

His Majesty set out secretly from his palace at Whithall on the night of Monday—Tuesday one hour after midnight, crossed the Thames in a small boat and arrived on the other side at Vauxhall, where he found the horses waiting for him. From there, with only two companions, His Majesty crossed the river Medway at Alisford Bridge. Two or three miles further on he found a relay of six horses with Mr. Sheldon, one of his equerries, whom he had sent on ahead. The next day, Tuesday, at six o'clock in the morning, the King arrived at Emley Ferry, where there should have been a small boat ready for him, but it had not yet arrived. As soon as it turned up, the King went on board, and with him went Sir Edward Hales and Mr. Sheldon. The wind was fair, but it was strong, so that the master of the vessel told the King that he dared not set sail because he had not taken in any ballast. The King agreed, realising that without ballast the ship would not carry sail. They therefore made for Sheppey which lies west of Sheerness, and there they ran ashore, the tide being almost low, with the intention of setting out with the tide for the first French port which they could make. But round about eleven o'clock at night, when the ship began to float, three fishing-boats from Faversham, carrying 50 to 60 men, boarded their ship by force. Their captain, with his sword in one hand and a pistol in the other, leapt straight into the cabin where was the King, with the two gentlemen who were accompanying him. He told them they were his prisoners, that they were suspicious and dangerous characters and that he was going to hale them in front of the Mayor of Faversham for examination. The King realized that none of those who had entered the cabin recognized him, and he thought quickly enough not to give himself away, hoping to find means of escape out of their hands. While the captain, whose name was Ames, examined them in the cabin, Sir Edward Hales took the opportunity, while the rest were not looking, to put into his hand fifty guineas and to whisper to him that there would be another hundred, if he called off his men before they came to Faversham. The captain took the money and promised to do so.

In the meantime there was enough tide to float the ship, which they steered to the mouth of the river at Faversham. Here they dropped anchor and waited for the full tide to carry the ship in. Captain Ames left them there to go, as he pretended, to find means of escape for them, but before he parted from them, he went down into the cabin where the King was and told him and those with His Majesty that the people he was leaving behind were only rough folk who were well capable of plundering them in his absence : therefore he advised them to put into his hands what money and other valuables they had, so that he could take care of them and return them when they had been discharged. Thereupon the King and the other two gentlemen gave him their money and their watches in front of some witnesses and received from him a receipt : but the King kept three large diamond bodkins which belonged to the Queen, and the ring which he had worn at his coronation, which was a valuable ruby, and slipped them down his trousers, hoping thus to save them. In the event, the captain's warning proved only too true.

Meanwhile the captain went to Faversham. On his return he told Sir Edward Hales that they could not escape, but they would have to go in front of the Mayor of Faversham to be interrogated. It was already day, and Sir Edward Hales had been recognized, although they had not yet recognized the King. The captain then returned to arrange for a carriage to take them into the town. While he was away the sailors rushed into the cabin and said they must search them because they had reason to believe that they had not given the captain everything. The King and his two companions told them they had given up all the money they had and they could search them if they wanted to. The sailors looked into their hands, their pockets, searched everywhere, but they did it so carelessly that they found nothing on them. One sailor, however, who was searching the King, only just missed a fine prize, for he felt near the King's knee one of the diamond bodkins, and as he tightened his grasp, he shouted out that he

P. I

had found something. He had already found in the King's pocket his scissors, case and some small keys. The King therefore told the sailor that he had only to put his hand into the King's pocket and he would find that what he was feeling was one of the things he had already seen. The king spoke so casually that the sailor let go his prize and, thrusting his hand into the King's pocket, he was fully persuaded that what he had felt was something in the pocket. Thus was this diamond, and the others, saved. These men were so ignorant that, when they found the King's diamond buckles wrapped up in paper in his pocket, they gave them back to him, saying that they were glass buckles.

While all this was going on, the carriage which the captain had sent to take them into the town arrived at the water's edge. They went from their ship to the shore by a small boat. They climbed into the carriage and were guarded by a man named Edwards and some of the populace. They went to an inn, and the King was not recognized at all until he went to a room upstairs. Although he was disguised by wearing a black wig, some of those present spotted him. When His Majesty perceived this, he made no more attempt to hide his identity, whereupon the populace dispersed. On being told that Lord Winchelsea and the greater part of the gentlemen of the county were gathered at Canterbury, the King sent to them to come to him. . . .

THE CAPTURE OF JAMES II AT FAVERSHAM

WEDNESDAY, DECEMBER 12TH, 1688

Source : A letter from one of the gentlemen who came to the King, when he was taken, to his friend in London. Printed in a footnote on pp. xxii sqq. of vol. 1 of Tindal's Continuation of Rapin's *History of England*, 2nd ed., 1751.

The night was attended by something more extraordinary, for the seamen, armed with a sort of emulation at the success of the landmen, were resolved to have a frolic in their way ; and about seven at night, under the conduct of William Ames and James Hunt, with about fifty more, chiefly seamen, put off in quest of a prize, and about eleven at night they took a Custom-house boat, in which proved to be the King, Sir Edward Hales and Ralph Sheldon. The King was in a particular disguise and so not known that night ; but as if his destiny designed to be severe upon him, the seamen treated him very roughly above the rest, though *incognito*. One cried out 'twas Father Petre ; they knew it to be so by his lean jaws. A second called him old hatchet-faced Jesuit. A third swore 'twas a cunning old rogue, they would warrant him. And all night long they welcomed him with these rough salutations, and perfuming the room with tobacco, the smell whereof the King hates. His Majesty was taken at the west point, not above a quarter of an hour before the flood would have carried him off ; and it was his own fault that they stopped there for ballast, which the pilot was against : but the roughness of the sea made his Majesty fear they were not safe in so small a boat without ballast ; whereby they lost six or eight hours, and so were providentially taken. He was detained at sea all night, and brought up from Owse, where he landed, to Faversham about twelve, Wednesday the 12th. Then he was suspected as he came up the town, and within a quarter of an hour after he was in the inn, fully discovered. He was willing by all arts at first to conceal himself, and at his first coming in he called for bacon and eggs, as if he were some ordinary man in his diet, whereas he takes no meat that is in the least salted, as it afterwards appeared. He seemed cast down somewhat at the noise of the rabble, but after some recollection, called for some ink and paper to write to the Earl of Winchelsea ; but was so discomposed that he wrote, and tore, and begun again, as if he were overcome with disorder or fears. Inasmuch as I was with him before he was discovered, he entered into some discourse with me. He thanked me and commended my prudence for not discovering him with the first, though I knew him as soon as anyone. He told me that the rage of the people was up, and now that of the Psalmist was true : ' I, who still the raging of the sea, must still the rage and madness of the people ', for he could not, therefore he (*blank in the MS*). He complained heavily of fears and jealousies blown about by ill men, and too many of the black coats had done him that ill office they could never make amends for. He insisted on his integrity, said he had a good conscience and could suffer and die. He told me he read scripture much and found great comfort in it. He declared he never designed to oppress conscience, alter the government, or destroy the subjects' liberties ; and at last asked me plainly, ' What have I done ? What are the errors of my reign? Tell me freely.' To which you may be sure I made no answer. He insisted much upon going off after he was taken, and I believe he put the question to every layman and churchman in the room to get him a boat and let him escape. He said the Prince of Orange fought his crown and life, and if he were delivered up, his blood would lie at our doors, for he seemed persuaded they would murder him. ' Now,' said he, ' the opportunity is in your hand, but if you miss this, it will not be in your power to help me.' He argued much upon these words, ' He that is not with me is against me,' and sermonised half an hour, making reflections on men's coldness to serve him in that extremity. Whilst he insisted upon going off, and used all motives proper, as he thought, in begging, praying, tempting, arguing, persuading, reproving, etc., which was above three hours, the rage of the seamen took fire apprehending he would prevail with some to let him escape secretly, and thereupon arose some contemptuous words and no small insolences offered, which I almost think had not happened, if the fear of his escape had not run so much in their minds, or if his Majesty would have waived discoursing so much thereof. For the seamen much valued themselves on their charge, and did apprehend their own lives in danger if he went off, imagining they had done a singular piece of service to the nation, and resolving there to keep him till order from the Prince or the Lords at Guildhall. And the King himself undertook to discourse them, and asked the seamen, ' By what authority do you stand here? Am not I your King? And sure you will not hurt my life. Will you stand by me? I'll reward you. If you be my good subjects, you must obey me. Come and serve me and get me a boat, and I'll be off.' Afterward he went so far as to regulate their way of keeping guards, bid them stand further off, ' Go down and keep your distance,' which so enraged them that some of them forgot all decency and reverence to him, insomuch that Sir Edward Hales was desired to take the King from that discourse, which made him cheap and proved so unpolitic and unsuccessful. But still the rage of the seamen increased, and they shook hands and cried out one and all, ' We'll rather die than he shall go off ', got together in a full body, broke out into scornful huzzas, and for a while doubled their guard, suffered none to go to him but whom they well knew, loaded their muskets and made ready as if they resolved to fire upon any that opposed their measures. This indeed intimidated the King, and his spirits seemed much down, which made him keep his eye upon the door and watch all their motions narrowly, and desire not to be much alone, but the gentlemen to stay with him. Towards night the Earl of Winchelsea came, and then it was resolved to remove the King to a private house, which the seamen still opposed for fear of escape. But my Lord pawning his honour for the King's stay, the better sort of them consented, but the mobile still refused, and as the King came downstairs, I believe more than twenty swords were drawn over his head and some threats passed, and at the bottom of the stairs they stopped him near a quarter of an hour. At length the matter was compounded upon condition they only should be the King's guards whilst he stayed. So at length the King was suffered to walk down the dirty street to his private apartments, with the irregular, disorderly crew at his heels. . . .

Next day being Thursday the 13th . . . towards night Captain Crayford and another Captain came from Sheerness, declaring the resolution to deliver up to the Prince the fort and the ships in the Swale, which is a road under the protection of the fort. Upon the hearing of which he said he would consent to anything to prevent bloodshed, but seemed extremely afflicted thereat. He was really very melancholy at times and often shed tears. His guards were so severe upon him, and pursued him from one room to another, and pressed upon in his privacies, so that he had scarce the civilities from the seamen that was due to a gentleman in restraint, scarce leisure to be devout or retire to the calls of nature, so over officiously did they guard him. Fresh rumours oft were raised of his going off, which fetched the scattered seamen together, and were the occasion of fresh heats and insolences. In this tumultuous manner was the poor King guarded, neither would they suffer the gentlemen to take their turns.

INDEX

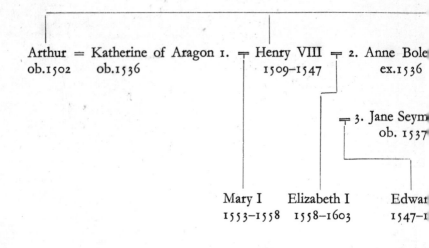

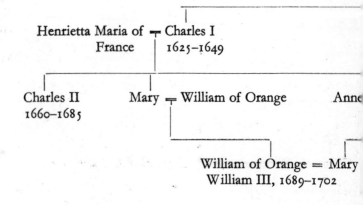

Arthur = Katherine of Aragon 1. ⊤ Henry VIII ⊤ 2. Anne Bole
ob.1502   ob.1536   1509–1547   ex.1536

⊤ 3. Jane Seym
ob. 1537

Mary I   Elizabeth I   Edwar
1553–1558   1558–1603   1547–1

Henrietta Maria of ⊤ Charles I
France | 1625–1649

Charles II   Mary ⊤ William of Orange   Anne
1660–1685

William of Orange = Mary
William III, 1689–1702